A HISTORICAL GUIDE TO

Edith Wharton

The Historical Guides to American Authors is an interdisciplinary, historically sensitive series that combines close attention to the United States' most widely read and studied authors with a strong sense of time, place, and history. Placing each writer in the context of the vibrant relationship between literature and society, volumes in this series contain historical essays written on subjects of contemporary social, political, and cultural relevance. Each volume also includes a capsule biography and illustrated chronology detailing important cultural events as they coincided with the author's life and works, while photographs and illustrations dating from the period capture the flavor of the author's time and social milieu. Equally accessible to students of literature and of life, the volumes offer a complete and rounded picture of each author in his or her America.

A Historical Guide to Ernest Hemingway
Edited by Linda Wagner-Martin

A Historical Guide to Walt Whitman
Edited by David S. Reynolds

A Historical Guide to Ralph Waldo Emerson
Edited by Joel Myerson

A Historical Guide to Henry David Thoreau
Edited by William E. Cain

A Historical Guide to Edgar Allan Poe
Edited by J. Gerald Kennedy

A Historical Guide to Nathaniel Hawthorne
Edited by Larry Reynolds

A Historical Guide to Mark Twain
Edited by Shelley Fisher Fishkin

A Historical Guide to Edith Wharton
Edited by Carol J. Singley

A
Historical Guide
to Edith Wharton

EDITED BY
CAROL J. SINGLEY

OXFORD
UNIVERSITY PRESS
2003

OXFORD
UNIVERSITY PRESS

Oxford   New York
Auckland   Bangkok   Buenos Aires   Cape Town   Chennai
Dar es Salaam   Delhi   Hong Kong   Istanbul   Karachi   Kolkata
Kuala Lumpur   Madrid   Melbourne   Mexico City   Mumbai   Nairobi
Sao Paulo   Shanghai   Taipei   Tokyo   Toronto

Copyright © 2003 by Oxford University Press, Inc.

Published by Oxford University Press, Inc.
198 Madison Avenue, New York, New York 10016

www.oup.com

Oxford is a registered trademark of Oxford University Press

Library of Congress Cataloging-in-Publication Data
A historical guide to Edith Wharton / edited by Carol J. Singley.
p.   cm.—(Historical guides to American authors)
Includes bibliographical references and index.
ISBN 0-19-513590-3; ISBN 0-19-513591-1 (pbk.)
1. Wharton, Edith, 1862–1937—Knowledge—History.
2. Wharton, Edith, 1862–1937—Criticism and interpretation.
3. Literature and history—United States—History—20th century.
4. Women and literature—United States—History—20th century.
I. Singley, Carol J., 1951–   II. Series.
PS3545.H16 Z663   2002
813'.52—dc21   2002034613

1 3 5 7 9 8 6 4 2

Printed in the United States of America
on acid-free paper

For the Edith Wharton Society

Contents

Abbreviations

Ethan Frome, Summer, Old New York (False Dawn, The Old Maid, The Spark, New Year's Day), The Mother's Recompense, A Backward Glance, "Life and I"]. Ed. Cynthia Griffin Wolff. New York: Library of America, 1990.

SF   *A Son at the Front.* New York: Scribner's, 1923.

TS   *Twilight Sleep.* New York, Appleton, 1927.

UCW   *Edith Wharton: The Uncollected Critical Writings.* Ed. Frederick Wegener. Princeton: Princeton University Press, 1996.

V   *The Valley of Decision.* 2 vols. New York: Scribner's, 1902.

WF   *The Writing of Fiction.* New York: Scribner's, 1925.

A HISTORICAL GUIDE TO

Edith Wharton

Introduction

Carol J. Singley

Edith Wharton is by critical and popular acclaim one of the United States' finest novelists and short story writers. A consummate stylist and astute critic of late nineteenth- and early twentieth-century American social life, Wharton often ridiculed the upper-class New York society of which she herself was a member. She also turned her sharp eye to New England and Europe, creating incisive portraits of characters deeply affected by their social and physical environments. Wharton's ability to combine such cutting satire and irony with compassion for human suffering results in a unique American realism that elevates her characters' struggles against restrictive conventions and circumstances beyond comedy of manners to pathos, and even tragedy. Today Wharton's critical reputation has never been higher; indeed, her place in American letters as one of the premier practitioners of realism seems assured.

Wharton has not always enjoyed such high esteem. Indeed, her relationship to literary history has been uneven. Although she was a best-selling and critically lauded author during her lifetime—at one point she was the highest paid living American novelist—throughout most of the twentieth century her reputation suffered from excessive comparison to Henry James. Her work also languished under the approbation, "society fiction," a term that implied narrowness of scope, and from a tendency plaguing American literary criticism generally: a reluctance to equate literary excellence with female authorship. Wharton, keenly aware of the obstacles she faced, pursued her craft with energy, conviction, and professionalism. Yet even after receiving numerous literary commendations, including the Pulitzer Prize for *The Age of Innocence* (1920), Wharton worried about her place in literary history, confiding to a friend in 1925: "as my work reaches its close, I feel so sure that it is either nothing, or far more than they know. . . . And I wonder, a little desolately, which?" (*L*, 483).

Today Wharton would be gratified by many signs that confirm positive reception of her work: scholarly books, articles, and dissertations about her life and writing; reprinted editions of her novels, short stories, and nonfiction; inclusion of her work in college and university curricula; film and theatrical adaptations of her fiction; and allusions to her life and writing by a host of contemporary authors. As a woman interested in culture, art, and history, as well as literature, she would also be pleased by other acknowledgments of her stature as a major American figure. These include publicly and privately funded projects to restore her homes and gardens in the United States and in France, recognition of her independent organization of massive World War I relief efforts, the centennial reprint of her co-authored book *The Decoration of Houses*, and even a line of Edith Wharton designer fabrics. Clearly, Wharton occupies a significant place in literary and cultural history. It is time now to explore the extent to which, through her life and writings, she also affected the course of events around her.

Edith Wharton changed history—her own, her family's, her society's, and the literary world in which she wrote for fifty years. Although shy as a child and lacking self-confidence as an apprentice writer, she nevertheless had one consuming passion: to "'make up' stories" (*Backward, NW*, 809). She pursued this desire with fierce determination even when discouraged by friends and family. Whether living in New York, New England, or Europe, Wharton remained committed to a life surrounded by art and beauty, and she worked to develop the creative as well as the professional aspects of her craft. The results of her efforts are lasting contributions to American literature in general and to women's writing in particular.

When Edith Newbold Jones was born in January 1862, into a fashionable New York family near Fifth Avenue and Madison Square, she forever altered her family's predictable routine. The third and final child of the socially prominent Lucretia Rhinelander Jones and George Frederic Jones, she had two older brothers, one sixteen and the other eleven. The surprise of Edith's birth, occurring long after her mother had left the nursery, seemed perhaps more inconvenience than benefaction to Lucretia Jones, who prized social standing and fashionability above other aspects of domesticity. In fact, so unexpected was Edith's arrival that it gave rise to rumors that she was the offspring of her brothers' tutor or a Scottish nobleman. These speculations reflect not so much biographical evidence, as a striking difference in sensibility between Wharton and her clan. More serious than they, and more alive to the nuances of art and culture, Wharton was from the beginning an anomaly, even an embarrassment to her conventionally minded family and society.

Wharton's family represented a class of American aristocrats made comfortable from inherited wealth, steeped in traditional values, and well practiced in patterns of ritualized behavior. Members of her society socialized with one another and shunned the ostentation of the nouveau riche, who after the Civil War were making their way into the social ranks of Old New York. From her mother, reputedly the best-dressed woman in New York and the inspiration for the phrase "keeping up with the Joneses," Wharton learned social graces, a flair for fashion, and reverence for proper usage of the English language. From her father, a more quiet, reflective man, she absorbed a love of poetry. But neither parent was inclined or equipped to nurture sufficiently their daughter's driving ambition for writing. Like the heroine in Wharton's short story "The Mission of Jane," about a precocious adopted daughter who offends her parents' sense of good taste, Wharton confounded her family, who struggled to make accommodations for her.

Wharton's voracious appetite for reading and writing challenged the Jones household. As was customary for girls at the time, she received no formal schooling. Eager to learn, however, she eavesdropped on the threshold of her father's library while her brothers were tutored. She stole surreptitiously among the books there, immersing herself in the classics, as well as in novels and romances her mother had forbidden her to read. Desperate to compose stories but provided with no writing paper, she was "driven to begging for the wrappings of the parcels delivered at the house" (*Backward, NW,* 39). In 1878, when she was sixteen, her parents—hostile toward contemporary literature and especially scornful of writers such as Poe and Whitman—privately published her first collection of poems, *Verses,* hoping to assuage their daughter's current literary ambitions and forestall future ones. This same year, Lucretia Jones, concerned about Edith's excessive intellectualism, arranged for an early social debut that eventually led in 1885 to marriage to Edward (Teddy) Wharton, an upper-class man of leisure of whom Lucretia approved but with whom Wharton was fundamentally incompatible.

Wharton inherited a strong sense of social tradition, but she felt willing, even compelled, to disrupt comfortable patterns in order to follow her chosen path as a woman and a writer. Her marriage to Teddy initially survived because of the couple's shared love for travel and entertaining, but as Wharton began to write seriously and to experience success from her efforts, she felt more alienated from him and from the world of her youth. She increasingly sought the company of like-minded intellectuals and artists, chose to summer in New England as well as the fashionable Newport, and was drawn to the creative life of Paris rather than New York. Her marriage floundering, she engaged in an extramarital affair with Morton Fullerton in 1908. Wharton—who had been raised in a society that revered marriage and shunned scandal at all costs, and who herself had lamented the poverty of love outside marriage—obtained a divorce in 1913. Although she seldom discussed her private life, Wharton showed by her example that women could achieve strength and self-sufficiency without the conventional supports of marriage. She also pointed the way for women's autonomy from restrictive families of origin. Wharton often struggled alone to establish herself as a writer. Even after she gained a foothold in the literary world, no family member except a distant relative ever spoke to her about her work. The pretense of family cohesion finally dissolved when she became estranged from her mother and one brother. To replace these ties, Wharton developed a tight network of friends, servants, and associates to whom she remained loyal and generous. Wharton created this alternative family model from necessity, but the fact that she was also a well-adjusted, independent woman, who enjoyed a satisfying and well-paying career as well as close, rewarding relationships, prefigures a type of modern womanhood not widely seen until well into the twentieth century.

In these and other ways, Edith Wharton changed the image of the woman writer. A consummate professional, she wrote on a daily schedule and took charge of literary business as few female authors of the generation before her had done. She oversaw each stage of the publishing process and spoke forcefully for adequate publicity and compensation. She produced a large corpus of work: twenty-five novels, including best-sellers such as *The House of Mirth* and the Pulitzer Prize–winning *The Age of Innocence*, eighty-six short stories, three books of poetry, a book on interior design, numerous volumes of travel literature, a study on the theory of fiction, an autobiography, and countless articles, essays, and reviews—an impressive accomplishment, all the more so because she did not launch her career fully until she reached her forties. She was a serious intellectual, well read in science, religion, and philosophy, as well as in horticulture, art, and architecture. She pursued avid interests in the world around her while at the same time upholding the domestic arts and principles of good taste. Posing for publicity photos in pearls and furs, Wharton combined the image of the professional female author and the fashionable lady in unique ways. She never apologized for her wealth, using her earnings and inheritances to build elaborate homes and gardens in the United States and France, to take extensive and often exotic trips, and to create warm environments for friends like Walter Berry, Henry James, and Bernard Berenson.

Wharton transformed American fiction of the late nineteenth

and early twentieth centuries. Her life (1862–1937) spanned a long period in the nation's history and marked great changes in its literature. The post–Civil War era into which Wharton was born was a Victorian one. Wharton inherited a domestic, often sentimental, literary tradition from her female predecessors such as Harriet Beecher Stowe, Louisa May Alcott, and Sarah Orne Jewett. Acknowledging her debt to them but rejecting the "rose-coloured" lenses through which some of these writers saw the world (*Backward, NW,* 1002), she aimed instead for moral depth and ambiguity more associated with Nathaniel Hawthorne. Wharton helped to transform nineteenth-century romantic literature into a twentieth-century realism that confronted directly and critically the pressing issues facing men and women at the turn of the century. Her realism is at once more uncompromising than William Dean Howells's and more rooted in physical passion than James's. Wharton takes special interest in women. In novels as different as *The House of Mirth* and *The Custom of the Country,* she documents the effects of an increasingly consumer-based culture, shifting sexual relations, and changing urban and rural demographics on women of all classes. With her penetrating portraits of people negotiating the requirements of place and custom, Wharton also makes original contributions to the school of literary naturalism. Her characters, like those in Theodore Dreiser's and Frank Norris's fictions, are often trapped by biology or circumstance. But as novels such as *The Reef, Summer,* and *The Age of Innocence* show, Wharton probes more deeply than many writers the complex interplay of training and temperament. Possessing a strong moral sensibility, she holds her characters accountable for choices made ever under severe constraints.

Edith Wharton also made her mark on literary modernism. Because she wrote with a lucid, conventional style and disliked the experimental prose of high modernists such as James Joyce, it has been easy to overlook her role in the development of this innovative literary form. Yet as early as 1911, in *Ethan Frome,* Wharton developed techniques to probe a character's inner consciousness and incapacitating sense of isolation. Like many other modernist writers, Wharton was an expatriate with first-hand experience of the devastating effects of war, who feared for the demise of civilization itself. Like Ernest Hemingway, she describes the trauma of battle; like F. Scott Fitzgerald, the social hilarity and rootlessness of the post–World War I era. A sense of discontinuity and lost purpose, hallmarks of modernism, characterize Wharton's late fiction. Novels such as *The Glimpses of the Moon, Twilight Sleep,* and *The Mother's Recompense* chart a precipitous cultural fall into moral relativism which, lacking an ethical safety net, puts individuals and institutions at risk. Wharton's modernism, however, unlike Ezra Pound's or T. S. Eliot's, is neither anti-romantic nor impersonal. On the contrary, Wharton foregrounds the experiences of desire and disappointment, especially as they relate to women's sexuality. Although she was critical of old mores that restricted women's freedoms, she was equally skeptical of new dispensations that left women without secure boundaries. As the late novels illustrate, Wharton confronted prospects for twentieth-century women with ambivalence. Ahead of her time in exploring the limitations that women faced, she nevertheless hesitated to venture too far from familiar conventions when charting their alternatives. It is ironic that a quality lauded in an acclaimed modernist such as Eliot—concern for tradition—should have led to Wharton being considered old-fashioned or shrill, for Wharton no less than Eliot searches for stable structures of meaning amid unsettling cultural change.

Wharton also made her mark on national and world history. Few casual readers of fiction know, for example, of her civic leadership. She was a strong supporter of what became the Society for the Prevention of Cruelty to Animals, and she organized dozens of charities during World War I. Her workrooms, hospitals, and shelters gave assistance to thousands of French and Belgian refugees and soldiers. She worked tirelessly to enlist American support for the war and had the ear of President Theodore Roosevelt, a longtime friend. When the United States entered the conflict in 1914, the Red Cross struggled to absorb Wharton's immense charitable operations. She was also an expert in horticulture, architectural design, and eighteenth-century French and Italian art and architecture, and she made original contributions in several of these fields. An expatriate and a world traveler, she spoke five languages, wrote in at least two, and infused her life with a globalism only now appreciated. Always politically engaged, Wharton seems from today's perspective to have had a limited perspective on some issues; most troubling are her views on eugenics and race. But Wharton also staunchly believed in basic human dignity, and she worked through her fiction and in her life to give expression to the pain of the misunderstood and defenseless, whether they wore working clothes or Doucet gowns.

Edith Wharton's significance, therefore, must be understood in the context of her literary, social, and political roles: her views of changing gender relations, her position in movements such as realism and modernism, her engagement with and influence on broad historical events like World War I. The chapters in this volume celebrate the variety of Wharton's achievements in such arenas and speak to her indisputable importance in American literary history. All of the essays appear for the first time and have been written expressly for this series. The contributors are well known not only for their scholarship on Edith Wharton but also for their expertise in the fields of art, film, and culture, as well as American literature. Taking a variety of interdisciplinary approaches and enlisting a broad spectrum of critical methodologies, the authors chart new territory in Wharton studies. They expand our understanding of Wharton's relationship to literary movements of her time, especially realism, naturalism, and modernism. They also explore her relationship to other important intellectual and literary figures of her day, and they explain the cultural developments that affected her writing and were, in turn, affected by it.

Shari Benstock, one of Wharton's acclaimed biographers, sets Wharton's life and work in historical context. She describes Wharton's birth, in 1862, into a nation challenged by civil war and on the brink of unprecedented social, economic, and cultural change. Benstock weighs the benefits and disadvantages of Wharton's affluent but insular New York upbringing; chronicles the development of her interests in literature, art, and design, begun when the family sojourned in Europe to escape the effects of a post–Civil War recession; and charts pivotal figures and events in Wharton's long literary apprenticeship through the 1890s. At an young age, Benstock argues, Wharton developed the keen observational skills and distanced, often ironic perspective that distinguish her social satires. She also acquired early on a sense of history and a visual approach to literature and landscape. Place—whether it be New York City transforming itself from small town to major metropolis, New England blanketed with snow, or elegant brownstone interiors—is the dominant metaphor in Wharton's fiction. Benstock also demonstrates how Wharton, in novels concerned with social mores and social reform, reflects the extremes of the Gilded Age and the anxieties of the modern era. Never shrinking from controversial subjects, Wharton records the effects of World War I, tensions leading to World War II, accelerating rates of technological innovation, and rapidly changing social institutions such as marriage and divorce. Throughout her life and work, Benstock notes, is an abiding concern for the psychological, social, and economic well-being of women.

In her essay, "Wharton's Women: In Fashion, In History, Out of Time," Martha Banta explains how Wharton's use of material culture reveals the social and psychological realities of her female characters. Wharton's detailed accounts of late nineteenth- and early twentieth-century life—of forms of communication, transportation, architecture, and design—offer important clues to the dispositions and fates of her heroines. Trains, carriages, steamliners, electric currents, and clocks, for example, all underline the quickening pace of modern life and its pressures. Of particular importance is fashion, a marker that allows Wharton to trace women's shifting social positions. Clothes "speak" to where women are, Banta argues, not only in relation to social hierarchies, but also in relation to a larger sweep of history. Citing texts ranging from short stories to novels such as *The House of Mirth, The Custom of the Country,* and *The Age of Innocence,* Banta demonstrates how Wharton's chronicles of fashion do more than enhance her realism. Fashion operates as a powerful metaphor that makes manifest the social laws affecting women at particular moments. Women who follow or resist fashion reveal the extent to which they are aligned with, behind, or ahead of their times.

Wharton is a writer concerned, Banta asserts, not just with trend, but with pattern; not just with localized changes in style, but with a more "seamless" concept of history in which process and progression may also be regression. For many of Wharton's women, who remained trapped despite social change, time can flow backward as well as forward. Wharton thus proposes a historical realism that acknowledges events in the long and short run, that locates the colossal in the apparently minuscule, and that favors consistency and coherence over hectic renovation.

In "Emerson, Darwin, and *The Custom of the Country*," Cecelia Tichi investigates Wharton's engagement with two key figures of the nineteenth century, linked together as early as 1901 in her short story "The Angel at the Grave." Noting Wharton's use of Darwinian thought to express tensions between survival and extinction in novels from *The House of Mirth* (1905) to *The Age of Innocence* (1920), Tichi focuses on *The Custom of the Country* (1913). *Custom* is patterned on the multiple binary formulations found in Darwin and Herbert Spencer, in which organisms struggle to survive and lower natures are subordinated to higher natures. According to this paradigm, the character of Ralph Marvell represents an attenuated aristocratic race vanquished by the nouveau riche, embodied by Undine Spragg. Ralph's name also evokes that of Ralph Waldo Emerson, which connotes poetry and spirit, as well as polarities in nature and human nature. But whereas Emerson's binary divisions resolve into wholeness, Wharton's novel exploits Emerson to demonstrate an enduring dualism, in which larger natures capitulate to smaller ones, gender inversions allow masculine women to overwhelm feminine men, and self-reliance deteriorates into self-interest and disregard for others. The gross appetites and crude appearances of invaders like Undine and Peter Van Degen align them not only with a lower order of organisms but also with the nonhuman. Tichi concludes by observing that Wharton's deliberate misreading of Emerson demonstrates not only her Darwinism but also her bleak outlook for the future, an outlook only partially mediated by her complimentary depiction of Ralph and Undine's son Paul, in whom Wharton tentatively places hope for a more humane, refined society.

Dale M. Bauer, in "Wharton's 'Others': Addiction and Inti-macy," explores the intersection of Wharton's modernism and portrayals of female sexuality. While critics have described objec-tification in Wharton's fiction in terms of a racial, ethnic, or class otherness, Bauer theorizes the "other" in order to explain sexual expression as a form of modernist alienation rather than inti-macy. She locates this alienation not only in Wharton's heroines but also in Wharton herself. Resisting outmoded Victorian mores as well as competing movements that embraced either Freudian psychology or Christian reform, Wharton understood alienation not as the repression or absence of passion, but as pas-sion misdirected or degraded by a consumer-based culture. In novels about women's failed desire on which Bauer focuses, *The House of Mirth*, *The Fruit of the Tree* (1907), and *Ethan Frome*, (1911) heroines substitute drugs for sexual expression. Wharton repre-sents her characters' longing for connection as an addiction, even literalizing this trope in her fiction. Her women become es-tranged from themselves, from their own internalized sense of themselves as other. Although Wharton yearned for women's sexual freedom, she was wary of simple formulas for liberation. Following a "pay for pleasure" principle practiced by realists such as Howells, James, and Dreiser rather than a more unfettered view of sexual expression espoused by modernist women writ-ers, Wharton ultimately rejected women's sexual power because it resulted in personal as well as cultural alienation.

Nancy Bentley continues the emphasis on Wharton as a writer concerned with twentieth-century issues in "Wharton, Travel, and Modernity." Bentley investigates Wharton's love of mobility, evident in her incessant travel and embrace of technol-ogy, contrasted with her equally strong appreciation of reflective stillness, manifested in her cultivation of homes, gardens, and habits of writing. These contrary impulses, Bentley argues, frame Wharton's life. They also speak directly to the question of her modernism, addressing on the one hand her conservative misgivings about the erosion of traditional values and on the other hand her forward-looking attitudes about personal free-doms. In novels such as *The House of Mirth*, *The Custom of the Country*, *Twilight Sleep* (1927), and *The Children* (1928), Wharton subjects her characters to the increasing velocities of modern life—experienced through modes of transport such as trains, ocean liners, and automobiles—and to the risks of disaster that modern speed entails. These depictions of mobility index changes in family structures as well more global forces. Noting the irony that Wharton, wealthy enough to travel, was often blind to the effects of modern life on poor and colonized people, Bentley also observes that Wharton's imperialist impulses are more preservationist rather than expansionist, more aesthetic than political, and more aligned with European tradition than American progressivism. Perhaps herself decentered by the forces of modern life, Wharton hoped paradoxically for global access made possible by commercialized technology and for simultaneous resistance to the recklessness that such modern forces engendered.

The next two chapters direct attention to Wharton's participation in sister arts. In "Wharton and Art," Eleanor Dwight focuses on Wharton's keen sense of the visual and on the development of this aesthetic in her life and writings. Early on, Dwight explains, extensive travel in Europe nurtured Wharton's innate picture-making abilities, beginning a lifelong love of art, architecture, and landscape, especially French and Italian. Like many writers of her time, Wharton identified with traditional European, rather than American or modern, styles and forms. In novels beginning with *The Valley of Decision* (1902), she extols European art of the past and praises sensitive characters who find solace and inspiration in beauty around them. In other novels, *The Custom of the Country,* for example, she denigrates crude Americans, especially the nouveau riche, for bad taste, extravagance, and the inability to distinguish authentic from inauthentic art. Wharton's capacity to see the world as a series of pictures results in a signature arrangement of fictional elements. She frequently evokes spectacle, positioning characters amid others in revealing settings. In the tableau vivant scene in *The House of Mirth,* Wharton protests the objectification of women by representing Lily Bart as a work of art whose value is determined by viewers. In *The Age of Innocence,* in contrast, she depicts Ellen Olenska as an artist who creates her own life. Wharton also thematizes portraiture. "The Portrait," "The Moving Finger," and *A Son at the Front* (1923) explore relationships between outer and inner representations of self. Wharton's use of the visual, especially to portray character and setting, links her to artistic contemporaries such as John Singer Sargent and Walter Gay and helps to define her unique literary aesthetic.

In "Wharton and the Age of Film," film and literary critic Linda Costanzo Cahir analyzes Wharton's fiction in relation to cinematic art. She attributes the unusually large number of film and television adaptations of Wharton's work, beginning with the adaptation of her novel *The House of Mirth* in 1918, not to Wharton's immense literary and analytical powers, but to the fact that her strong linear narratives, upscale settings, and rounded, differentiated characters have broad commercial appeal. Cahir notes, however, that the complexities of Wharton's work are often compromised in the process of film translation. Such is the case in the 1929 adaptation of *The Children* (*The Marriage Playground*), which reduces the darker undertones of Wharton's novel about a middle-aged man's crush on a fifteen-year-old to a rompish comedy with a Hollywood happy ending. A 1990 release of *The Children* suffers from a common opposite problem, a deadening faithfulness to Wharton's text. Wharton's *The Old Maid* (1924), adapted in 1939, fares better. Filmmakers and censors negotiated topics of illicit sex and illegitimacy in this novella to produce a "women's film" that draws not only on the sentimental but also conveys the nuanced passion and repression so important in Wharton's work. Cahir also assesses recent box-office adaptations of Wharton's work: the visually beautiful *The Age of Innocence* (1993), which despite its opulence fails to achieve a wider import than that of ill-fated love story; the prosaic *Ethan Frome* (1993); and the intelligently composed and executed *The House of Mirth* (2000). Wharton's writings offer filmmakers challenges which, when met, result in films that both illuminate her texts and depart from them in rewarding ways.

Clare Colquitt addresses the extensive, rapidly growing body of work by and about Wharton in "Bibliographic Essay: Visions and Revisions of Wharton." She describes Wharton's development into a world-class novelist, beginning with the publication of her poems and short stories in the 1880s and her first novel, *The Valley of Decision,* in 1902, through the posthumous publication of her novel, *The Buccaneers,* in 1938. Wharton, Colquitt notes, had a long, successful career, highlighted by best-sellers such as *The House of Mirth* and *The Glimpses of the Moon* (1922) and the Pulitzer Prize-winning *The Age of Innocence.* Numerous in-print editions of her fiction and nonfiction testify to Wharton's stature; however, given her extraordinary achievements, it is "unfortunate"—one might add "astonishing"—that there is no complete edition of her work. Readers can consult useful primary and secondary bibliographies to acquaint themselves with Wharton, but there is need for an updated secondary bibliography, especially because so much material has been published in the past fifteen years. Wharton studies is thriving, Colquitt observes, citing not only books and articles about Wharton but also literary and visual adaptations of her work, the *Edith Wharton Review,* and the efforts of organizations such as the Edith Wharton Society and Edith Wharton Restoration. Biographers and critics continue to expand and revise our understanding of this remarkable writer, with approaches that range from formalist to cultural, from psychological to social, from traditional to feminist, deconstructive, and new historicist.

A historical emphasis gives scope and pattern to Edith Wharton's accomplishments. During her long life—seventy-five years—Wharton witnessed unprecedented social, economic, and political transformations at home and abroad. She experienced post–Civil War Reconstruction, the Gilded Age, the Progressive Era, World War I, the flapper decade, and the coming of World War II. A citizen with global as well as New York ties, Wharton immersed herself in issues of her day and produced fiction about the effects of change at all levels of society. She constantly sought new experiences through reading, writing, travel, and friendships, calling herself a "life-wonderer & adventurer"(L, 598). However, she also craved social and moral stability. As she put it, the most striking feature of being born into a world without "telephones, motors, electric light, central heating . . . X-rays, cinemas, radium, aeroplanes, and wireless telegraphy" was not the daily impact of innovation, but "a more vital change" "in national point of view" that led away from European tradition and culture. Concern over this cultural shift permeates Wharton's life and work, creating a tension between preservation and reform, between tradition and innovation. Wharton's multiple perspectives on history make her at once an "assiduous relic-hunter" of the past (*NW,* 781), an observant chronicler of the present, and a compelling voice for the future.

I thank Elissa Morris at Oxford University Press for her editorial acumen and support. I also thank T. Susan Chang for bringing me aboard the Oxford Historical Guides to American Authors series. My appreciation extends to Shari Benstock for encouragement, especially at early stages of the project, and to Susan Elizabeth Sweeney for insightful comments and review. I thank Ellie Dwight for providing photographs, some of which appear in her *Edith Wharton: An Extraordinary Life* (Abrams, 1994). Finally, I am grateful to fellow Wharton scholars, with whom my work is in constant dialogue.

Edith Wharton
1862–1937

A Brief Biography

Shari Benstock

Edith Newbold Jones, who became the writer Edith Wharton, was born on January 24, 1862, in her parents' New York City home, a spacious brownstone at 14 West Twenty-third Street, just off Fifth Avenue and the fashionable Madison Square. She entered a country divided by a war whose consequences would touch her own life and become part of her literary subject matter. Descended from Anglo-Dutch merchant families, she was born in a period of social, economic, and cultural transition. Her extended family was distinguished by its social status. The Joneses belonged to an elite group called the "society of birth"; George Frederic Jones and his wife Lucretia lived on inherited Manhattan real estate investments from the estates of George Frederic's father and grandfather. They created a life of ease for themselves, their family, and friends that included their civic and charitable responsibilities as members of the New York elite.

At the time of Edith's birth, the family divided their time between the New York City townhouse and their recently constructed Newport, Rhode Island, cottage. Lucretia oversaw a domestic staff of seven and participated in the social rituals expected of her class, which included making social calls, giving dinner parties, attending the opera, and supporting artistic and charity causes and church-sponsored events. George Frederic served on the boards of charitable associations—the Blind Asylum and the Insane Asylum—and Lucretia Jones conducted a sewing class during Lent that made goods for the poor (*Backward, NW,* 828). Edith was expected to follow her mother's example in accepting such responsibilities as a legacy of her social standing.

Edith's mother, Lucretia Stevens Rhinelander, was descended from prominent Anglo-Dutch families, but her personality and outlook were shaped by the financial hardship that dominated her teenage years. Her father, a dreamy young man with literary interests, did not manage his Long Island estates well, and after his premature death at age forty, his farms were managed even less well by his brother. Lucretia, the eldest of five children, became responsible for the care of her younger siblings and was subjected to the criticism of her demanding mother. The family's straitened circumstances meant that Lucretia came out into society in hand-me-down dresses and borrowed shoes, humiliations she remembered her entire life and compensated for after her marriage to George Frederic Jones. The phrase "keeping up with the Joneses" is said to have referred to George Frederic's family.[1] George Jones was forty-one years old when his daughter was born. His elder son, Frederic, was about to enter college; his younger son, Henry, was being tutored at home by a graduate of Cambridge University, a man rumored to be the baby's father. There is no confirming evidence of the truth of the story. Moreover, a second rumor, which circulated in Edith's middle years, purported that her real father was a Scotsman, Lord Brougham, chancellor of Edinburgh University at the time of her birth. The Joneses had met him during winter vacations in the south of France. With her red hair and lively intelligence, Edith did bear a marked resemblance to the old man. Although these stories were false, they suggest that Edith's mother was the subject of gossip, perhaps caused by jealousy of her social position. Lucretia took pride of place as *the* Mrs. Jones among a large family. The story may also have been at the expense of the rather ineffectual George Frederic.[2] In any case, Edith grew up to fear gossip and on occasion to be the focus of it. She distrusted her mother and loved her father. He became the model for many of her male characters, men with cultural interests but little ambition or desire to improve the world around them.

When Edith was four years old her parents, like many of their social class, left the United States for the continent in response to the economic depression that followed the Civil War. They rented their New York and Newport homes and traveled for six years in Europe (1866–1872), spending substantial time in Spain, Italy, France, and Germany. These years were formative for Edith, who between the ages of four and ten discovered the values, behaviors, languages, and aesthetic principles that would underwrite her art and her way of life. Her quick eye for geography, the line and scale of buildings, her attention to customs and the rhythms of daily life, became her standard of culture.

The family's return to New York in 1872 created in Edith a powerful reaction to the ugliness of the city, especially the brownstone houses and the ironwork of the city's industrial areas. The architectural confusion of the city depressed her, as did the mock-European chateaux erected by the newly rich, whose money was made in the thriving industries of transportation, mining, and construction. Lower Manhattan, where her seventeenth-century Anglo-Dutch ancestors had built their first homes, was now a thriving commercial center and busy entry point for immigrants, who would provide the skilled labor for America's industrial boom of the 1880s and 1890s and into the new century.

The transformation of New York City from a port town surrounded by lush farmland to a financial metropolis that attracted financiers, industrialists, real estate developers, and venture capitalists would provide Edith Wharton primary literary subject matter. Plotting the tensions between Old New York wealth, represented by her grandparents' generation, and the nouveau riche entrepreneurs of the West and Midwest, Wharton would chronicle the shifts in social structure and cultural values at the turn of the twentieth century.

In the 1870s and 1880s, Edith began a literary apprenticeship that constituted her primary education. Her father nurtured her literary interests, allowing free access to his "gentleman's library," the primary source of her early learning. Stretched out on the rug, she read volumes of history, philosophy, poetry, translations of classical texts, religious history, and medieval literature. These were the beginnings of her lifelong effort of self-education. The pleasures of reading, however, are recalled in her novels and stories, where books are stacked on tables alongside literary magazines, these scenes lit by a reading lamp. Reading is invoked in virtually every story and novel by Edith Wharton, a sign not only of her own love of reading but also of the importance of cultural literacy in her scale of values—values that she accords to her literary subjects.

Edith's mother, who had few literary interests but had grown up in a family that appreciated well-spoken English, encouraged accuracy of language. As a young child Edith delighted in making up stories, pacing the floor, a book in hand, as she made up the story aloud. When she was older, she wrote her fictions on sheets of brown parcel paper. One of these stories, written when Edith was eleven years old, was a domestic narrative that opened with a bit of dialogue: "'Oh, how do you do, Mrs. Brown?' said Mrs. Tompkins. 'If only I had known you were going to call I should have tidied up the drawing-room.'" Lucretia, who had a keen eye and ear for social behavior, remarked to her daughter: "Drawing-rooms are always tidy" (*Backward, NW,* 839). Heartless as the comment may seem, Lucretia Jones was teaching her daughter that social observation is based in accuracy of detail—a lesson Edith never forgot.

In "Life and I," a revealing memoir that remained unpublished in her lifetime, Edith recalled her fondness for her young "good little governess," Anna Bahlmann, who ignited her love for German literature, but who "never struck a spark" in response to the passion for learning in the young girl who hungered for knowledge (*NW,* 1089). Edith was befriended in this period by the rector of New Calvary Episcopal Church, where the Jones family worshiped. E. A. Washburn was a cousin of Ralph Waldo Emerson and had participated for many years in the New England group of intellectuals that included Bronson Alcott, Henry David Thoreau, and Margaret Fuller. Dr. Washburn's ideas of education for women were very different from the attitudes of Edith's parents. Rather than worrying that "bookishness" might compromise a young woman's marital possibilities, he believed learning was an asset in its own right. He gave his daughter a "gentleman's" education, hiring a German tutor for her.

Emelyn Washburn passed on to Edith the fruits of her learning. She introduced Edith to the works of German poet and philosopher, Johann Wolfgang von Goethe, to the Anglo-Saxon Icelandic sagas, and also tutored her in languages. Edith first read Dante's *Divine Comedy* with Emelyn on summer afternoons on the upstairs balcony of the Washburn home. Dr. Washburn encouraged Edith's desire to write professionally, suggesting that she begin with translation exercises. Together they chose a poem by Heinrich Karl Brugsch, *Was die Steine Erzählen* ("What the Stones Tell"). Edith prepared a translation that he approved, and they sent it off to a new literary magazine. It was printed over Emelyn's initials because Edith's parents did not want her name to appear in print, Old New York society following the custom that a woman's name appear in the newspaper only three times in her life—at birth, marriage, and death. In this single act of encouragement and activism, however, Dr. Washburn and his daughter showed Edith, who was then fifteen years old, that writing for publication was possible for a young woman of her social class. Edith's parents, who held Dr. Washburn in high regard, accepted his encouraging support of her work.

Edith's informal education contrasted markedly, however, with the educations that her father, brothers, and her future husband received. George Jones and his son Frederic graduated from Columbia College in New York City; Henry Jones was educated at Trinity College, Cambridge, England; and Edith's husband, Edward Wharton, was a graduate of Harvard University. Leading lives of leisure, these men did not practice professions, and one might conclude that they made little use of the educations they received. By contrast, Edith contributed to the advancement of arts and letters. Edith's niece, Beatrix Jones, daughter of Frederic, who also had no formal education, became an internationally known landscape architect. In her long career, she created welcoming spaces for reading and quiet thought on a number of American university campuses, including three prestigious academic institutions—Yale, Princeton, and the University of Chicago.

The direction of Edith's work as a social satirist is evident in much of her youthful writing. She evaluated the delicate distinctions between the surface of society and its background, often drawing on her own family history to evaluate changing social norms. She wrote her first satire, a novella entitled *Fast and Loose*, in 1876 at age fourteen under the pseudonym "David Olivieri." The story combines various modes of satire, effectively satirizing the literary genre itself. She appended to the story several mock literary reviews that disparaged the novel's literary methods, written in the style of the *Nation*, a noteworthy intellectual magazine that Edith probably first read in the Washburn household. *Fast and Loose* shows that even in her youth Edith had a distanced perspective on her work.

Although her parents did not want her to publish work under her name, they did arrange to have privately printed a small book of her poetry entitled *Verses* (1878). In this volume she again used the device of parodying or copying standard subjects and poetic forms as a way of analyzing poetic method. In 1880, she published five unsigned poems in the *Atlantic Monthly*, the most prestigious of American literary magazines of the period. A family friend had sent some of her poems to the aging poet, Henry Wadsworth Longfellow, stating that her work was "remarkable," not only because of her youth but also because, as he noted, her upbringing "in fashionable surroundings [was] little calculated to feed her taste for the Muses." Longfellow enclosed the poems with a letter of praise to William Dean Howells, then the editor of the *Atlantic*, and Howells printed them. Indeed, this recognition of Edith's writing skills was a remarkable event in her young life.[3] One effect of such praise was her increased striving to meet the highest literary standards of her day and increasing self-criticism when she felt that she had fallen short of the standards she set for herself. This struggle dominates her efforts to produce her first volume of short fiction, *The Greater Inclination* (1899), and the detailed historical research she undertook for *The Valley of Decision* (1902), her first novel.

In the late 1870s, the Jones family was occupied with the failing health of George Frederic. The financial markets in this period were volatile, and the effect of several market crashes had led to a collapse of real estate prices. Anxious about Edith's future and the diminishing family wealth, Lucretia advanced Edith's coming out party by almost two years to winter 1879, when Edith turned seventeen. The party was held at the home of friends, the guests including members of the extended family and friends of Edith's older brothers. Among the guests was Edward Robbins Wharton, a longtime associate of her brother Henry. Six years later Teddy would become Edith's husband.

In this period, George Frederic tried unsuccessfully to cover Lucretia's household expenditures and curb her desire to remodel and redecorate their New York and Newport homes. In 1881, his doctors recommended that he move to a warmer climate and the family went to the south of France, hoping that he might recover. When George Frederic died of a stroke in 1882, Edith was devastated. The only child at home, she became the companion to her mother, who, in the months following her husband's death, stopped attending church and became entirely dependent on her daughter.

During this period, Edith was courted by Harry Leyden Stevens, the twenty-three-year-old son of a widowed socialite, whose late husband had been a successful hotelier in Boston and New York City. Edith was about to marry "new money," and her mother and uncle approved the match. The young couple's wedding plans were announced in October 1882, and two months later were abruptly retracted for reasons that had to do with Mr. Stevens's inheritance. By the terms of his father's will, Mrs. Stevens had sole control of her son's property—estimated at more than one million dollars—until he married or reached the age of twenty-five. Mrs. Stevens forced her son's hand, but the gossip papers suggested that Edith's literary ambitions had thwarted the relationship. Dismayed by this turn of events and concerned that Edith's marriage possibilities would be compromised, Lucretia quickly took her to Europe. For Edith, the broken engagement and especially the public remarks about her literary interests, undermined her confidence. Three years later, Harry Leyden Stevens was dead of tuberculosis, and Edith was about to be married.

Between these two events, Edith met the man who years later she described as the love of her life. In summer 1883, during a stay at Bar Harbor, she met Walter Van Rensselaer Berry, a young lawyer who was her distant cousin. Their friendship bloomed, and while it appeared to their friends that he might ask for her hand in marriage, he did not propose. It was some years later that he took his place as her confidant and advisor. Along the way, he tried to justify his behavior by saying that in 1883 he was then just entering the law profession and had nothing to offer her. This was perhaps a lame excuse, given that he had considerable inherited wealth.

Lucretia wanted to see her daughter married and to someone who would be a good son-in-law to her. She was fond of Edward Wharton, who was thirteen years older than Edith, a man without substantial means and with no professional interests or ambitions. At the time of their marriage, he was living with his mother and maiden sister in the family home in Boston. Edith and Edward shared few interests, except their love for the outdoor life, but in some ways Teddy was a version of Lucretia's father, Frederic William Rhinelander. Affable and kindly with a sunny disposition, Teddy had traits that Lucretia valued. She described him as "sunshine in the house."[4] Given the sadness and loss of the past years, both mother and daughter appreciated Teddy's gentle humor and sincere concern for the happiness of both his fiancée and his mother-in-law to be. He proposed marriage to her in January 1885, and they were married in April.

There was a cloud over their prospective union, however. Teddy's father, William Craig Wharton, then in his seventies, was suffering from manic depression. He had been confined numerous times at McLean Hospital north of Boston because of his illness, and his erratic behavior and emotional states were well known to members of his Boston social circle. Concerned that his condition might be hereditary and pose a risk to the children Edith and Teddy hoped to have, Lucretia spoke with Teddy's mother about his illness. She was assured by the Wharton family physician that the risks she feared were improbable. Six years after their marriage, in May 1891, at age eighty, Mr. Wharton committed suicide in the McLean hospital.

Edith and Teddy were married in Trinity Church chapel, located across the street from the Jones home on Twenty-third Street, at noon on April 29, 1885. It was a small, "very quiet" wedding, according to the *New York Times,* the guest list limited to the immediate relatives of the two families. Having no money for a honeymoon, the couple went directly to Newport, settling into Pencraig Cottage, a little house on the Jones family estate that they rented from Lucretia for the next several years.

Edith was a nervous bride, wondering about the intimate side of married life. On her wedding eve, she shyly approached her mother with this question, only to receive a coldly dismissive response. Lucretia made reference to the sexual act by reminding her daughter of the differences in physiology between men and women as represented in statues in art museums. When Edith looked puzzled at this explanation, Lucretia accused her of false naiveté. This event, which caused an emotional paralysis in Edith around issues of sexuality in her marriage, had a variety of consequences: she and her husband had a companionate marriage without children; Lucretia did not have more grandchildren, as she had hoped. Edith did not experience sexual pleasure until more than twenty years later, when she had a clandestine affair in her mid-forties.

The Whartons established a domestic routine in Newport, in which they traveled in Europe from late winter to early spring and participated in Newport society in summer and fall. Three years after their marriage, they were invited by their friend James Van Allen on a four-month cruise of the Aegean, a voyage that opened Edith's eyes to the ancient world. Aboard the steam yacht *Vanadis,* they traced part of Odysseus's voyage home from Troy to Ithaca. Midway through the trip, Edith, then twenty-six years old, received a letter notifying her that she was to receive a substantial legacy from the estate of Joshua Jones, a second cousin of her father. The inheritance not only more than paid their costs but also gave Edith financial independence. The trip began in Algiers and traced an elongated loop in the Aegean. In total, they visited forty islands.

Edith equipped the yacht's library with books relevant to their itinerary. She included Villiers de Lisle Adam's writing on

Rhodes; Theophile Gautier's aesthetic treatises and travel accounts of the journey from Constantinople to Athens; and the Butcher and Lang translation of Homer's *Odyssey,* from which Edith read aloud after dinner by the light of a gas lamp. She recorded the trip in a diary, describing Greek and Roman amphitheaters, catacombs, temples, monasteries, hermitages and burial grounds, cities and small towns. On a few occasions, the three travelers entered places no Westerner had yet visited. Edith's diary, which constitutes the first of her travel writings, was for many years assumed lost or destroyed. Discovered in the library in Hyères, France, Wharton's Riviera home in the 1930s, it was published in 1992 under the title Wharton had originally given it, *The Cruise of the Vanadis.* In 1926, when she was sixty-four, Edith made the trip again on a rented steam yacht, taking with her a group of friends. This cruise lasted ten weeks, the group traveling as far as Alexandria, Egypt.

It was in the first years of marriage that Edith began to study the history of architecture, design, and house decoration. She quickly learned the language of architecture and articulated with precision the relation of form, balance, and proportion. Her primary tutor was art collector and connoisseur Egerton Winthrop, a widower who had returned to Newport in 1885 after a long residence in Paris. He systematized Edith's reading, taught her elements of literary analysis, discussed French literature and history with her, and introduced her to nineteenth-century scientific thought through the writings of Charles Darwin, Alfred Wallace, and Thomas Henry Huxley. She credited him as the first person that "taught my mind to analyze and my eyes to see" (*Backward, NW,* 855–56). Winthrop accompanied Edith and Teddy on two trips to Italy during these years and helped her really see Renaissance and *settecento* art and architecture in perspective.

From her childhood memories of Italian architecture, Edith's sense of design always incorporated the perspectives and proportions of Italy, effects that are evident in the remodeling of the house and grounds at Land's End, the Newport house she purchased in 1893, in the design of The Mount, the home she built in Lenox, Massachusetts in 1901, and in the two country homes she owned in France in the 1920s and 1930s. Her interest in house design led to the writing of her first book, *The Decoration of Houses* (1897), which she co-authored with Boston architect Ogden Codman. This work promoted classical European design as the model for American home design and decoration. Wharton and Codman argued for classical proportions and subtle details as an antidote to the design excesses of the "Gilded Age." The book found a new readership one hundred years later, when it was reprinted in 1997, during a similar period of affluence and exuberant bad taste in the United States.

Wharton's interest in house and garden design led her back to Italy in the first decades of the twentieth century, where she did research for two books. The first, *Italian Villas and Their Gardens* (1904), a text illustrated by artist Maxfield Parrish, examined the relationship of architecture to the surrounding landscape. The second book, *Italian Backgrounds* (1905), was the result of Wharton's travels through various areas of the country, including the Pennine Alps, Milan, and Tuscany. In this book, Wharton analyzes regional differences in art, design, and local customs. These works reveal important elements of her aesthetic approaches to both landscape and literature: she took in the world through her quick eye and finely tuned ear, then translated sight and sound into words, as if she were a visual artist. Her first published novel, which is informed by her long experience of Italy, provides a good example of this process.

The Valley of Decision (1902) is a historical work set in late eighteenth-century Italy in the time of struggle for democratic reform of the corrupted city-state system. The novel charts the life of a boy caught in the power struggles that characterized this tumultuous time. Wharton's abiding interest in history and her particular interest in Italian culture led her to this subject. She carefully set the local scenes that provide the background of the story and just as carefully created the characters that represent the social and political issues that carry the plot and meaning of the book. She was delighted when literary critics praised the authenticity of her narrative, comparing it favorably to *The Charterhouse of Parma* by French writer Stendhal, a novel that treats the same time period and similar subjects in France.

The Newport years constitute an intense period of Edith's literary apprenticeship. She was writing daily, mostly short stories, and organized her domestic life to accommodate her literary work, a practice she continued throughout her life. She wrote in the morning in her bedroom, her public life beginning at the luncheon hour. She wrote four of her most important pieces of short fiction in this period, stories with deeply personal subject matter reflected through psychological studies of her women characters. Living in a wealthy community already famous for its seaside mansions built by the newly rich, Edith was writing about poverty, loneliness, and emotional paralysis. The first story published under her name appeared in *Scribner's Magazine* (July 1891), when she was twenty-nine years old and was reprinted the following year in a Scribner's collection entitled *Stories of New York*. "Mrs. Manstey's View" is a seven-page sketch of a lonely woman living in a boarding house. Two years after its publication, Edith wrote a much longer work in a similar vein that did not appear in print until twenty-three years later because it was too long to be printed in a single issue of a literary magazine. When *Bunner Sisters* was finally published in the collection *Xingu and Other Stories* (1916), Charles Scribner's Sons paid her $2,000 for the story, the highest amount she had yet been paid for a novella. *Bunner Sisters*, a poignant novella of urban life, was perhaps drawn from scenes Edith witnessed in New York City in the early 1890s, when she purchased two narrow, adjoining houses on upper Park Avenue, an area that was not yet fashionable. Although she disliked the social whirl of the city, Edith needed its artistic and intellectual stimulation, especially theater productions, as well as its street life, which she observed on long walks and, in the 1890s, on bicycle rides.

"Mrs. Manstey's View" and *Bunner Sisters* are important not only because they analyze urban poverty but also because they reveal Wharton's narrative method: the sense of space, light, and architectural details of the settings are entryways to subject matter and the emotional content of the story. These elements are also the building blocks of the plot and resolution of the stories. In these two tales, dark rooms and narrow views onto the outside world symbolize the confinements of space and of mental and emotional liberty. They also, importantly, delineate the realities of life for women alone.

The best-known example of architectural metaphors for human experience among Wharton's fiction is found in "The Fullness of Life," a story written in 1891 and published in *Scribner's Magazine,* December 1895. Its source was Edith and Teddy's Easter week visit to Florence in the spring of their tenth wedding anniversary. In the tale, a woman dies, and when she meets the Spirit of Life in Paradise she admits that she has never experienced "that fullness of life which we all feel ourselves capable of knowing." In response to the spirit's question about her feelings for her husband, the woman offers an elaborate image, the most famous in all of Wharton's fiction:

> I have sometimes thought that a woman's nature is like a great house full of rooms: there is the hall through which everyone passes in going in and out; the drawing room, where one receives formal visits; . . . but beyond that, far beyond, are other rooms, the handles of whose doors perhaps are never turned; no one knows the way to them, no one knows whither they lead; and in the innermost room, the holy of holies, the soul sits alone and waits for a footstep that never comes. (*CSS,* 1:13–14)

"The Fullness of Life" is a highly layered text that opens to a variety of interpretations, but the central metaphor of the house as woman's nature reveals more of Edith Wharton's personal situation in these years than she wanted the public to know. She refused to let her publishers reprint the story in a collection, describing it as "one long shriek" (*L,* 36–37).

The fourth story of this crucial period of Edith Wharton's literary development is "The Lamp of Psyche," published in *Scribner's Magazine,* October 1895. The story's title is drawn from the myth of Cupid and Psyche; it portrays a wife's disillusionment with her second husband when her aunt, a Boston philanthropist, suspects that Delia Corbett's husband Laurence avoided military duty during the Civil War (1861–1866) and cannot explain either to himself or to his wife the reasons for his behavior. These revelations cause Delia to lose her "Ideal" of him.

This story, written in 1893, on the thirtieth anniversary of the National Conscription Act, represents Edith's effort to understand her father's behavior during the war. The 1863 act required men between the ages of twenty and forty-five to register for the military draft. George Frederic Jones, then age forty-two, did not register. On the first day of mandatory conscription, he was at his summer residence in Newport, Rhode Island, far from the anti-conscription riots led by German immigrants in lower Manhattan, who protested the law on the grounds of ethnic and class prejudice. As a gentleman, George Jones had little to fear by avoiding the draft; if caught, he would have paid a relatively modest fine, or he could have procured someone else to serve in his place for a fee of $1,000. Those who agreed to be mercenaries were usually immigrants or former prisoners.

By the time she wrote the story, Edith knew of the guilt Theodore Roosevelt, Sr., a member of her parents' social set, had suffered from his decision to buy a substitute who took his place in battle. His son, Theodore Roosevelt, Jr., a lifelong friend of Edith, also felt his father's shame and compensated for it in 1898 by resigning his post as assistant secretary of the navy and joining the cavalry forces in the Spanish–American War (1898–1899), to support the effort to remove Spanish dictators from Cuba. The other colonialist war of the period was the Boer War (1899–1902) in South Africa, a brutal conflict between British forces and Dutch settlers in the Transvaal and Orange Free State. These conflicts, which forecast the eventual end of European colonialism, received wide press coverage. But the news that rocked the European continent in summer 1899 was the announcement that a military court in France had court-martialed for a second time Alfred Dreyfus, a Jewish army captain, who in 1894 had been falsely convicted of treason for supposedly selling secrets to Germany. French novelist Emile Zola had a year earlier agitated for the trial and accused those who brought Dreyfus to trial of being the actual traitors. Charged with libel, Zola was forced to flee to England.

The news of the second court-martial, with mandatory imprisonment, sparked riots in France and its colonies, raised the profile of blatant anti-Semitism in the French military, and forecast the political climate that would lead to the holocaust and World War II. Edith and Teddy read the news of the trial while traveling in Italy with their friends Minnie and Paul Bourget. Edith felt the unspoken tensions between the Bourgets—Paul was an outspoken anti-Dreyfusard; his wife, who was Jewish, said little about the latest turn in a case that would have international import. It was not until 1906 that Dreyfus was fully exonerated. In 1906, in a ceremony at the courtyard of Napoleon's tomb, only a few blocks from the Whartons' Paris apartment, Dreyfus was reinstated into the French army and enrolled in the Legion of Honor, the highest honor the government could extend.

At the turn of the twentieth century, with the publication of the first of a dozen short story collections and her first novella, *The Touchstone* (1900), Edith Wharton was firmly established as a writer of short fiction, her work already acclaimed by critics on both sides of the Atlantic. The Whartons visited Paris in summer 1900, the year of the Paris International Exposition, a technology fair at which the Paris Metro system was officially opened to the public. Although Edith welcomed most forms of new technology, she did not attend the fair, which brought thousands of people to the city, or is it recorded that she ever used the Paris metro system. A thoroughly modern woman, she was enamored of motor cars, telephones, the telegraph, radio, gramophone and record player, high-speed transatlantic steamers, and paved roads. We do not know for certain whether she ever saw a movie, but several of her novels were produced in film versions. She did not fly in an airplane, but she was thrilled by Charles Lindbergh's 1927 nonstop transatlantic flight from Long Island, New York, to Le Bourget, France.

Edith's primary interest during summer 1900 was in Minnie Bourget's progress in translating Edith's story, "The Muse's Tragedy," the first of her works to appear in French. Edith was also working hard to finish *The Valley of Decision* (1902), the work that established her credentials as a writer of historical fiction. During her stay, Edith visited her bedridden mother, a duty Edith dreaded. Minnie Jones's divorce from Edith's brother in 1896 on the grounds of adultery had divided loyalties among family members. Her mother's death in June 1901 led to a challenge of Lucretia's will by Edith and her brother Henry. They successfully argued that Frederic had encouraged his mother to restrict Edith's inheritance as punishment for her siding with Minnie in the divorce. Although Edith won this legal battle, her niece Beatrix would challenge the will after Edith's death. The Jones family history was marked by bitterness, greed, self-interest, and favoritism—themes that appear frequently in Edith's writing.

In the early years of the new century, she began a friendship with Henry James, a literary and personal companionship that she regarded as the most important of her life. James, twenty years older than Edith and a longtime friend of Minnie Jones, had met her briefly some years earlier, but it was only when Edith was in her early forties that the friendship deepened. He encouraged her in various ways to explore what he called the "New York" subject, and by 1905, when *The House of Mirth* was serialized in *Scribner's Magazine,* Edith and Henry were already very good friends. Her critique of high society is represented by the fate of Lily Bart, the heroine of *The House of Mirth,* a woman who has been too long on the debutante circuit and gambles away her inheritance in a desperate effort to snare a rich husband. Compromising her reputation and encumbering her finances, Lily is abandoned by her nouveau riche friends and dies from an overdose of a sleeping potion.

This modern tragedy captured a readership that extended from the east to the west coasts. Within the first two weeks of publication, the book sold 80,000 copies. Edith Wharton and her heroine were literary celebrities. The novel was adapted for the theater by playwright Clyde Fitch and opened first at the Detroit opera house in autumn 1906 and later at the Savoy Theatre in New York City. New York critics pronounced it "too doleful" because Edith refused to rewrite the story and let Lily live.

By the time *The House of Mirth* reached the stage, Edith was trying to duplicate its literary success in *The Fruit of the Tree* (1907), a social reform novel that portrays class tensions in a New England mill town. The hoped-for financial and critical success did not arrive. A moralist who wore the label proudly, Edith

Wharton belonged to the tradition of French novelist Honoré de Balzac and English writer George Eliot (Mary Ann Evans), whose writings examined the social mores of the emerging middle class of the nineteenth century. *The House of Mirth* and *The Fruit of the Tree* represent two sides of Wharton's literary interests in relation to the Gilded Age, which was marked by great wealth and terrible poverty, the result of boom and bust economic cycles. Economic profiteering, common in the late nineteenth century, continued through World War I, when the United States prospered by its isolationist foreign policy. The European and American market collapse in the late 1920s resulted in an economic depression that was caused, in part, by the strict requirements of the 1919 Treaty of Versailles, requiring payment of war reparations by Axis nations.

The theme of financial security in relation to women's possibilities for independence emerges in Wharton's writing during this period, often linked to another primary subject in her writing, the consequences of cross-cultural marriages. Her 1907 novella, *Madame de Treymes,* is a study of an unhappily married American woman whose French husband agrees to a divorce only on the condition that she renounce her rights to custody of their son. Henry James, who was jealously following Edith's literary and financial successes in this period, thought the story was "beautifully done," but he warned her not to go too far with the Franco-American subject: "The real field of your extension is *here,"* by which he meant New York (*JWL,* 67).

By late 1907, Edith was reevaluating her relationship to Europe, in large part because she was falling in love with William Morton Fullerton, an American correspondent for the *Times* of London in Paris. She had met him the previous January, and sought his help in finding a publisher for a French translation of *The House of Mirth.* Their relationship lasted for more than three years. Only a few close friends knew of it. Among those was Henry James, a longtime friend of Fullerton. The love affair included a brief period of sexual passion in 1909, while Teddy Wharton was away from Paris on a rest cure for his manic depression. Throughout the relationship Edith planned day trips to villages nearby Paris in order to meet Fullerton privately. These romantic outings, documented in her diary and in letters to Fullerton, became part of the "romance of the motor car" that also underwrote her travel literature in this period.

In 1906 and 1907, she combined her love for the French countryside and her desire to write travel narratives into one of her most charming works, *A Motor-Flight Through France* (1908), a work that provided itineraries for three excursions that travelers can make even today. On the first trip, in March 1906, Teddy and Edith were accompanied by her brother Henry. Their itinerary circled from Boulogne on the north coast of France through the Seine valley to Nohant, the former home of French novelist George Sand, a writer Wharton greatly admired. On the second trip, in May 1907, Henry James, who had already explored western Massachusetts with the Whartons, was their guest on the longest journey they had yet made—more than 2,000 miles, from Paris to Poitiers, through the Pyrenées, and Provence.

Wharton and James were particularly taken with the Pyrenées. Edith jotted down her impressions of the passing countryside, taking note of changes in landscape and flora, and paying particular attention to architecture. Edith's visual memory, eye for detail, and fluency in the language of architecture make *A Motor-Flight* something more than a travel narrative. As in her works on Italian gardens and villas, she provided a cultural history of French life and the influences of the ancient world, for example, the layering of Greek and Roman cultures on modern life.

The third trip, an effort to raise Teddy's spirits as his illness became more pronounced, took place over Easter weekend in 1907 and was an exploration of northeast France, a region that Edith would later describe in her collection of World War I essays, *Fighting France, from Dunkerque to Belfort* (1915).

During the period from 1907 to 1911, the year she sold The Mount and separated from Teddy, Edith was restless, finding it increasingly difficult to endure the effects of her husband's illness, worried that Fullerton was seeing other women during her absences from Paris (concerns that were valid), and torn between her American subject matter and her desire to live permanently in Europe. Her novel *The Reef* (1912) treats the complexities of family and romantic loyalties. This is her most intellectual novel and one of two works in which she constructs a heroine most like herself (the other is Ellen Olenska in *The Age of Innocence*). By the time *The Reef* was published, Edith had ended her affair with Fullerton, had decided to divorce Teddy after twenty-eight years of marriage, and had renewed her longtime friendship with Walter Van Rensselaer Berry, who moved his law practice from Washington, D.C., to Paris after her divorce. He would be her traveling companion and closest friend until his death in 1927. In 1913, she published *The Custom of the Country*, generally considered a highly cynical estimation of social mores. She was fifty-one years old and on her own for the first time in her life.

Intellectually and emotionally starved in the long years of her marriage, Wharton sought out friendships among a wide range of people in diverse fields—politics, creative arts and design, publishing, and the academy. Friends from her early adulthood, when she was trying to redress the inadequacies of her home tutoring, included American professors and intellectuals Charles Eliot Norton, Harvard professor of aesthetics and the translator of Dante's *Divine Comedy*, and his colleague historian Barrett Wendell. Her Newport and Lenox, Massachusetts friends included connoisseurs James Van Allen, Egerton Winthrop, and literary editor Richard Watson Gilder. In England, her group included Henry James, Percy Lubbock (who became her first biographer), art historian Kenneth Clark, art connoisseur Bernard Berenson and his wife Mary, and Cambridge University tutor Gaillard Lapsley, a specialist in English medieval history, a field of particular interest to Edith. Her women friends included Elisina Tyler, who was crucial to the success of Edith's efforts on behalf of refugees in World War I, Margaret Terry Chanler, whom she had known since childhood, and her sister-in-law, Mary Cadwalader Jones, Elizabeth Cameron, and Elizabeth and Sara Norton.

In her later years, Edith Wharton cultivated friendships with younger writers, including novelist Aldous Huxley, cultural historian Cyril Connolly, and French writer André Gide, all of whom frequented the south coast of France, where Wharton then lived.

In 1913, Edith hoped to create an entirely new life for herself and was seriously considering the purchase of a country house in England. Before she could realize these desires, German forces invaded Belgium in August 1914. Within days Edith Wharton was organizing relief efforts from Paris. Over the next four years she created hostels, schools, workrooms, and various supporting services for women and children refugees. She made public appeals for financial support, raising funds from wealthy friends in New York, Newport, and Philadelphia. Her first war book, *Fighting France* (1915), was drawn from her visits to the western front to deliver food and hospital supplies. She also edited *The Book of the Homeless* (1916), a collection of stories, essays, and poems illustrated by a group of international artists.

This work was intended to raise the consciousness of Americans to the devastating effects of the war on the civilian populations in Belgium and France. It was sold as a gift item for the Christmas season, and the original art and literature included in it were auctioned in New York City as a fundraiser for relief organizations. Wharton's friend, former president of the United States, Teddy Roosevelt, commiserated with her in her outrage at U.S. isolationist policy that forbade American participation in the war. Although Edith did not renounce her citizenship in response to American policy on the war, as did Henry James, who took British citizenship in 1915, the year before his death, she took every opportunity in the American press to describe the effects of the war. Her efforts on behalf of refugees from the invaded regions began within days of Germany's assault on Belgium and continued even beyond the end of the war.

In the first years of the war, she worked with Charles du Bos, translator of *The House of Mirth*, and writer André Gide in creating the "Foyer Franco-*Belge*, a clearing house for refugees. With another group of friends, Edith established the "American Hostels for Refugees," which began its work with $250 cash, three donated houses, and some furniture, but soon included a free clinic and medical dispensary, a restaurant, and a clothing depot. Edith Wharton was the primary fundraiser in these enterprises, raising $100,000 in the first five months of the war. She also created workrooms (*ouvoirs*) in which Belgian women made lingerie and knitted goods that were sold in the United States to raise further money for refugees. A crucial part of Wharton's work was the establishment of schools for Belgian children. In addition to the standard curriculum, girls learned traditional lace making and boys were schooled in trades. During the years of the stalemated war, Wharton focused her energies on containing the spread of tuberculosis, which had infiltrated the military. In summer 1916, she established her third charity, the Maisons Américaines de Convolescences, rest homes for tubercular patients. Wives and children of ill soldiers returning from the battle regions were trained to recognize the symptoms of tuberculosis and to practice hygienic measures to prevent its spread in the family. By 1917, Wharton and her American colleagues were managing twenty-one hostels and rest homes in Paris and outlying regions.

Despite these administrative and supervisory responsibilities, Edith continued to write fiction. In winter 1915, she returned in her imagination to the rural beauty of western Massachusetts to write *Summer* (1917), a love story that reverses the contrasts in season and sensation to the frigid New England setting of her earlier story *Ethan Frome* (1911). *Ethan Frome* was written in Paris as an exercise for her French tutor in 1909. It is a story of doomed love and frozen emotions. Despite the sensuality and lyric beauty of *Summer,* it is less well known than *Ethan Frome,* primarily because in the mid-1930s *Ethan Frome* became part of the literature curriculum in American high schools, where it held a firm place for several decades. The tragic circumstances that destroy the possibility of happiness for young Mattie Silver and the unhappily married Ethan have historically been interpreted through the lens of American Puritanism: infidelity is a sin, and those who indulge in it must suffer. By contrast, *Summer* is a story of sexual awakening that does not deny social responsibility but also does not punish its lovers. The emotional arc of this tale is figured by the landscape itself—the long vistas over the hillsides, the fragrance of wild flowers, and the heat of the sun. These scenes in memory contrasted dramatically with the devastation of the muddy, pitted, and scarred battlefields of northern France. The destruction of the French countryside was for Wharton one of the most distressing elements of the war. In a 1915 letter to Henry James, she described the surroundings of an emergency medical facility near Verdun, where she delivered food and supplies:

> a hamlet plunged to the eaves in mud, where beds had been rigged up in two or three little houses, a primitive operating-room installed, etc. Picture this all under a white winter sky, driving great flurries of snow across mud-&-cinder-coloured landscape, with the steel-cold Meuse [river] winding between beaten poplars . . . poor bandaged creatures in rag-bag clothes leaning in doorways, & always, over & above us, the boom, boom, boom of the guns on the grey heights to the east. It was Winter War to the fullest. (*L,* 351)

It was only at the end of the war that Wharton could begin to analyze the meaning of its enormous consequences for the future of Western society and culture. She wrote two war novels, *The Marne* (1918) and *A Son at the Front* (1923). These stories reveal her belief that the future of civilization was at stake in the war. Neither of these books was enthusiastically received by critics because there was a prevailing prejudice that women could not write authoritatively about the war because they served as noncombatants.

Wharton's relief work during the war left her exhausted and eager to leave Paris for the countryside north of Paris, where she bought a small estate, St. Brice-sous-forêt. She was fifty-seven years old when the Treaty of Versailles was signed and had suffered two heart attacks caused by emotional stress and bouts of pneumonia occasioned by absence of adequate heat during the winters.

Wharton's decision to write of the past rather than the present was based on her desire not only to provide a record of a lost period in American culture but also to contrast the values of an earlier American culture against those of the postwar period. She turned to early nineteenth-century subjects in *The Age of Innocence* (1920), which won the Pulitzer Prize in 1921, and a collection of four novellas, *Old New York* (1924), that represents Edith's parents' generation.

She developed a technique in *The Age of Innocence* that allowed her to treat themes of infidelity, greed, and cold-heartedness within the framework of a historically distant time period that appears to be simpler than contemporary life. The *Old New York* tales are organized chronologically, beginning with "False Dawn," set in the 1840s. This story recounts a version of her parents' courtship and the good luck of a poor bride to marry for love and fall into wealth as well. "The Old Maid," set in the 1850s, unravels a dark story of unwed pregnancy in which the birth mother is forced to play the role of a maiden aunt. The two other stories in this collection treat women's economic dependence on their husbands and a child's first glimpse of deception through lies. Rather than being shocked by this subject matter, the reading public found these stories quaint and nostalgic.

The Age of Innocence recreates a world bound by form and convention. Edith wrote the novel in seven months, drawing freely on memories of her family and friends, mixing and matching their qualities and life experiences as needed. The three principal characters are Newland Archer, a man of leisure from an Old New York family of high standing; his fiancée (and later his wife) May Welland, a girl of the same social set; and May's cousin, Ellen Mingott, a woman in her late twenties unhappily married to a Polish count, who has returned from Europe to create a simpler life in the New York of her friends and family.

The subject and shape of the story echo Wharton's 1907 novella *Madame de Treymes*. The plot of *The Age of Innocence* is predictable, in that Newland and Ellen fall in love. He is drawn to her European ways (for example, her decision to live in an "artistic" district of the city and entertain men in her home without a chaperon) that shocks Old New Yorkers. The novel contrasts European and American customs, creates smoldering passion between the two principal characters, but does not deliver the predictable ending in which Ellen and Newland would elope together. The moral of this story is that there is no space for illicit love within the bounds of a society such as New York of the 1870s.

The novel was serialized in *The Pictorial Review* magazine, which paid $18,000 for serial rights. When published in book form, *The Age of Innocence* sold 115,000 copies in the United States,

Canada, and Great Britain. That the Pulitzer Prize would go to Edith Wharton was not at all a "given," despite sales and excellent reviews of the book. Its primary competition was Sinclair Lewis's *Main Street*, a novel of middle America. The prize was awarded through Columbia University; no record of the committee vote was made public; and we do not know how many votes were cast for *The Age of Innocence*. Sinclair Lewis considered himself robbed of the prize, and Edith Wharton became the first woman to receive the Pulitzer Prize in fiction.[5]

Edith initially took the prize lightly, as if unaware of its prestige. But this recognition and the popular success of the novel—which was adapted for the New York stage in 1928, starring Katherine Cornell, and also made into three separate films in the 1920s and 1930s—encouraged Wharton to turn again to modern topics, the analysis of contemporary life that had always been her primary subject matter. In particular, she needed to find a way to update her critique of the Gilded Age society of the 1890s and 1910s for the post-war world. The best example of this strategy is *The Glimpses of the Moon* (1922), a novel of modern marriage in which the young couple pledge themselves to absolute honesty in the relationship but find themselves "tripped up by obsolete sensibilities and discarded ideals," as Wharton explained to Bernard Berenson.[6] Susy Branch and Nick Lansing were 1920s versions of Lily Bart and Lawrence Selden from *The House of Mirth*, and Wharton hoped that the novel would be as successful as the earlier story had been. Her wish came true. The 1920s spirit of the story made it a runaway best-seller, selling 60,000 copies in three weeks and garnering a $15,000 film contract from Warner Brothers studios. The silent film version of the novel, starring Bebe Daniels and David Powell, opened in the United States to enthusiastic reviews. Wharton herself never saw the film, although she learned from friends that it was of high quality. English writer Somerset Maugham considered adapting *Glimpses of the Moon* for the theater, a plan that did not materialize and that Wharton was skeptical about from the outset. She considered "updating" *The Age of Innocence* by tracing the contemporary life of Dallas Archer, an idea she quickly abandoned.[7]

In the 1920s, Wharton commanded top prices for her short stories. Her novels were serialized in popular magazines such as *The Delineator*, which was owned by the Butterick sewing pattern company, and *The Pictorial Review*, both of which paid "top dollar." *The Pictorial Review* paid $18,000 to serialize *Glimpses of the Moon* in their magazine and also paid $27,000 for a sequel to this novel. Including the Warner Brothers contract and allowing for inflation, she earned $600,000 on *Glimpses of the Moon* prior to any royalty payments from book sales and in the absence of any written proposal from Wharton as to what the subject of the "sequel" to the novel would be.

From 1922, when she was sixty-two, until 1936, the year before her death, Edith Wharton wrote faster and worked harder than ever in her career, earning literally millions of dollars at today's rates. Rutger Jewett, her editor at Appleton, successfully placed her fiction in magazines—*The Woman's Home Companion* and *The Ladies' Home Journal*, among other women's magazines. In 1927, Wharton fulfilled contracts to the *Pictorial Review* and *Delineator* magazines that netted her $132,000, the equivalent of almost two million dollars today. Wharton never retreated from controversial subject matter. Against the prevailing norms of her generation, she explicitly revealed the price women pay through their bodies as they try to meet society's standards of beauty and sensuality. Her fiction exposes the greater psychological and intellectual costs to women in societies that restrict their development and freedom of expression. These themes, first announced in her early fiction—*The House of Mirth* and *The Fruit of the Tree*—formed the core of her thematic interests. *The Reef* (1912) and *The Mother's Recompense* (1925) examine the dangers and rewards for women who act on their desire for self-fulfillment.

Edith Wharton's writing of the mid to late twenties set a new standard of moral outrage as she satirized the irresponsibility and self-indulgence of the rich. *Twilight Sleep* (1927) treated the then controversial practice of anesthetizing women in childbirth. *The Children* (1928) tells the story of divorce and child abandonment among the newly rich. Some critics objected to this broad satire of modern life (as they had to the "cynicism" of *The Custom of the Country* in 1913), but a retrospective analysis of *The Children* reveals Edith Wharton to be a vigilant social historian and

careful observer of human behavior who paid particular attention to the changing customs of everyday life. The book was a
huge commercial success, a Book-of-the-Month club selection,
and was made into a Paramount movie entitled *The Marriage
Playground,* starring Fredric March.

Wharton's financial success in this period is reflected in her expansive lifestyle, which included the additional purchase of a
chateau in Hyères on the Mediterranean. She divided her time
between her two residences, taking her entire staff with her, a
group that included a butler, chauffeur, housekeeper, gardener,
several maids, and a secretary who typed her manuscripts and at-
tended to business items. In Hyères, she often had guests who
stayed for weeks at a time, but her writing schedule never varied:
she wrote in the mornings, walked through her gardens before
lunch, and took motor excursions in the afternoon. This daily
routine allowed the balance of activities so important to her creative work and prevented the loneliness and isolation that writers
often experience.

This period of Wharton's writing reveals the extensive range
of her literary interests and abilities. *The Mother's Recompense*
(1925), a text that examines the emotional price of motherhood,
explores a theme she had analyzed in *The Reef* and more recently
in *A Son at the Front* (1923). She completed a collection of essays
on literary technique, *The Writing of Fiction* (1925), in which she
traces the history of literary method in the English novel and
contrasts the experimentalism of Modernist writing with "classic" styles and subjects. This work, unique in her oeuvre, was
suggested by her Appleton editor Rutger Jewett but was serialized in *Scribner's Magazine* and published in book form by Scribner's. The reference points of this text are nineteenth-century
English and French writers who influenced her own writing and
whose works filled her library shelves—Honoré de Balzac, Gus-
tave Flaubert, Jane Austen, George Eliot, George Meredith, and
Henry James.

The 1920s and early 1930s was the age of acclaim for Edith
Wharton. In 1923, she was the first woman to receive an honorary degree in letters from Yale University, an award arranged
by Beatrix Farrand and her husband Max, who was a member of

the Yale Law faculty. Wharton made her final trip to the United States, after an absence of ten years from her native country, to receive the honor. In 1925, she became the first woman to be awarded the gold medal for literature from the American National Institute of Arts and Letters and in 1926 was elected to the Institute, as its first female member. In 1927, she was nominated for the Nobel Prize for literature for lifetime achievement in literature. She had little hope of receiving the coveted prize, but she was thrilled by the nomination, which was arranged by her longtime friend Robert Woods Bliss, then ambassador to Sweden. In 1929, she was inducted into the American Academy of Arts and Letters, her accomplishments defined by the category "special distinction in literature." In 1930, she entered the American Academy, the second woman to be inducted.

Edith Wharton's energy in the 1920s did not flag, despite the onset of health problems. She produced five volumes of short stories between 1926 and her death. Between 1929 and 1932, she published two large, linked "epic" novels that discuss issues of creativity. *Hudson River Bracketed* (1929) is a story of love for one's profession, in which Wharton uses the architecture and scenery of upstate New York, where her ancestors had built country estates, to capture the emotion of her theme. She repeats a method that worked well in *Summer*, allowing architecture and landscape to reveal human psychology. *The Gods Arrive* (1932), a novel of a young New York writer's growth, employs a familiar technique in Wharton's fiction, in which aspects of her own self are infused into a character of the opposite sex. Neither of these novels was well received in their time, perhaps because their subject was the commitment to a profession rather than to family or a love relationship.

In the early 1930s, Edith Wharton's health began to fail. Her expansive lifestyle, however, required that she keep writing to support herself and her domestic staff and to provide for her former sister-in-law, Minnie Jones, who depended on Edith and Beatrix for financial support. Edith's income, like that of most Europeans and Americans, was diminished by the global economic depression, and she had difficulty paying taxes on her properties. Publishing houses and magazines could no longer pay the sums for serial rights and advance contracts on literary royalties that she had been accustomed to receiving, but some of this loss was made up by payments of film rights to her works and receipts from the New York theater production of *The Old Maid*, which won the Pulitzer Prize for drama in 1935, and the Philadelphia production of *Ethan Frome*, starring Raymond Massey and Ruth Gordon as Ethan and Mattie.

Edith's autobiography, *A Backward Glance* (1934), received praiseworthy reviews but slow sales, and *The Ladies' Home Journal* was forced to decrease its contract price for the serial rights. When Henry Paine Burton, editor of *Cosmopolitan*, rejected Edith's asking price of $50,000 for serial rights to her novel *The Buccaneers* (left incomplete at her death), offering instead a $1,000 option on the work, she was outraged. She wrote Jewett: "I have never before been treated as a beginner, and I do not like it."[8] She put her hopes in the possibility of a London tour of *Ethan Frome* and continued work on *The Buccaneers*, a story set in the mid-1800s, in which rich American entrepreneurs marry their daughters to land-poor English aristocrats, in effect trading money for titles.

In February 1934, as she worked at the new novel, Edith listened to her "wireless" in Hyères for the latest information on the Paris riots in which fascists and communists battled in the streets. Like many others, she feared civil war and declined to leave France to accept an honorary degree in literature from Columbia University. By 1936, Spain was engulfed in civil war between the forces of dictator Francisco Franco and the socialist loyalists. Germany was arming for war under the leadership of Adolf Hitler, who was making overtures to the fascist leader of Italy, Benito Mussolini. Like many of her social class, Wharton was more frightened of Communism following the Bolshevik revolution in 1917, with its enforced appropriation of personal property, than of fascism. In the last years of her life, during the period that France was governed by the socialist party of Léon Blum, Wharton worried that her literary earnings and possibly her real estate might be taken from her. These fears never became reality, but they did have dilatory effects on her psychological state. Clearly, Europe was headed for another world war, and she, like others of her generation who had lived through the 1914–1918 world war, believed that she would not survive the rigors of another conflict of such scale.

By December 1936, in the last months of Edith Wharton's life, Madrid was under siege, and Italy and Germany were giving support to Franco's troops. German troops occupied the Rhineland and the Ruhr valleys. Nazi violence in Austria presaged Germany's annexation of that country. In Germany, Hitler was enforcing laws against Jews and other "non-Aryan" groups. Writer Thomas Mann, along with ninety other Germans, was deprived of his citizenship and forced to flee to Switzerland. As all this was happening, Edith presided over the last meeting of the Sainte Claire Christmas club, a group of her closest friends who gathered yearly at her Riviera home for the holiday. In the months ahead, she suffered a series of small strokes. In June, while visiting architect Ogden Codman at his French villa, where they were planning to revise and update their 1897 book *The Decoration of Houses,* Edith suffered a heart attack from which she could not recover. She died at Pavillon Colombe in St. Brice-sous-forêt on August 7, 1937, and was buried at the Cimetière des Gonards, Versailles, nearby the grave of her lifelong friend Walter Berry, who had died in 1927. She was buried with all the honors of a war hero and a chevalier of the Legion of Honor.

Her death received attention in the international press both for her literary achievements and for her World War I work. Scholars and literary critics praised the beauty of her writing style and her success in providing through her works a historical analysis of American life that encompassed a century, from her parents' youth in the 1830s to the Great Depression of the 1930s. For almost thirty years after her death, Wharton's work was overlooked, and many of her works fell out of print. In the 1970s, with the advent of second-wave feminism and the founding of Women's Studies programs in colleges and universities, her work captured the interest of a new generation of students and scholars interested in her social critique of American mores.

Today, Edith Wharton is considered by literary scholars in the United States and Europe to be one of the most important writers and cultural critics of the twentieth century. Students in schools and universities study her writings, her novels and stories attract new readers among the general public, and scholarly investigations of her life and work continue to open new perspectives on the period in which she lived and the subject matter of her literary and critical writing.

NOTES

1. Shari Benstock, *No Gifts from Chance: A Biography of Edith Wharton* (New York: Scribner's, 1994), 26.

2. The rumor that Edith Wharton's father was Lord Brougham was spread by her friend Ogden Codman (Benstock, *No Gifts from Chance*, 377).

3. Benstock, *No Gifts from Chance*, 39.

4. Emelyn Washburn to Elisina Tyler, 8 December [1938], Benstock, *No Gifts from Chance*, 482 n.6.

5. Benstock, *No Gifts from Chance*, 364.

6. Ibid., 369.

7. Ibid., 371.

8. Ibid., 439.

WHARTON IN
HER TIME

Wharton's Women

In Fashion, In History, Out of Time

Martha Banta

Nothing Changed but the Fashions

This could well be the heading Edith Wharton might attach to her own "Historical Guide." As someone in Wharton's 1925 novel, *The Mother's Recompense,* observes about plans for a proposed wedding, "with the cut of everything changing every six months, there's no use in ordering a huge trousseau . . . whatever people say, it *is* more satisfactory to get the latest models on the spot" (*NW, 697*). This is the situation that numbs the heart of the heroine, Kate Clephane, the woman most affected by "the latest models" for marriage whose cut seems to be "changing every six months."

Look in vain for a Whartonian guide to laws regarding woman's suffrage, to references to women entering male-bound professions, or to the rise of female enrollments into institutions of higher learning. *Those* markers by which women defined their march through history between the 1840s and 1930s are absent from Wharton's pages. Her life and writings offer excellent notations on the ways in which women are affected by historical events, material changes, and shifts in social and legal matters, but her true subject is Time, not History. History provides the subtext and necessary background for her tales, but the alterations upon which historians concentrate come to Wharton's readers by means of subtle, oblique narrative references, reflected, as it were, in mirrors or by glimpses of city streets out distant windows. Wharton's imagination takes responsibility for recording the psychological relations between past, present, and future that impose themselves on the nerves and heartstrings of the women who populate her fictional world.

It is not frivolous, therefore, to claim that Edith Wharton viewed women's fashion as one of the more important markers by which she traced shifts in the social habitus occupied by her fictional characters in the final decades of the nineteenth century and the first three decades of the twentieth century. The clothes with which her female protagonists adorn themselves *speak* (a crucial term in this essay) to *where they are.* That is, where they are in relation not only to the physical geographies mapped by prevailing social strictures, but also to chronologies experienced by three generations of women on the move through history.

In certain instances, the chronicles of dress that Wharton transcribed testify to the ambiguous status accorded to women by the freaks of fashion. Think of the confusion felt by Mrs. Lidcote in Wharton's 1916 tale, "Autre Temps . . . ," about a woman cast out by her "set" for having left her husband to go off with her lover.[1] As she sits on the deck of the *Utopia* which is bringing her back to America after a twenty-year exile in Italy, she listens to "two lively young women with the latest Paris hats on their heads and the latest New York ideas in them." She cannot tell from the hats she sees or the ideas they express

> whether they were married or unmarried, "nice" or "horrid," or any one or other of the definite things which young women in her youth and her society, were conveniently assumed to be. . . . But in the present fluid state of manners what did anything imply except what their hats implied—that no one could tell what was coming next? (*CSS*, 2:259)

On other occasions, Wharton pressed the point that fashions do more than confuse the onlooker; costumes erase the unique personalities of their wearers. On board yet another ocean liner (traversing the neutral zone between France and America), the narrator in "The Temperate Zone" of 1924 eyes a handsome young couple. The woman "had the air of wearing her features, like her clothes, simply because they were the latest fashion, and not because they were a part of her being. Her inner state was probably a much less complicated affair than her lovely exterior." Strolling nearer, the narrator receives an answer to "what the Olympian lovers in fashion plates found to say to each other"— such as "I haven't seen my golf clubs since we came on board" and "I do hope Marshall's brought enough of that new stuff for my face" (*CSS*, 2:458).

Wharton was too shrewd to make the mistake of automatically equating the wearing of the newest fashions with the living of superficial lives, but like Gertrude Stein, Wharton knew the validity of studying the surfaces upon which women reside.[2] Whereas the obtuse among Wharton's fictional characters are misled by the outer look of the women they eye, the more alert pay close attention to the clues clothing offers to a woman's inner nature. As for the readers of Wharton's fictions, it is essential to let her tutor them in the ways that current fashions show laws at work in each particular social moment and propel Wharton's women toward either good endings or ill.

The "Josephine look" of the dark blue velvet gown, "rather theatrically caught up under her bosom by a girdle with a large old-fashioned clasp," in which Ellen Olenska first appears in the opening scene of *The Age of Innocence* (1920) is deemed "unusual" by members of Old New York society (*N*, 1021). It brings "a rush of indignation" to Newland Archer when he sees May Welland, his betrothed, dressed all in white, with "a modest tulle tucker fashioned with a single gardenia," seated next to a woman who is causing unseemly "excitement" in a social set for whom "excitement," together with "the unusual" and "the unpleasant," are not terms with which ladies of the mid-1870s ought to be associated (*N*, 1024, 1019, 1021, 1094). On the one hand, Ellen's gown, styled à la Josephine, and seemingly made doubly out-of-date by the presence of an "old-fashioned clasp," harkens back to the earliest days of the nineteenth century. On the other hand, Ellen's gown is shockingly new in that it not only anticipates the scandalous look projected by John Singer Sargent's portrait of Mme. Gautreau of 1884, but also approximates the neo-Directoire fashions Paul Poiret introduced in 1908.[3] Ellen Olenska's personality as imaged by her attire can be called "retro avant-garde," according to what is now in vogue at *Vogue* and other fashion journals. She is a woman whose look draws inspiration from the past and calls attention to itself in ways unacceptable to the present standards of New York society, yet will find approval at a future time authorized by Parisian high society.[4]

Archer is drawn to Ellen by the very fact that she does not fit "the times," whose regulations are laid down by his class. He is entranced when he sees her attired in a robe that comes straight out of a "portrait by the new painter, Carolus Duran, whose pictures were the sensation of the Salon." In his New York, "it was usual for ladies who received in the evenings to wear what were called 'simple dinner dresses': a close-fitting armour of whaleboned silk, slightly open in the neck, with lace ruffles filling in the crack, and tight sleeves with a flounce uncovering just enough wrist to show an Etruscan gold bracelet or a velvet band." Ellen—"heedless of tradition" as codified by Fifth Avenue society—"was attired in a long robe of red velvet bordered about the chin and down the front with glossy black fur. . . . There was something perverse and provocative in the notion of fur worn in the evening in a heated drawing-room, and in the combination of a muffled throat and bare arms; but the effect was undeniably pleasing" (*N,* 1099). Although Archer knows what he *should* be seeing, he is fascinated by the sight of a woman in a fashion that is, by Old New York standards, both out of place and ahead of the times.

The Age of Innocence uses a number of devices to indicate the nature of changes in the status of women over the span of the novel's narrative time (from the mid-1870s to the early 1900s). Women's fashions are but one of the ways Wharton's readers, along with Archer, discover that Ellen is "different" and May Welland is not; but Wharton did not consider this way a negligible one. Lawrence Selden in Wharton's 1905 novel, *The House of Mirth,* senses that the clothes Lily Bart wears make it difficult to know her—the sign of a woman who is "different." When Selden assumes the spectator's protective self-detachment, he enjoys the "luxurious pleasure" of her dress and appearance. Although Lily may stand out "from the herd of her sex" because of the success of her calculated artifice, she is not a disturbance to him as long as he can categorize her as yet another example of the society creature of "vulgar clay" glazed over by "beauty and fastidiousness." He becomes troubled at moments when he wonders if she might be a special case, a woman whose true "material was fine" (*N*, 5). Later, Selden sees Lily representing Reynolds's portrait of "Mrs. Lloyd" in the *tableaux vivants* at the Welly Brys, attired in "pale draperies" that heighten "the long, dryad-like curves that swept upward from her poised foot to her lifted arm." He is suddenly overwhelmed by the feeling "that for the first time he seemed to see before him the real Lily Bart, divested of the trivialities of her little world." The perspective of that world, which causes Ned Van Alstyne to gloat over Lily's figure yet sneer at her exhibitionism, angers Selden since he perceives "the whole tragedy of her life" that interprets her "difference" in terms "cheapened and vulgarized" (*N*, 142). Unfortunately, the "whole tragedy" of Lily's life and death will be sealed by the fact that Selden keeps wavering between the comfort of believing she is just like all the others in her set and the troubling responsibility of treating her as a woman of exceptional worth.

As an author who applied her social criticism to historical events spanning almost four generations, Wharton was particularly careful to trace the time-lines that separate generations. The fashions worn by daughters and by mothers help suggest that the gains and losses in personal power are fixed and compelled by the other markers of history that write themselves into our consciousness.

Wharton knew what clothes have to tell us. Lily Bart's first slow dip down the social ladder comes when she admits with a sigh to Gus Trenor, "I have had to give up Doucet [dresses]; and bridge too—I can't afford it" (*N*, 86). Wharton's own complex psychological narratives, absorbed as they are with recording History's impact on women's lives, are layered by additional subtexts devoted to the timeless effects of Time's vagaries. In the introduction Wharton prepared for the 1936 edition of *The House of*

Mirth, she fends off possible objections to the fact that she "dated" her characters by "an elaborated stage-setting of manners, furniture and costume" keyed to the early 1900s. Proudly announcing that "the book still lives," Wharton continues: "Of course bustles and leg-o'-mutton sleeves date! . . . Everything dates in a work of art, and should do so; and to situate a picture or a novel firmly where it belongs in the unrolling social picture is to help it draw vitality from the soil it grew in" (*UCW,* 267).[5]

Wharton's attention to "the passing fripperies of clothes and custom" underscores her concern with Time as History (that which changes over the years), but just as much her dedication to seamless Time—"the other, and supreme, preservative of fiction," which is devoted to tracking "unchanging human nature," the "essential soul" that is "always there," however much "it is modified and distorted by the shifting fashions of the hour" (*UCW,* 267). The connections (and disjunctures) in Wharton's writings between "the shifting fashions of the hour" and "unchanging human nature" are also what this essay is about: in particular, the way Wharton presents women whose narratives question their ability to share the same time-scheme which their adversaries enlist to define rules of the game that Wharton's heroines are expected to obey.

Wharton identifies her (oft-times suffering) heroines as those whose look strikes others as "different" and as "always new."[6] This fact marks an Ellen Olenska or a Lily Bart not only as Wharton's ideal but also as women who are anathema to the social set for which difference and newness are only acceptable if converted into conformity with the tastes of the times.

Mrs. Mingott comments that because of "modern sports" May Welland's hand is larger than her own hand which was much admired in her youth (*N,* 1038). A generation later, May's daughter Mary is

> as tall and fair as her mother, but large-waisted, flat-chested and slightly slouching, as the altered fashion required. Mary Chivers's mighty feats of athleticism could not have been performed with the twenty-inch waist that May Archer's azure sash so easily spanned. And the difference seemed symbolic;

the mother's life had been as closely girt as her figure. Mary, who was no less conventional, and no more intelligent, yet led a larger life and held more tolerant views. There was good in the new order too. (*N*, 1292)

These are allowable "differences" because they blend in with the conventions accepted by Archer's set. But Ellen Olenska's look never was, is, or will be quite right for those who live according to the time-scheme currently sanctioned by the social register. Rather than virginal white, Ellen wore black satin at her coming-out ball. She is best represented by "the fiery beauty" of yellow roses rather than the placid purity of May's lilies of the valley (*N*, 1079). She commanded the attention of Europe's portrait painters who limed her likeness nine times over, yet few appreciate her look in New York. Most disturbing of all, she bears a highly trained look in full sight of her watchers, whereas May's highly trained demeanor is disguised as unknowing naturalness.[7]

Wharton was equally fascinated, if often skeptical, about the women whom she placed as indicators of the Modern Moment. Each in her own way, Clemence Verney (*Sanctuary*, 1903), Sophy Viner (*The Reef*, 1912), and the Princess Estradina (*The Custom of the Country*, 1913), possess the restless, boyish look of youth that pulls away from the static, statuesque, full-bosomed girlish maturity which earned May Welland the approval of earlier generations.[8] Nonetheless, Wharton continued to lavish her attention on women like Ellen, whose "look" is both ahead of their times and seemingly outdated. This is the fate of Treeshy Kent of *False Dawn*, whose inner being and outward appearance fail to mesh with Old New York of the 1840s. She is likened to a Piero della Francesca portrait and a Venetian Saint Ursula, models of painterly beauty rejected out of hand by New York's established preference for "fashions" inherited from Carlo Dolci, Guido Remi, the Carraccis, and other late Renaissance masters.[9] Years after Treeshy's death, her "look" and that of the early Renaissance painters gain such great value (both in social and market terms) that the husband of one of her descendants will forego divorcing his wife once the family's Treeshy-like paintings, collected long ago, are found to be worth their weight in Rolls Royces, pearls, and a new Fifth Avenue abode.

Material Markers of Change

Bless Wharton for taking such care with all the props she used to reveal the inner lives of her women; inner lives—whether empty or rich and complex—written for all to see, and perhaps to misread, on their faces and their bodies; inner lives that result in each woman's "look."

A wide range of material markers are endlessly in view—useful tabulations by which to measure the acceleration of changes on the social scene that inform the "historical guide" created in Wharton's novels and tales. Fashions remain foremost, as exemplified in *The Age of Innocence* by the difference between a lady of "old-fashioned" New York society who sets aside her Worth gowns for two seasons and a member of the rebellious younger generation who is wont "to clap her new clothes on her back," even at the risk of emulating loose women such as Beaufort's mistress, Fanny Ring (*N*, 1221). But Wharton made deft use of other points of reference that get at the evidence upon which cultural historians rely, such as alterations in modes of transportation and methods of communication; the refurbishing of domestic interiors and updated tastes in architecture; the changing role played by hotels and other public spaces; electricity, clocks, and the quickened pace of city life in America and abroad—all the accouterments that highlight fluctuations in the social scene.

We date the events between 1875 and 1905 in *The Age of Innocence* according to whether its protagonists use brougham, hack, ferry, train, or Cunard liner; hand-delivered notes, telegram, or long-distance telephone. In following Lily Bart's fatal decline in *The House of Mirth* through the first years of 1900, we glimpse trains in and out of Grand Central Station, ocean-going steam yachts, and the dash along Fifth Avenue of Norma Hatch's flashy new electric victoria. Motor cars in the hands of Peter Van Degen figure in *The Custom of the Country* (1913) as a seductive force that matches Undine Spragg Marvell's restless desire to keep on the move. A decade later in *The Mother's Recompense* (1925), all New York has become one with "the crepuscular motor-dashes that clear the cobwebs from modern brains"—part of "the day, so full of outward bustle, of bell-ringing, telephone calls, rushings back and forth of friends, satellites and servants" (*NW*, 735).

Wharton's concentration on city life does not cause her to overlook similar patterns of change located beyond urban boundaries. The frozen tragedy of the crippled lives of Ethan, Mattie, and Zeena in *Ethan Frome* can be situated within the twenty-four years that separate the period when the stage ran from Bettsbridge to Starkfield in "pre-trolley days" from "the degenerate day of trolley, bicycle and rural delivery, when communication was easy between the scattered mountain villages, and the bigger towns in the valleys" (*NW*, 63, 65). Wharton also takes a hard look at the modern country club placed at a bucolic re move from the city's center. In *The American Scene* (1907), Henry James lauded this newly established institution as a bastion of secure family life, settled within continuities of closeness (and exclusivity). But in Wharton's *Twilight Sleep* (1927), the country club has been transformed into the trivial world of "the blatant club restaurant, noise, jazz, revolving couples, Japanese lanterns, screaming laughter, tumultuous good-byes" (*TS*, 269).

Without doubt, however, Wharton's focus is placed on the material, symbolic alterations taking place within city space that represent crucial shifts in the relation of the individual to the social group. The complex of architectural designs and interior decors considered "in fashion" at a given time figure hugely in *The Age of Innocence*. This is what New York City in the 1870s has to offer. Mrs. Mingott's house on the northern reaches of Fifth Avenue, with its mix of "Mingott heirlooms," "the frivolous upholstery of the Second Empire," and a bedroom shockingly located on the ground floor, is visibly out of place and almost scandalously ahead of its times (*N*, 1036). However, Mrs. Mingott has money, patience, audacious self-confidence, social status, and the shrewdness to know the rest of her world will soon wish to catch up with the new fashion she has sanctioned. There is also the outdated old-money gentility of West Twenty-eighth Street, where Mrs. Archer and Janey fend off any "trend" that might threaten their safe little world, Julius Beaufort's nouveau riche mansion flaunting its own ball-room and "enfiladed drawing-rooms," and Countess Olenska's hideaway on West Twenty-third Street—"not fashionable" but truly new because its rooms strike Archer as "unlike any room he had known" (*N*, 1220, 1032, 1074, 1071). Then there is the domestic box into which Newland Archer is placed by his marriage to May Welland, given material presence by the house her parents had built for the bridal couple in the still "remote" neighborhood of East Thirty-ninth. Constructed of "ghastly greenish-yellow stone that the younger architects were beginning to employ to protest" against the brownstones of the older generations, the house may appear to be modern but it only imposes a different set of conventions upon its occupants. Archer had hoped to provide himself with a personal sanctuary, set apart from society's conventions, old and new, by furnishing his study "with 'sincere' Eastlake furniture, and the plain new book-cases without glass doors" to house the newest books sent him from London; but his private interests are overwhelmed by the social banalities of the house itself (*N*, 1072).

Through Wharton's use of similar narrative strategies, *The House of Mirth* contains the mélange of physical settings available in the early years of the twentieth century that play a significant role in the descent into social hell experienced by Lily Bart: the "modern" enticements of Judy and Gus Trenor's Bellomont estate; the nouveau riche marble and gilt of the Welly Brys's ballroom; the Gormers' outpost—a "caricature approximating the real thing"; and Mrs. Norma Hatch's Emporium Hotel suite—"a world over-heated, over-upholstered, and over-fitted with mechanical appliances for the gratification of fantastic requirements" (*N*, 244, 288). And in *The Custom of the Country*, the rapid shifts taking place in the early 1910s that oppose the decorum authorized by the French aristocracy to the rising power of the American business ethic are tellingly registered by the removal of the family tapestries from the de Chelles's ancestral home to the ballroom of Elmer Moffatt's newly appropriated Paris hotel.

Wharton is just as attentive to the resistance to change found in the materials by which wealth and status are declared, set in contrast to displays of chic on view elsewhere in the same narrative: Mrs. Peniston's gloomily outmoded parlors in *The House of Mirth*, left over from the sixties (black walnut, purple satin curtains, malachite vases), and the fixed decor Kate Clephane of *The Mother's Recompense* finds on her return to the house in which she spent her dreary marriage, twenty years before. The overly melodramatic scene that upsets the fictive legitimacy of the conclusion of *Twilight Sleep* still insists on a certain logic once we compare Arthur Wyant's flat ("a faded derelict habitation in a street past which fashion and business had long since flowed") with "the elaborate social and domestic structure" of the household of Pauline Manford, his former wife ("the glitter of glass and silver, a shirt-sleeved man placing bowls of roses down the long table"), and the Art Deco boudoir of Lita, his son's errant wife ("this half-lit room, with its heaped-up cushions still showing where she had leaned, and the veiled light on two arums in a dark bowl"), whom Wyant later tries to kill because she has dishonored the family by her outrageous behavior and suspected infidelities (*TS*, 40, 68–69, 119).

Wharton may have overdone her critique of the historical/ social/psychological chasm between Wyant's stale quarters, Pauline's clinically perfect entertainment area, and Lita's sensuous inner sanctum, but her passionate distaste for the kind of women who put their flighty energies into fashioning an acceptably chic "personality" is reechoed in her obsessive return to the scene of the Hotel Nouveau Luxe to make her point about the lives of women lived in the newly erected public establishments where new money flaunts itself.[10] In "The Last Asset" (1904), "Les Metteurs en Scène" (1906), *The Custom of the Country* (1913), and "The Temperate Zone" (1924), women freely come and go in Paris and along the Riviera, but each stopover raises the question of what such freedom means within the terms of the times.

Such is the plight of Kate Clephane in *The Mother's Recompense* (1925). Kate's sensibility should make her "better" than her environment, but the conditions of her life-in-exile as a runaway wife lead her to join those "plunged into cards, gossip, flirtation, and all the artificial excitements which society so lavishly provides for people who want to forget" (*NW,* 554). Kate dislikes the Riviera crowd that "lived in a chronic state of mental inaccuracy, excitement and inertia, which made it vaguely exhilarating to lie and definitely fatiguing to be truthful" (568). When her daughter calls her back home to the society that had once shunned her, Kate believes all will now be well. She finds out differently. Her Old New York is now reconfigured as a more socially respectable version of "the hotel life" she has been living.

The hotel scene is embellished by the advent of electricity, another of Wharton's vivid historical markers. Thanks to Thomas Edison's innovations in electric lighting, by 1900, its ruthless glow reflected in a boudoir mirror was a threat to a woman like Lily Bart, whose "last asset" is a waning physical beauty more kindly set off by "candle-flames" (*N,* 29). Compare, however, what incandescent lighting does for the new kind of beauty possessed by Undine Spragg, which is capable of meeting modern technological advancements more than halfway.

> So untempered a glare would have been destructive to all half-tones and subtleties of modelling; but Undine's beauty was as vivid, and almost as crude, as the brightness suffusing it. Her black brows, her reddish-tawny hair and the pure red and white of her complexion defied the searching composing radiance; she might have been some fabled creature whose home was in a beam of light. (*N,* 635)

Clocks stand in contrast to the newness of electrical technologies. As a mechanism for measuring time's passage, methodical tickings have been with us for a long time, but Wharton inserts its sounds into certain scenes to suggest certain troubling facts about the kinds of time inflicting her characters' lives in ways both old and new. The remorseless beat of time's passage over which one has little control permeates the Wellands' world of convention. The narcotic effect on Newland Archer of his marriage union with May's family is summed up for him by "the perpetually reminding tick of disciplined clocks" in the Wellands' Newport cottage that chide him for his lack of "foresight in planning his days"(*N,* 1187, 1191). The clock's tick marks the Bunner

sisters' drift out of dull, limited contentment into tragic economic, physical, and emotional decline. The existential nothing-
ness that seeps through the country house of *Twilight Sleep* is
made vivid by the fact that, even though "all the clocks agreed to
a second, one could never believe them," since—as Lita Wyant
asks in one of her Daisy Buchanan moods—"what's the use of
knowing what time it is in the country? Time for *what?*" (*TS,* 291).

Time's passage can hunt you down wherever you are, city or
country, America or abroad. It is, however, time defined by the
hectic, quickening pace of New York's urban street-life and social
affairs that becomes one of Wharton's signature-markers for the
conditions through which her women must make their way
while trying to skirt disaster.

Ellen Olenska's early impressions of the city to which she returns in the mid-1870s are that of a refuge, laid out along gridded
streets apparently as easy to traverse as the mores of the social
world in which she now functions. This woman—whose little
house on West Twenty-third carries the scent of far-off Samar-
kand and whose walls are filled with pictures which "bewildered"
Archer, "for they were like nothing that he was accustomed to
look at"—is at first reassured by the thought of New York's
"straight-up-and-downness, and the big honest labels on everything" (*N,* 1071, 1076). But the seeming simplicity by which New
York once defined itself had been swept away in the years after
the Civil War. The newer "Old New York" is a dangerous site for
Ellen, a Europeanized American, whose responses have been tutored by other places and other time-schemes. This "New New
York" also imposes its changing will on Lily Bart in 1905 and Kate
Clephane in 1925, encasing them within different zones of behavior that affect their looks, their aspirations, and their achievements. The special qualities Wharton values in these women
is threatened by the accelerated pace of city life that undercuts
the principles—continuity, consistency, simplicity, coherence, and
rationality—to which Wharton adhered even as she threw herself forward into modern times. Ellen, Lily, and Kate are lost in a
world where the social markers that ought to help them make
meaning of their lives are impossible to read with accuracy.

Wharton did not overlook the alterations in the social and

material settings of her beloved Europe. She leaves it open whether the physical settings have changed, thus affecting the responses of different generations, or whether it is those altered responses that have the power to transform Eternal Cities into places-of-the-moment. In her short story, "Roman Fever" (1934), she shrewdly incorporates what "Rome" has meant to three generations of women. "To our grandmothers, Roman fever; to our mothers, sentimental dangers—how we used to be guarded!—to our daughters, no more dangers than the middle of Main Street" (*CSS*, 2:837). But it would be New York—ultimate symbol for her of the abhorrent pace imposed by the modern city—that figures as one of her ruling indices for the dangers of change that form a woman's fate.

The Problem of Being "Edith Wharton"

Ever-shifting models for the latest fashions, technologies, and looks that mark a woman as *in or out of time* are matched in Wharton's narratives by considerations of the degree to which they function *in or out of place*.[11] Take, for example, the tenuous position(s) Wharton was assigned because of her inherited social space as a woman, as a woman who was not pretty, as a woman who wrote, as a woman who expatriated to Europe, and as a woman who married and divorced. As she explains in *A Backward Glance*:

> I could not believe that a girl like myself could ever write anything worth reading, and my friends would certainly have agreed with me. No one in our set had any intellectual interests. . . . I never dreamed that I was in any way their superior. Indeed, being much less pretty than many of the girls, and less quick at the up-take than the young men, I might have suffered from an inferiority complex had such ailments been known. (*NW*, 852)

Having been "alive and young and active," Wharton remembers her young womanhood as a fine time, since she was not plagued by "an inferiority complex," a malady for which her generation had yet no name. She was aware, however, that she fulfilled neither category of "pretty" girl nor "quick" young man. A few years later, her out-of-placeness became more apparent. She was considered a "failure in Boston" because "they thought I was too fashionable to be intelligent, and a failure in New York because they were afraid I was too intelligent to be fashionable" (*NW,* 873). The problem of "being Edith Wharton" sharpened on the two occasions in the late 1880s, when she was placed in the same company as Henry James. With no literary credentials of her own, she hoped to impress the revered writer by appearing as pretty and fashionable as possible.

> I could hardly believe that such a privilege could befall me, and I could think of only one way of deserving it—to put on my newest Doucet dress and to try to look my prettiest! I was probably not more than twenty-five, those were the principles in which I had been brought up, and it would never have occurred to me that I had anything but my youth, and my pretty frock, to commend me to the man whose shoe-strings I thought myself unworthy to unloose. I can see the dress still— and it *was* pretty: a tea-rose pink, embroidered with iridescent beads. But, alas, it neither gave me the courage to speak, nor attracted the attention of the great man. The evening was a failure, and I went home humbled and discouraged. (*NW,* 913)

Shortly afterward, she had another chance to meet James.

> Once more I thought: How can I make myself pretty enough for him to Notice me? Well—this time I had a new hat; *a beautiful new hat!* I was almost sure it was becoming, and I felt that if he would only tell me so I might at last pluck up courage to blurt out my admiration for "Daisy Miller" and "The Portrait of a Lady." But he noticed neither the hat nor its wearer—and the second of our meetings fell as flat as the first. (*NW,* 913)

Later, when Wharton and James were the closest of friends, she asked him if he recalled those two occasions, but he had no memory of having met her. Fortunately, for their relationship,

Doucet frocks and beautiful hats were replaced by expressions of intelligence and literary force. Unfortunately, however, these factors never brought Wharton into relation with her New York set.[12] She flung herself even more drastically out of synchronization with her native land by eventually choosing to live abroad. Notwithstanding the liking Wharton had for Theodore Roosevelt, a fellow member of Old New York society, Roosevelt's 1894 essay, "True Americanism," casts expatriates into the outer darkness and obliterates them from the annals of "American History"—a fate which, in theory, Wharton later shared with Henry Adams and Henry James, as that nonentity which was "nothing at all."[13]

Marrying and Divorcing

Where one is physically situated in her married life—the material locales from which she seeks to break free, or the alternative social settings she enters as an accepted divorcée or as an outcast adulteress—makes a great deal of difference to the women involved. Wharton astutely makes note of this fact, as in "Souls Belated" (1899), *Madame de Treymes* (1907), *The Custom of the Country* (1913), "Autre Temps . . ." (1916), and *The Mother's Recompense* (1925)—in *all* her stories of marriage, illicit love, and divorce, whether dated 1899, 1925, or the years in between. But time factors are just as important, perhaps more so, since they are even more bewilderingly mixed and unstable than is space viewed in isolation.

In the years annotated by *The Age of Innocence*, society with its collective force held to the truth that "our legislation favors divorce—our social customs don't" (*N*, 1103).[14] Individual women might also have mixed feelings about the legal rights that allowed them to divorce as they pleased. Wharton's own reactions to the termination in 1913 of the stale *marriage blanche* into which she had entered with Teddy Wharton in 1885 were as complicated as those narrated in the stories she wrote just before and after her divorce. The pain she felt when Morton Fullerton broke off their ardent affair in 1910 came not from feeling the stigma society imposes on adultery, but from personal remorse over lost love and the sense that she had betrayed cherished principles regarding responsible action.[15]

Even though a full generation separates Franklin Ide from Leila Lidcote Pursh Barkley in "Autre Temps . . ." blushes of equal strength flood the embarrassed countenances of both the old-fashioned suitor and the modern-age daughter of Lydia Lidcote over the shamed existence Lydia endured for twenty years because she chose adultery over imprisoning marriage. In this 1916 tale, Ide initially reassures Mrs. Lidcote upon her return to New York "that things are different now—altogether easier" (*CSS,* 2:260). Leila leaps from husband to husband, her social standing enhanced rather than hurt by her divorce and remarriage, but her mother, fated to be forever out-of-time, finds it necessary to return to her long exile in Florence, kept at a safe remove from good society.

> It's simply that society is much too busy to revise its own judgments. Probably no one in the house with me stopped to consider that my case and Leila's were identical. They only remembered that I'd done something which, at the time I did it, was condemned by society. My case had been passed on and classified: I'm the woman who has been cut for nearly twenty years. The older people have half-forgotten why, and the younger ones have never really known: it's simply become a tradition to cut me.And traditions that have lost their meaning are the hardest of all to destroy. (*CSS,* 2:279)

Smart magazines like *Vanity Fair* called meaningless traditions (marrying *and* divorcing) to mind in order to satirize them. In January 1920, a wit like Dorothy Parker was up to the minute when reporting on society's commitment to "Our Great American Sport: Divorce Ranks First Among National Pastimes." Parker's text, which accompanies the sketch of "The Endless Chain" by "Fish," *Vanity Fair's* favorite female cartoonist, points out:

> Only the shortage of white paper prevented the artist from prolonging the above idea indefinitely. It is the motif for a

frieze entitled "Matrimony"— a rather quaint little conception, isn't it? If you are at all married—or even if you are only
an innocent bystander—you will get the idea without a struggle. As soon as divorce mercifully looses one set of shackles,
a change of partners is rapidly effected, new bonds are
formed—and there they are, *right back at the beginning again.*
That's the way it has been for generations. Enormous strides
have been made in every other direction, but matrimony is
practically *where it was when it started.*[16]

Dorothy Parker is of "the more things change, the more they
stay the same" camp. We shall see how Edith Wharton positioned herself over this all important time-issue in regard to what
was happening around her to women and other members of the
human race; but first, more needs to be said about the nature of
the markers her narratives supply as a "historical guide" to acts of
marriage and divorce.

One thing readers can count on: the personal value Wharton
accords to staying married or getting divorced differs in individual cases. The legal and social conditions offered by one or the
other could be "in time" or "out of place," depending on particular situations, as is evident in three sample narratives published
over a period of fourteen years. Divorce is an asset for Undine
Spragg in *The Custom of the Country* (1913), just as holding on to a
dead marriage proves to be Mrs. Newell's "Last Asset" (1908).
Documents certifying one's divorce are a terrifying "thing" for
Lydia in "Souls Belated" (1899) and a triumph for Mrs. Cope in
the same story.

Matters are even more complicated in *The Age of Innocence.*
Not only Ellen and Newland are agitated by their inability fully
to resolve the question of whether divorce would aid or thwart
their desires. Readers of the novel can also be grievously upset
by the pain the story inflicts on both themselves and the lovers
through the double-bind into which Wharton places them all.
The line she takes denies Ellen and Archer the possibilities offered either by acceptance of European mores (stay married,
have an affair) or by rejection of American moral imperatives
(stay married, adjure having an affair), based on the shared no-

tion that divorce must be avoided because it places a taint on the Family and introduces the "unpleasant" into its worlds of convention. In contrast, Ellen had wished a divorce for the sake of her freedom; but once she loves Archer, she cannot free herself from the desire never to hurt others. Because they love one another, they must remain apart; because they obey a highly personal code of behavior, they (and the novel's readers) must suffer.

Would the time ever come in Wharton's sense of history when being married or divorced becomes neither a woman's necessity nor her trap? Would not the social upheavals of World War I, which Wharton experienced first-hand in France, end the pressures to marry that drove Lily Bart to her death circa 1905 or prompted Undine Spragg to dive in and out of successive marriages and divorces prior to 1913? Not necessarily. A scene from *A Son at the Front* (1923) centers on the fact that

> mothers had to take their daughters wherever there was a chance of their meeting young men. . . . You had to take them there, Mme. de Tranlay's look seemed to say, because they had to be married (the sooner the better in these wild times, with all the old barriers down), and because the young men were growing so tragically few, and the competition was so fierce. (*SF*, 326)

As for the sons at the front: out of a new sense of urgency, they take "the new view" that rejects "the old barriers" which spurned a marriage bond as unfashionable. In George Campton's mind, "well, everything's different nowadays, isn't it?" When he speaks of his wish to end an elicit affair in order to insist on marriage with his lover, he decries "the old ideas [that] have come to seem such humbug. That's what I want to drag her out of—the coils and coils of stale humbug. They were killing her." George in 1917 on the eve of returning to the front is not Newland Archer in the 1870s, eager to escape to Japan with Ellen, freed from "the old ideas" of his generation that holds one to marriage ties. George wants to save his love from "the secrecy, the underhandedness" of "the sacred humbug" of irresponsible liaisons lacking in personal commitment, as well as to save himself by finding continuities in the midst of a fragmented universe at war (*SF,* 351, 361).

But oh, the trapped women! History defined as the whiggish promise of progress toward social and personal perfection is mocked by Wharton's novels and tales about women suffocating in unsatisfactory marriages. She provides no promises that things will ever be better as succeeding generations move through the chain of time. There is no guarantee except one: Whatever the decade, whatever the century, women who think they possess the means to escape are in for a great shock. For characters in Wharton's fictive world, such shocks can be tragic.

Wharton's stories are populated by the wrong men whom women marry. Readers are quickly provided with the physiological signs by which to recognize the men who will make life miserable for the women who fall under their control. Look for rolls of flesh that spill over the edges of a man's shirt collar; hear his loud voice; notice a florid, glossy complexion. Witness the husband in "The Long Run"—"a large glossy man with straw-colored hair and red face" who speaks with "a booming voice" (*CSS,* 2:305). There you have the type Wharton regularly portrays with mounting degrees of brutal meanness: Gus Trenor in *The House of Mirth*; Peter Van Degen in *The Custom of the Country,* Brympton in "The Lady's Maid's Bell," and Yves de Cornault in "Kerfol." Then there are the bores, the banal versions of Gilbert Osmond in James's *The Portrait of a Lady,* who live and let others die by their perverse subservience to society's rules: Fraser Leath in *The Reef,* who wears a "symmetrical blond mask," drops a kiss on Anna Leath's cheek "like a cold smooth pebble" and possesses a "neatly-balanced mind [that is] contentedly absorbed in formulating the conventions of the unconventional" (*N,* 416); and John Clephane in *The Mother's Recompense,* who coats his marriage with "the thick atmosphere of self-approval and unperceivingness which emanated . . . like coal-gas from a leaking furnace" (*NW,* 562).[17]

Husbands such as these often have a retinue of prison guards to aid them in keeping their wives entrapped. Some are likened literally or figuratively to the ghostly Mr. Jones, in the story by that title, who in 1818 imprisons the young mute and deaf wife, the captive of an arranged marriage who must sit alone, "day after day, month after month," until she is finally erased from her husband's history by the words on his funeral plaque—"Also His Wife" (*CSS*, 2:613, 612). Often it is the women of the family (the dragonish mother-in-law, the household old maid, the tyrannical aunt) who keep the keys to the prison gates. Witness the fate of Anne de Cornault in "Kerfol," played out in seventeenth-century Brittany. Upon the murder of her cruel lord by the ghostly dogs whom he had slaughtered, she is "handed over to *the keeping of her husband's family*, who shut her up in *the keep of Kerfol*, where she is said to have died many years later, a harmless madwoman" (*CSS*, 2:299–300, my italics). Then leap forward to the late 1920s in New York City, the setting for "Atropy."[18]

> What nonsense to pretend that nowadays, even in big cities, in the world's greatest social centers, the severe old-fashioned standards had given place to tolerance, laxity and ease! You look up the morning paper, and you read of girl bandits, movie star divorces, "hold-ups" at balls, murder and suicide and elopement, and a general welter of disjointed disconnected impulses and appetites; then you turned your eyes onto your own daily life, and found yourself cribbed and cabined, as beset by vigilant family eyes, observant friends, all sorts of embodied standards, as any white-muslin novel heroine of the [eighteen] sixties! (*CSS*, 2:501)

Wharton's women are also caught within confined lives if they figure as old maids. Consider the doom imposed upon Gerty Farish in *The House of Mirth*, Ann Eliza Bunner in "Bunner Sisters," and Charlotte Lovell (although Wharton allows *this* "Old Maid" a history of strong passion and anger). Such is the fate of Miss Mary Pask, in the 1925 story of the same name, never to have a man who "took a fancy to you" (*CSS*, 2:381). Long since thought to be dead and a ghost, the living Mary Pask seems to be "like hundreds of other dowdy old maids, cheerful derelicts content with their innumerable little substitutes for living" (*CSS*, 2:374). Initially shocked to encounter Mary in the flesh, the narrator is forced to recognize "the unuttered loneliness of a lifetime" and all that "the living woman had always had to keep dumb and hidden" (*CSS*, 2:382). Nonetheless, the conclusion is chilling. Realizing that Mary is not a literal ghost but someone who exists somewhere "between being dead and alive," the narrator hastens to forget this living "dead" woman, concluding, "I felt I should never again be interested in Mary Pask" (*CSS*, 2:383, 384).

Ever the practicing realist (although one who faltered at times and gave herself over to ripely romantic language and scenes verging on the melodramatic), Wharton sought to expose the tendency to romanticize and idealize the object of love. Males are not immune. Think of Ralph Marvell's wild misreadings of what marriage with Undine Spragg would have to offer. But Wharton is particularly critical of women who entrap themselves within dreams of male perfection, as in *The Reef, The Mother's Recompense, Twilight Sleep,* "The Letters," and "Sanctuary." Wise is the woman who replaces "passionate worship" with "tolerant affection" for the man in her life, as in the 1895 tale, "The Lamp of Psyche" (*CSS,* 1:57).

Wise, also, is the woman like Kate Clephane, who discovers what happens when she takes flight into the arms of a lover, in her escape from a bad marriage in which she "couldn't breathe." Often the consequence is that "asphyxiation was of a different kind, that was all" (*NW,* 562). On the one hand, flight into an affair entails the risk of taking a lover (even the rare man who is worthy of one's passion) who will come to feel bound "to a lifelong duty which has the irksomeness without the dignity of marriage"—a truth which Paulina Trant in "The Long Run" is quick to recognize (*CSS,* 2:316), as is Lydia in "Souls Belated" and Mrs. Lidcote in "Autre Temps . . . ". On the other hand, the consequences are dire if one foregoes the experience of ecstasy. Paulina urges her lover to take her without delay, the consequences be damned. The "other way" is "*not* to do it! To abstain and refrain." Her lover chooses that other way by refusing Paulina's generous offer of love. Trapped by "the rage of conformity," he submits to "timidity and inertia" (319, 321). He puts off life in the belief that only "the long run" will reveal whether taking risks is wise. As Wharton ponders whether her characters are "in" or "out" of time, whose force might save rather than destroy, she suggests that "the short run" of the heart's impulses may be better than "the long run" ruled by rationality and tradition. *Or not*—note the sad fate of Ellen Olenska and Newland Archer!

Seamless Time / Historical Time

It has been remarked that Dorothy Parker's caustic *Vanity Fair* piece exposed "the endless chain" by which the mechanisms of bourgeois divorce in 1920 merely reforged the manacles of marriage. Time in the world of "Vanity Fair" is, to put it politely, cyclical; to be more blunt and politically critical, it is reactionary. We have seen enough of Wharton's plots to know how readily they appear to reveal their author as a rank conservative, a creature trapped by breeding and class who only superficially escaped the conventions of an outworn society, an anti-feminist who voiced contempt for women who sought full political and economic independence, and an intellectual betrayed by a retrograde belief in fatalism that denies a woman the chance to direct her own destiny. There is truth here, but an overly simplistic one.[19]

This essay has indicated the consummate effort by which Wharton embedded her stories with the material markers that refer to the irreversible jolts and disjunctures which historians are wont to label as "epochs" and "eras" through their commitment to projects of periodization or sliced-out decades. This essay has also suggested the presence of another concept of time— seamless, continuous, capable of flowing backward as well as forward through the years, lacking allegiance to the notion that "process" is the same thing as "progress."[20] Wharton does *not*, I maintain, play the game by which, up front, radical changes deceptively appear on the social scene, while, behind the scrim, such changes (radical or not) are the big lie. Nor does she rely on cheap shots against the vapid women abroad in the Country of the Modern, while extolling the vanishing values of the Land of Tradition. As we shall see, over against the Litas and the Paulines who rush forward into a future imaged horrendously in terms of "twilight sleep," she also tells cautionary tales about Evelina Jaspar in "After Holbein," Louisa Dagonet van der Luyden in *The Age of Innocence*, and Mrs. Clingsland in "The Looking Glass"—grotesque figures pathetically fixed in fantasies of the past. And when, as in "Confession" of 1936, the story opens by stating, "This is the way it began; stupidly, trivially, out of nothing, as fatal things do," Wharton proposes a historical realism that acknowledges that "small incidents can become Colossal Events against the empty horizon of your idleness" (*CSS*, 2:801).

Any accurate "historical guide" to Wharton's women must take into account both "the short run" and "the long run." The former is the time when things happen about which her characters are aware; the latter is the period during which accumulations of consequences slowly, quietly build up into meanings which, if ever, can only be understood "afterward." It is at this point that the pleasure Wharton took in writing ghost stories, and the skill she had in serving the eager *"ghost-feeler"* (the reader "sensible of invisible currents of being in certain places and at certain hours"), are the same pleasures and skills she applied to her "real" tales of social life (*CSS*, 2:875). The 1910 story Wharton titled "Afterward" sets down the archetypal situation: a ghostly visitant representing a crucial action that a person made in the past will appear one day at her or his threshold, but "nobody knows it's a ghost" "till long, long afterward." "And then suddenly . . . suddenly, long afterward, one says to one's self '*That was it?*'" The readers of Wharton's narratives and many of Wharton's fictive protagonists (from Lily Bart to Ellen Olenska, from Anna Leath to Kate Clephane) learn the inflexible truth that "one just has to wait" to receive answers to questions that "all along have been there, waiting their hour" (*CSS*, 2:153, 158).

The preface Wharton appended to the 1937 edition of *Ghosts* acknowledges that the ghost figure exists in two time frames. In a world invaded by modern advances in technology (the wireless, electricity, the cinema), the ghost may feel very much a "nothing at all," but in the world where time runs seamlessly, the ghostly presence that defines our existence is very much at home. Craving only "continuity and silence," ghosts offer the author the gift of narrative continuity; after all, they *are* the past—*our* past—that runs through the present and predicts the future. In turn, the author's gift to her ghost are words that affirm its silent presence, sensitive to the fact that the ghost's "only chance of survival is in the tales of those who have encountered him" (*CSS*, 2:877).

Think of the silent objects—labeled "Use unknown"—that lie encased in the museum where, in *The Age of Innocence*, Ellen Olenska and Newland Archer meet on the eve of deciding their future together (*N*, 1262). It was Wharton's obligation in all her fictions to endow silent, silenced artifacts (themselves representative of long-ago lives, loves, fears, choices) with a history that became possible only if she let unspoken words be heard through her narrative powers. It is hardly necessary to note the many fictions in which Wharton's characters strive (and often fail) to say the right "word" at the right "time." And never more necessary when it is a woman for whom Wharton must break the silence, lest her fate be forever marked "Use unknown" or "Also His Wife" (as in "Mr. Jones"). Many of Wharton's tales speak the needed words "now," in immediate historical time. Many allow the establishment of a long continuity of seamless time, abruptly broken "long afterward" in her reader's consciousness, through the realization, "*That was it.*"

Women Racing against Time

Julia Westall's story in "The Reckoning" is a perfect example of the Wharton heroine who finds out "long afterward" what it means to have formed her life's choices both ahead of the times and behind the times. She demonstrates the pleasures, then shocks, felt by the woman who experiences two radically distinct marriage relations and comes to two diametrically different views regarding divorce. At the opening of "The Reckoning," Julia, the former Mrs. John Arment, has been Mrs. Clement Westall for ten years. In terms of the time frame offered by Wharton's story, which first appeared in 1902, Julia has been ahead of the curve since the mid-1890s.[21] It was then that she discarded her first husband to take up with Westall. As a very early disciple of the "marriage law of the new dispensation," she discarded her first husband for Westall in the name of "The New Ethics" (*CSS*, 1:420). As the narrative opens, however, Julia is experiencing social whiplash. Hitherto, Westall had been "almost pusillanimously careful" not to express commitment to "the new creed." It was Julia who had committed herself far in advance of the general run of society to the call "*Thou shalt not be unfaithful—to thyself*," but now, as Westall avidly promotes the "ideas" of "the immorality of marriage" before "the mentally unemployed" members of the Van Sideren set, Julia "felt differently" (*CSS*, 1:420–21). At one time, she gave

> adherence to the religion of personal independence, but she had long ceased to feel the want of any such ideal standards, and had accepted her marriage as frankly and naturally as though it had been based on the primitive needs of the heart, and required no special sanction to explain or justify it. (*CCS*, 424)

Julia's great shock comes when Westall tells her he is going to leave her for a much younger woman who "interests" him, as Julia no longer does. Julia reviews the feelings that earlier led her to take up the new creed now being cruelly turned against her. Without question, life with John Arment "was impossible," as the "world she adorned agreed" (*CSS*, 1:425).

> Her husband's personality seemed to be closing gradually in on her, obscuring the sky and cutting off the air, till she felt herself shut up among the decaying bodies of her starved hopes. A sense of having been decoyed by some world-old conspiracy into this bondage of body and soul filled her with despair. If marriage was the slow lifelong acquittal of a debt contracted in ignorance, then marriage was a crime against human nature. (*CSS*, 1:427)

Because of this experience, Julia comes to the belief in time defined as evolutionary. "People grew at varying rates, and the yoke that was an easy fit for the one might soon become galling to the other. That was what divorce was for: the readjustment of personal relations" (*CSS*, 1:427). Convinced that staying with an unsatisfactory marriage was the "new adultery"—"unfaithfulness to self"—Julia and Westall married as "champions of the new law, pioneers in the forbidden realm of individual freedom." Unfortunately, Westall chooses to obey this law by dismissing Julia from his life because he has tired of her and wants something "new." His action is met by her own "reversion, rather, to the old instinct" that honored union and unity (*CSS*, 1:427–28). She had once rebelled against that "old instinct" in her original struggle against the backward pull of her society. She now finds she is "the prisoner of her own choice; she had been her own legislator, and she was the predestined victim of the code she had devised" (*CSS*, 1:431–32).

Wharton's novel of 1913, *The Custom of the Country*, also harkens back to the mid-1890s, through flashbacks to Undine Spragg's early years in Apex, where she begins her own race against time that will eventually install her in a grand hotel in Paris, once again the wife of Elmer Moffatt. Compared to Wharton's other female protagonists, Undine may be said to beat the system, both the "old" one that crushes Lily Bart and wounds Ellen Olenska, and the "new" one that turns on Julia Westall. Undine has the supreme talent to act "in time" in order to be ahead of the curve of time which traps the likes of the Dagonets and the Marvells. Unbound by commitment to "the ideal standards" that drags down individuals like Lily, Ellen, and Julia, Undine swims free, buoyed by "her floating desires" (*N*, 653). She too, follows "the primitive needs of the heart"—but her primitivism has nothing to do with Julia's desire for union and unity. Nor is Undine's driving force limited to those money-needs which Wharton exposes as being time-bound to the ever-outmoded mores of the Hotel Nouveau Luxe or the machinations of Wall Street. In one sense, Undine cannot be harmed by the disconnect between human wishes and history's erratic movements. She exists outside historical time. She acts within archaic time, where the heart never stops aspiring to the "something she could never get, something that neither beauty nor influence nor millions could ever buy for her" (*N*, 1014). In another sense, *The Custom of the*

Country concludes—as do most of Wharton's narratives—with Undine unable to make it "in time," with *it* defined as becoming an ambassador's wife. In this case, historical changes long after Undine's era, and Wharton's, show what a woman can have "in time." "In time" there would be Pamela Harriman, another red-haired beauty, happy disciple of "the new dispensation" by which marriage, lovers, divorce, money, influence leads—not merely to figuring as the wife of an ambassador—to becoming an ambassador in her own right.

Twilight Sleep (1927) offers the case histories of three very different "modern" women, each placed at the mercy of Edith Wharton's razor-edged analysis. Wharton has pity for the moral confusions of Nona Wyant, caught in a vise of the "ideas" of her generation, but little sympathy for Pauline Manford's New Age altruism and Lita Wyant's atavistic amoralism. A generational divide marked by the fact of "the Great War" separates Pauline from Lita, her daughter-in-law, and from Nona, daughter of her first marriage. Lita and Nona figure among "the bewildered disenchanted young people who had grown up" since that historical cleft. As a consequence, their "energies were more spasmodic and less definitely directed" than those of Pauline's generation (*TS*, 6–7). Pauline's "energies" are almost ludicrously focused by her efforts to perfect society by means of Frederick Winslow Taylor's ultrafashionable principles of scientific time-management. However, she is driven like Lita (and Nona to some extent) to achieve perpetual youth, extol "personality," fend off worry, and fight off the "sin" of suffering. In a society that finds a haven in the obliteration of awareness through "twilight sleep," time's passage is a woman's greatest enemy. Pauline's generation strives to escape the threat of "an absolutely featureless expanse of time"—that "empty hour [that] stretched away into infinity like the endless road in a nightmare" and gapes "like the slippery sides of an abyss" (*TS*, 135).

However progressive Pauline's politics (though they oscillate—hilariously, in Wharton's telling—between a call to arms at a Mother's Meeting and leadership of the Birth Control Committee), she is not nearly as much "in fashion" as is Lita. Pauline's trouble is that she thinks too much about not having to think. Lita is wonderfully free of such constraints. Always "half-dancing, half-drifting"—possessed of "smiling animal patience," a "nature of spray and sunlight," and "goldfish-coloured hair, the mother-of-pearl complexion and screwed-up auburn eyes"—Lita is an advanced primitive version of Undine Spragg, doubly protected by her thoughtless expectation "that the matter should have no sequel" and actions no consequence (*TS*, 32, 14, 35, 95).

It is Nona whose relations to history, fashion, and time make her role in a Wharton novel both woefully problematic and wonderfully significant. Unlike either Pauline or Lita, Nona is "as firm as a rock." "If a woman was naturally straight, jazz and night-clubs couldn't make her crooked" (*TS*, 126–27). Yet Nona exists dangerously close to the land of twilight sleep dedicated to "escape by flight—by perpetual evasion" (*TS*, 362). Disappointed in love and in life, Nona causes her mother to worry (the very thing Pauline tries to avoid!): "at barely twenty," Nona seems "to be turning from a gay mocking girl into a pinched fault-finding old maid" (*TS*, 323). The members of Nona's mother's generation—"bright-complexioned white-haired mothers mailed in massage and optimism"—view themselves very much of "the times" (*TS*, 48). They "think away" sorrow and reject evil, those notions said to be "superannuated bogies, survivals of some obsolete European superstition, unworthy of enlightened Americans, to whom plumbing and dentistry had given higher standards, and bi-focal glasses a clearer view of the universe." Nona attempts to resist their "modern" ideas, which she takes as a betrayal of what human time actually means.[22] "After all, somebody in every family had to remember now and then that such things as wickedness, suffering and death had not yet been banished from the earth," else the "children had to serve as vicarious sacrifices" (*TS*, 47–48). Caught up in this murderous society, in which the newest forms of cruelty seem to crush the chance ever to create new forms of good, the knowledge to which Nona aspires may never come to her "in time." "I know most of the new ways of being rotten; I only wish I was sure I knew the best new way of being decent" (*TS*, 244).

Getting On

Lily Bart had no chance of survival. For one thing, her body exists in the current moment to be sold in marriage, while her heart exists in a time-lag defined by the romantic illusion that a woman has the freedom to live in the Republic of the Spirit. For another, she did not know how to win playing at bridge as the truly modern girl does. Take Miss Audrey De Peyster, "a young lady of Dutch heritage and courage," the heroine of "Getting on in New York Society," a *Vanity Fair* sketch of October 1916. Audrey has been hired by the Higgingbothams as their social secretary in their desire to move up in "good" society. Audrey does very well for herself, although not for the Higgingbothams.

> Audrey smokes, drinks and plays "cut throat"; she also knows how to get first-night tickets at the Follies and an inside table at Bustanoby's. She can mix eleven different kinds of cocktails with only one bottle of gin, one lemon, two bottles of Vermouth and a single olive. . . . The dinner has been cleared away and Audrey and her friends have just finished a little session with the cards. Net result: the T. Pennypacker Higgingbothams are minus $208.00.[23]

In the moments covered by Wharton's narrative, Lily is led to believe that she *must* marry and marry money; no choices allowed. Audrey De Peyster is not so limited, nor are the women who signed up for the three-hour seminar in 1991 on "How to Marry Rich" at the Independent Adult Learning Center in South Pasadena, California. They simply *want* to marry and to marry into wealth. As thoroughly modern women, their "idea" is that they possess the right to choose, thus are freed (as Lily is not) from the fatal determinant of "must."[24]

It is difficult to know with Wharton whether her women are stopped "dead" by the ephemeral nature of the questionable ideas that float in and out of their minds as fashionable vagaries of the times—ideas they have the obligation to judge as well as to choose—or whether they are caught by the fixed fate that denies choice. Wharton can be very Shakespearean in the narratives she relates of lovers destined for tragic ends. Think of Ophelia, victimized just because she happens to live while rottenness spreads throughout the state of Denmark; or Juliet, whose falling in love happens to coincide with a Verona torn apart by family feuds. Or consider Cleopatra. She may be a maker of history, in love with another history-maker; but both are fated to die because their personal passions represent the clash between Egypt and Rome at the particular moment when Augustus Caesar takes control and Antony's divorce from the emperor's sister cannot be abided. There is no way around the fact of Edith Wharton's ingrained sadness, the fact that removes her from the standard (and admirable) list of women reformers and feminists. Yet it is nice to remember the thought with which Wharton closes her autobiography: "Life is the saddest thing there is, next to death; yet there are always new countries to see, new books to read (and, I hope, to write), a thousand little daily wonders to marvel at and rejoice in" (*NW*, 1063–64). Perhaps, even a beautiful new hat to wear.

NOTES

1. "Autre Temps . . . ," published in Wharton's collection, *Xingu*, first appeared as "Other Times, Other Manners," in *The Century Magazine* in 1911.

2. Stein's pronouncements circle around the issue of surfaces in her own maddeningly opaque way (*Tender Buttons* is filled with them), but she felt that surface-writing-and-seeing was an important aspect of a writer's response to the things in the world around us, particularly those situated in the present moment. Excessive probings below surfaces tilt the writer's efforts toward the calculated, schematic, consistent *explanation* and away from the spontaneous immediacy of *clarity*. See "What Is English Literature," from *Lectures in America* (Boston: Beacon Press, 1985), 38. Stein likes "digging" and "doing" as opposed to acts of "organizing" that imply "jury" and "reward." See *Everybody's Autobiography* (Cambridge: Exact Change, 1993), 233. Stein praises Carl Van Vechten's "The Blind Bow-Boy" (1923) because "It's all the background and the background, as yet American life is the background. Others have tried to make background foreground, but you have made foreground background, and our foreground is our background." See *The Letters of Gertrude*

Stein and Carl Van Vechten, 1913–1946, vol. 1, ed. Edward Burns (New York: Columbia University Press, 1986), 86–87. Edith Wharton would not say all this in the same manner as Stein, but she too strove for clarity, doing, and mergers of foreground-background.

3. See Valerie Steele, *Fashion and Eroticism: Ideals of Feminine Beauty from the Victorian Era to the Jazz Age* (New York: Oxford University Press, 1985), concerning the advent in 1908 of the House of Poiret's version of the "straight but sinuous silhouette, with an easy and often raised waistline and narrow skirt," brought forward from the Directoire period (227).

4. Steele criticizes "the *Zeitgeist* theory" that imposes "a single attitude" upon the fashions of any one period. She argues the influence of "a multiplicity of competing and often contradictory world views." Changing styles "are related not only to changes in the larger culture, but are also reactions to previous fashions." Fashions seldom repeat themselves as they move from earlier to later times, since "the various forms, colors, and other 'expressive elements' of fashion tend to have different connotations in different times and places." In reference to the Josephine-cum-Poiret style that Ellen Olenska wears in 1875, Steele asserts, "The 'tubular' style of 1910 looked different and was perceived differently from the 'tubular' style of 1810" (*Fashion and Eroticism*, 21–23). Ellen's gown is a mixture of styles associated with specific periods and changing styles that flow from the past to the present and into the future.

5. On February 17, 1921, Wharton wrote about Zoë Akins's proposed staging of *The Age of Innocence* (an event that never took place). "I could do every stick of furniture & every rag of clothing myself, for every detail of that far-off scene was indelibly stamped on my infant brain." Wharton was also wary that a theatrical production of 1921 not place male actors representing "gentlemen" of the 1870s on stage attired like "'Summit Collar' athletes, with stern jaws & shaven lips"—in obvious reference to the style of advertising art made famous by J. C. Lyendecker (*L*, 439).

6. Steele notes that "appearance (a style of dress and adornment, a body and a mode of self-presentation) is more than a series of *statements* about social and psychological phenomena." Clothing helps "create a total visual image—a *look*" (*Fashion and Eroticism*, 147).

7. Steele claims that "the popular belief that fashion has pro-

gressed or should progress towards greater naturalness is antithetical to the phenomenon. Fashion is never 'natural'" (*Fashion and Eroticism*, 48). However inexperienced Evelina Bunner may be in the arts of erotic appeal, she "knows" to pin a crimson bow under her collar to attract the attention of Herman Ramy.

8. Steele rejects the notion that the fashions of the years prior to and following World War I expressed a woman's wish to look like a boy. Rather, women preferred to dress like little girls in order to take command of the freedoms of youth and to discard the restrictions placed on adults (*Fashion and Eroticism*, 230, 239, 241). Wharton had reservations regarding women who shirk the responsibilities that come with maturity.

9. In *Old New York: False Dawn (The 'Forties)*, Lewis Raycie's travels abroad (ostensibly in obedience to his father's command to collect Dolcis and Remis) "confirmed rather than weakened the family view of Treeshy's plainness; she could not be made to fit any of the patterns of female beauty so far submitted to him" (*NW*, 339). He discovers her face in a Venetian fresco: "a girl with round cheeks, high cheek-bones and widely set eyes under an intricate head-dress of pearl-woven braids" (*NW*, 343). To the outrage of his father and the bewilderment of his friends, he brings back to New York a Piero della Francesca—"a small picture representing a snub-nosed young woman with a high forehead and jewelled coif" (*NW*, 349).

10. In *Edith Wharton: A Biography* (New York: Harper & Row, 1975), R. W. B. Lewis cites Wharton's "anti-Ritz" views (335). In *A Backward Glance*, Wharton states that Riviera hotels were defined by "aimless drift" and "emptiness of life" (*NW*, 976). Claire Preston's *Edith Wharton's Social Register* (London: Macmillan, 2000) notes that Wharton situated characters considered unacceptable in such hotels, not only to measure their "index of restlessness" but also to "provide for these outcasts an exemplary geography of status" (63).

11. I refer to Preston's fine study, *Edith Wharton's Social Register*, regarding the social and psychological nature of the "displacements" that harm many of Wharton's female characters in ways that free me to concentrate on time issues without disregarding how material "places" mesh with the temporal "placements" that complicate any formulation of Wharton's "historical guide" to the fate of women. Making shrewd use of the formula "x" = "niceness," and "not-x" = "non-niceness" (2), Preston notes that Wharton's women are labeled

as outcasts once their society views them as one of the "not-x"—
their tragic narratives are driven by Wharton's application of the
"binary pattern of 'x/not-x' to the imagination of place" (61). I shall
do something similar in terms of the imagination of time.

12. As Wharton said, "I had to fight my way to expression
through a thick fog of indifference." "None of my relations ever
spoke to me of my books, either to praise or blame—they simply ig-
nored them; and among the immense tribe of my New York cousins
. . . the subject was avoided as though it were a kind of family dis-
grace which might be condoned but could not be forgotten" (*NW*,
875, 891). Wharton makes clear that the "not-x" of being a practicing
literary figure afflicted men as well as women. Ned Winsett in *The
Age of Innocence* is "a pure man of letters, *untimely born* in a world
that had no need of letters" (*N*, 1114, my italics). Wharton suffered
another kind of "out-of-placeness." As an upper-class "summer
person"—a seasonal visitor in the New England Berkshires—her
claim to understanding the economic and psychological travails of
the native residents immured in the worlds of *Ethan Frome* and *Summer* has been called into question.

13. Theodore Roosevelt, "True Americanism," in *American Ideals*,
vol. 15, *The Works of Theodore Roosevelt*. Memorial edition (New
York: Scribner's, 1924). Although Roosevelt's scathing remarks are
directed to uncentered males, they apply equally to Wharton. Just
as the European immigrant who fails to assimilate fully "becomes
nothing at all," any American-born individual who chooses expatriation "does not really become a European" but "only ceases being an
American, and becomes nothing" (22, 26). Preston does not refer to
the threat to American citizenry by the cosmopolite type in Roosevelt's terms, but her comments emphasize the dangers of Wharton's choice: "to step beyond the boundary is to leave the defining
conditions of tribal membership, to become marginalised or obliter-
ated, to become not-nice; it is to become, in essence, unknown, invisible, non-existent; 'not-x' is merely nothing at all" (5).

14. For two excellent studies of changes in legal actions taking
place during Wharton's writing career, see the chapter regarding divorce and the marriage market, centered on *The Custom of the Country*, in Debra MacComb's *Tales of Liberation, Strategies of Containment: Divorce and the Representation of Womanhood in American Fiction,
1880–1920* (New York: Garland Press, 2000), and the chapter on court

cases regarding privacy law played out in *The House of Mirth*, in William E. Moddelmog's *Reconstituting Authority: American Fiction in the Province of the Law, 1880–1920* (Iowa City: University of Iowa Press, 2000).

15. R. W. B. Lewis's biography argues that Wharton did not view the fact of adultery or divorce in terms of "abstract morality." Instead, she found these acts distressful when they violated "the civilized order of life." Even though she dramatized the dire effects of family traditions that had lost their meaning, she still cherished the vital traditions that give coherence to human relations, whether in the privacy of marriage or in society at large. Her highest praise was given to marriages in which each partner sees what the other is seeing. At one point, she cried out to a friend, "Ah, the poverty, the miserable poverty, of any love that lies outside of marriage, of any love that is not a living together, a sharing of all" (*Edith Wharton: A Biography*, 221, 317–18). It was this sharing which men like Fullerton fail to give a woman, either inside or outside of marriage.

16. Dorothy Parker, "Our Great American Sport," *Vanity Fair* (January 1920), 62, my italics. In the same piece, Parker and Fish include text and sketch for "Old Home Week," which cleverly speaks to Wharton's "The Other Two," written sixteen years earlier. "It is so nice for the new bridegroom to meet his wife's collection of former husbands. It is something for him to look forward to, all through the honeymoon. These little family gatherings are so delightfully homey—it is always reassuring to feel that you are all members of the same club" (63).

17. Wharton is noted for trapping her heroines in prison-like houses which represent stifling, outdated traditions. In *The Reef*, Anna Leath thinks of the French house, in Givré, as "the very symbol of narrowness and monotony" (*N*, 410). Undine Spragg of *The Custom of the Country* finally rebels against the de Chelles's château de Saint Désert, where her life seems as crushingly confined as it had been for Anne de Cornault in "Kerfol," locked up in her husband's Brittany château, "where the days were long, and it rained too much" (*CSS*, 2:293). The 1920s New York household in *Twilight Sleep* is just as disturbing in its expression of the modern marriage state. "It looked, for all its studied effects, its rather nervous attention to 'values,' complementary colours, and the things the modern decorator lies awake over, more like the waiting-room of a glorified railway

station than the setting of an established way of life. Nothing in it seemed at home or at ease" (*TS*, 30).

18. "Atropy" first appeared in *Ladies' Home Journal* in November 1927 and was reprinted in *Certain People*, 1930.

19. I have tried not to contribute to the notion that Wharton's narratives are hopelessly locked into a negative deterministic philosophy that kills both her female characters and her own imaginative power. My introduction to *The House of Mirth* (The World's Classics [Oxford: Oxford University Press, 1994], vii–xxxi) has much to say on this score, and, I trust, opens up the subject rather than closes it down.

20. As Evelina Bunner lies dying after her tragic sojourn into romance and marriage, two yellow jonquils are brought to her bedside. While her sister Ann Eliza sits at her sewing machine, "the click, click, click of the machine sounded in her ear like the tick of Ramy's clock [the man whom both women loved and who brought ruin to their quiet lives], and it seemed to her that life had gone backward, and that Evelina, radiant and foolish, had just come into the room with the yellow flowers in her hand." After Evelina dies, and Ann Eliza has lost all her worldly possessions, she sets out to find a job, only to learn that applicants must be "not over thirty, anyhow; and nice-looking." Ann Eliza trudges forth to her "end" while "the great city, under the fair spring sky, seemed to throb with the stir of innumerable beginnings" (*CS*, 2:246). Both "times" (Ann Eliza's time and New York's time) are real as they run along simultaneously, each indifferent to the other's destiny.

21. "The Reckoning" first appeared in August 1902, in *Harper's Magazine* and was reprinted in Wharton's 1904 collection, *The Descent of Man*.

22. If Newland Archer's mother feared trends, Wharton distrusted "ideas" even more, since they are often no more than rigid dogmas of "faith" and "belief," unrelated to human history and the complexities of time. Undine Spragg is devoted to such ideas as writing on "the new pigeon-blood note-paper with white ink" and becoming "an Ambassador's wife" (*N*, 633, 1014), just as Julia Westall originally gives herself over to the worship of ideas of personal self-fulfillment. Little wonder that Nona wishes to go into "a convent where nobody believes in anything" (*TS*, 373).

23. Anonymous, "Getting on in New York Society," *Vanity Fair* (October 1916), 60–61.

24. Miles Corwin, in a *Los Angeles Times* article, "How to Marry Rich: It May Just Take a Little Class and $39," 30 November 1992, details what takes place during this evening class (a form of "twilight sleep," perhaps). The women are instructed to repeat, "I want to be rich! I deserve to be rich! I am rich! I was born to be rich!" If anyone believes she is in love with a man who is already at his peak-earning years and "maxed out at $100,000," she is told, "forget it." Love will come after marrying a really rich man, for "How could you not love someone who is doing all these wonderful things for you?"

Emerson, Darwin, and
The Custom of the Country

Cecelia Tichi

> Do the races and species of men,
> whichever term might be applied, en-
> croach on and replace each other, so
> that some finally become extinct? We
> shall see that all these questions . . .
> must be answered in the affirmative.
> Charles Darwin, *The Descent of Man*, I,
> 2nd ed., 1877

> Ralph sometimes called his mother
> and grandfather the Aborigines, and
> likened them to those vanishing
> denizens of the American continent
> doomed to rapid extinction with the
> advance of the invading race.
> Edith Wharton, *The Custom of the
> Country*, 1913

Readers of Edith Wharton have for some years recognized her appreciation of—and affinity with—Darwin and Darwinism, which was a major part of her self-schooling in the sciences, especially between 1906 and 1908. Accordingly, in *The Custom of the Country*, Ralph Marvell's analysis of social dislocation employs a

Darwinian heuristic to present a precis of the plot dynamic. A son of Old New York and an important figure in the novel, Ralph declares traditional families like his own to be a species endangered by the late nineteenth-century nouveau riche "invading race," by which Wharton means a line of descent, not a genetic category. As a young aspirant poet-critic, who is newly appreciative of his heritage, Ralph understands his family and their cohorts to be casualties of a recent historical-evolutionary rupture. The new modern, invasive "race" of plutocrats, with their headquarters on Wall Street and their domiciles on Fifth Avenue, are fast conquering an enervated Old New York comprised of the ladies and gentlemen of Washington Square. Ralph assesses the invaders' "modern tendencies" as a deplorable "chaos of indiscriminate appetites" from the monetary to the gustatory, these over and against the moderate and temperate "coherent and respectable" ideals of his family's waning Old New York (*N*, 669). More than social change or a reversible decline in mores and manners, this phenomenon is a Darwinian process of encroachment and extinction. As a record of the contest between base and higher morality, *The Custom of the Country* is arguably Wharton's most thoroughgoing socially Darwinian narrative.

Wharton wrote exhuberantly of "the wonder-world of nineteenth century science," citing Darwin and Herbert Spencer among the "greatest" of her "formative influences" (*NW*, 856; *L*, 136).[1] From her memoir, *A Backward Glance* (1934), we know the writings of Charles Darwin were introduced to her by a valued family friend, Egerton Winthrop, who gave her *The Origin of Species* (1859) and Alfred Wallace's *Darwin and Darwinism* (1901), and also informed her of the work of Spencer (*NW*, 855–56). In a March 1908 letter to Charles Eliot Norton, Wharton cited as reportedly "admirable" Vernon L. Kellogg's *Darwinism Today: A Discussion of Present-Day Scientific Criticism of the Darwinian Selection Theories* (1907) (*L*, 131), and she reported being "deep" in the book three months later, on shipboard, to be followed, she wrote, by Robert H. Lock's *The Recent Progress in the Study of Variation, Heredity and Evolution* (1906) (*L*, 146). Wharton titled a 1904 collection of short stories *The Descent of Man*, in direct reference to Darwin's title (her title story condemning the popularization of science—and by extension debased literature too). As Carol Singley observes, "Darwin is the figure most closely associated with [Wharton] both because of the strong determinist strain in her fiction and because of the monumental position Darwin occupied in the nineteenth century."[2]

The Darwinian dimension in Wharton's fiction might seem *overly* familiar, first as a categorical fellow-traveler of the long-term rubric of naturalism in literary study. In its reductivist binary version of winners versus losers, in addition, Darwinism offers easy access to the tensions in Wharton's fiction, which from the 1905 *The House of Mirth* to the 1920 *The Age of Innocence* recurrently pit the social old guard against the ascendent crass arrivistes.

The Custom of the Country has understandably attracted recent attention in quite different directions, such as Wharton's evidently crucial exploitation of classical myth, particularly via Ralph Marvell's vision of his new bride, Undine, as "a lovely rock-bound Andromeda," which has seemed key to Wharton's "underworld" literary division between true and meretricious language, with one key to all this being Ralph's last name, Marvell, directly referent to the seventeenth-century lyric and pastoral poet, Andrew Marvell.[3]

The figure of Undine as Ralph's Andromeda has also prompted study of Wharton's coeval relation to contemporary, erotically evocative paintings (e.g., by Edward Burne-Jones and J. W. Waterhouse), expressing the subjectivity of the male gaze.[4] Critical studies in literature's links to business culture, in addition, have prompted inquiry into *The Custom of the Country* as an instance of Wharton's transformation of Undine "from an unregulated corporate force into a well-managed corporate employee."[5]

To some extent, these interpretive opportunities present themselves within the aesthetic claim for narrative superiority, which is Cynthia Griffin Wolff's emphasis: "*The Custom of the Country*—vexing, harsh, superbly polished, and utterly uncompromising—has now come to be regarded by many critics as Edith Wharton's best work."[6] Two of Wharton's biographers, Wolff and Shari Benstock, emphasize the importance of energy

("psychic energy—power, assertion, drive, ambition") as themati-
cally central to the novel.[7] Most recently, the novel has been
called "a contemporary jeremiad that rails against reckless materialism" and as Wharton's documentation of the replacement of
"traditional morality" and "common decency" by "gross materialism and selfish desire."[8]

This discussion redirects focus to a Darwinian design of *The
Custom of the Country*, specifically to argue that Wharton structured her narrative largely on a pattern of multiple binary formulations, encountered in Darwin and in the Darwinian thought
of Herbert Spencer. In addition, evidence suggests that we need
to pay closer attention to the utilization of binaries in another of
Wharton's favorite authors, Ralph Waldo Emerson. The apparently incongruous literary-scientific provenance of Emerson-
Darwin was, in fact, established in a 1901 Wharton story, "The
Angel at the Grave," in which a prolific but minor transcendentalist writer of the earlier nineteenth century is cited as a "friend
of Emerson" and a Darwinist as well. In youth, this fictional
Orestes Anson, in a phase of "anatomical ardor," had preco-
ciously advanced an evolutionary hypothesis based on study of
"the notochord of the *amphioxus* as a cartilaginous vertebral col-
umn" (*CSS*, 1:262, 267). Ironically, decades after Anson's death, his
prodigious multivolume *Works* have faded from public memory,
while his single pamphlet setting forth an evolutionary hypothesis proves key to the man's enduring significance. Though "The
Angel at the Grave" is rich in such ironies, it interests us here
as evidence that, several years before writing *The Custom of the
Country*, Wharton encompassed the disparate worlds of Emerson's and Darwin's thought in a single fictional site. The story
serves as a marker anticipating Wharton's fuller exploitation of
both writers' argumentive designs.

The Custom of the Country evidently drew upon Emerson's essays, not for transcendentalist themes but for a binary mode of
argumentation that was, for her rhetorical purposes, congenial
with that of Darwin. This is not to say that Wharton merely
transferred Emerson (and Darwin) per se into her narrative. On
the contrary, in ways crucial to the novel, she deliberately mis-
reads them for her own purposes. The Emerson-Darwin nexus

nonetheless provided Wharton the scheme of bifurcation by which to expose the crisis of sundered culture, which was the very crisis explored in her first major (and best-selling) novel, *The House of Mirth*, in which readers encountered a story line focused on the lethal social dislocations of aggressive new American wealth invading the traditional territory of landed gentility.

Wharton is tantalizingly cryptic about her specific responses to Darwin, whose *Descent of Man*, as we notice, argues the inevitable human extinction via "encroach[ment]" upon "races or species of men,"[9] but whose *Origin of Species* actually is optimistic in the societal expectation that "virtuous habits will grow stronger" because these "are founded on the social instincts, and relate to the welfare of others."[10] Darwin argued the evolutionary mandate for philanthropy by the stronger homo sapiens, cautioning in *Origin of Species* against the "neglect [of] the weak and helpless," which would provide only a "contingent benefit, with an overwhelming present evil."[11]

Within the realm of Darwinian thought, however, Wharton's other "greatest . . . formative influence," the political sociologist Herbert Spencer, emphasized a different evolutionary lesson. Spencer was, and continues to be, best known as "the man who coined the key phrase in social Darwinism—survival of the fittest."[12] The equation of "natural selection" with "survival of the fittest" was one Wharton possibly encountered in the sixth edition of *Origin of Species* but more probably in Spencer, perhaps the 1886 *Principles of Biology*,[13] and then again in Robert Lock's book on evolution, which she planned to read on shipboard in 1906.[14] Doubtless she also heard the phrase elsewhere in desultory reading and in conversation.

Conservative social Darwinians of Wharton's late-nineteenth and early-twentieth centuries had grounds for trepidation about the Spencerian position, as Jennie Kassanoff has shown in a recent essay on the staging of race and class in *The House of Mirth*, which demonstrates Wharton's preference, expressed in that novel, for extinction over eugenic degradation. Indeed, depending on class position, one could find terrifying Spencer's statement that "in animals of complex structures, inheritance of acquired characters becomes an important, if not the chief, cause of evolution."[15] To elites, the term, "inheritance" or its cognate, "heritage" could be cold comfort because, as Kassanoff states, "As cultural democratization, class mobility, and ethnic pluralism eroded the elite's belief in the social exclusivity of Darwinian fitness, hereditary distinction increasingly seemed neither permanent nor unique."[16] The Darwinian-Spencerian position that readers encounter in Wharton's fiction is one distilled by the historian Mike Hawkins, who states that "for Spencer, evolutionary progress entailed the continuous purging of the unfit; he had no vision of these latter improving their position and moving up the evolutionary ladder."[17] The degree of angst depended on the question of who was or was not "fit."

Social Darwinism in *The Custom of the Country* is best approached through a key passage in which Wharton crafts Ralph's analysis of his family's plight. The educated, well-traveled gentleman (Harvard, Oxford) frames encroachment-extinction in terms of the consignment of American indigenous peoples to reservations, which was itself a Spencerian fait accompli in recent American history. Ralph's postfrontier viewpoint presumes the conclusion of the fierce Indian wars of the later nineteenth century and subsumes the outcome of the U.S. Government Indian Peace Commission initiative, begun in 1867, charged with ending the Sioux wars and ending the causes of Indian wars, in general. As historians George Tindall and David Shi state, "Congress decided this was best accomplished at the expense of the Indians, by persuading them to take up life on out-of-the-way reservations."[18] Ralph's own tribe, facing extinction by the "Invaders" (*N*, 673), prompts the designation of Ralph's Washington Square friends and family as tribal "Aborigines," their homes the "Reservation" (*N*, 669). Christopher Gair has examined Wharton's connections between Native Americans and the New York genteels, arguing that just as the Indians' "demise had been guaranteed by the ascendency of the next generation of the pioneer," so "the latter are now condemned to the same fate by the ascendency of the next generation of pioneers, that is, the new capitalist hegemony of speculators."[19] Ralph's irony thus deepens against such late-nineteenth-century statements as that of an Indian commissioner who wrote of the reservations, "They consist, for the most part, of ground . . . suited to the peculiar habits of the Indians . . . [and] unfitted for cultivation."[20]

Ralph's analysis has to date failed to capture readers' proper attention because it seems of a piece with Wharton's broadest satire—with barbs at hotels with names like The Incandescent and Stentorian (with its "Looey suites") (*N*, 623, 624, 638), at a society newspaper named the *Radiator*, at American place names such as the Spraggs' hometown of Apex City and the summer resorts of Potash Springs, and indeed at the very name, Undine, chosen by her parents, not from the water sprite of classical myth but a commercial hair-curling product, together with Spragg, the kind of surname Wharton assigns to outlanders, a name distinctly unsuited to monogrammed stationary. Wharton's reflexive satirical barrage per se elicits a response as undifferentiated as the satirical promiscuousness of the author.

Peppered by satire, then, one easily can miss the extension of Wharton's critique—via ironic inversion—from Ralph's awareness of the imperialist, public exhibitions of inferior "others" at such world's fair expositions as those in turn-of-the-century Paris, Chicago, St. Louis. Like Henry Adams, another gentleman self-identified as superannuated in the new era and himself also a devotee of world's fairs, Ralph knows something about the expositions' display of primitive peoples. He imagines the imperialist staging of his own "vanishing" race "exhibited at ethnological shows, pathetically engaged in the exercise of their primitive industries" (*N*, 669).

Within the early twentieth-century age of plate glass and electrification, Wharton's readers are thus invited to imagine crowds gawking at exhibited gentlemen, who are reading case law or displayed at writing desks penning volumes of history, the ladies pouring tea while planning social events to benefit charities. As humorously fey as such an image may be (and also disquieting enough to elicit a nervous laugh from many self-identified genteel readers), Wharton also makes clear that the soon-to-be-extinct old guard of Ralph's lineage is not simply vestigial but also seriously "racially" flawed. Ralph's reference to the tight "restrictions and exclusions of the old code" (*N*, 670) indicates its political quiescence, its rigidity, its provincialism, including want of inventiveness in art, architecture, culinary opportunity. To some extent, Old New York is complicit in its imminent extinction. Wharton had revealed the gravity of this social dislocation in a 1902 fictional fragment, "Disintegration," in which she used "penal settlement" as the term later converted to the ironic "reservation" and "ethnological shows."[21]

Possibly Wharton withheld Darwin's name from Ralph's musing in order to permit what in *The Custom of the Country* she describes as "the undisturbed amusement of watching the picture compose itself" (*N*, 802). If so, readers see a Gilded Age genre painting, in which Ralph falls in love with the beautiful young Midwesterner, Miss Undine Spragg, who is newly moved to New York City and living in a hotel suite with her mother and businessman-father, who have relocated from their Midwestern hometown of Apex in order to further their daughter's social ambitions.

Mistakenly, Ralph believes Undine to be an innocent in need of rescue and protection from the predations of the insouciant, barbarous rich male, an Invader epitomized by Peter Van Degen. In the course of the novel, we find that Marvell's rescue-by-marriage to Undine is fatal, that his love, decency, and sense of responsibility are no match for her boundless, aggressive self-interest. Conducting marriage as a business opportunity for ascent into high social position and wealth, and correlatively regarding divorce as a necessary expedient in that ascent, Undine successively marries and divorces Ralph (with whom she has a son, Paul, from an unwanted pregnancy) and then a Catholic French nobleman, Raymond de Chelles, before finally marrying one of America's newest business titans, Elmer Moffatt, the very man with whom Undine had eloped back in Apex City, when Elmer was poor and Undine's father easily able to have the marriage annulled. The novel ends at a pause, not a conclusion, for Undine's careerist thirst is unslakable, and indications are she will bolt this most recent marriage for yet another she perceives as a new height to scale.

The plot of *The Custom of the Country* is thus cyclical, but the axis of the novel is a socially Darwinian fault line, which is based precisely on Ralph's presupposition of Darwin's binary distinction between lower and higher moral natures. Darwin had cited the "higher . . . social instincts [which] relate to the welfare of others" in opposition to the "lower [i.e., selfish] moral rules."[22] Ralph and Undine represent the extremes of this polarity: Undine totally self-interested, Ralph self-sacrificing to a fault, ruining his health and indefinitely postponing his own literary career as he attempts business dealings to underwrite his wife's expenses for travel, seasonal wardrobes, portraiture, jewelry.

Ralph's grasp of the Darwinian binary moral division, accurate in its broad contours, is thus fatally myopic in specifics, a disjuncture which the novel exploits profoundly in the lethal relationship between him and Undine. Their two racial groups, one of high moral development, the other base, are fundamentally incompatible. The doomed Ralph Marvell proves to be the recording secretary of the cultured Aborigines' demise and of the low, that is, self-interested, Invaders' hegemony.

In literary association, Ralph's given name may call to mind the kindly invalid, Ralph Touchett, in Henry James's *The Portrait of a Lady*. A different connection, however, is central to *The Custom of the Country*. Just as "Marvell" is the surname summoning a host of poetic associations from seventeenth-century England, as Candace Waid shows,[23] so the given name, Ralph, directs us to Ralph Waldo Emerson. While Darwinism provided Wharton a social paradigm useful for fictional design, Emerson was the American literary figure who served Wharton as an important argumentive precursor to Darwin and Darwinism and also proved influential in the development of the narrative structure of *The Custom of the Country*.

In Wharton's thought, Emerson may seem an improbable predecessor to Darwin. His transcendentalism has been understood to be one facet of her search for spirituality and has been recognized as a philosophical counter to Darwinian determinism.[24] As with her admiring but unspecific references to Darwin and Spencer, Wharton's remarks on Emerson are less explicit and extensive than might be wished; though the record of her interest is clear, her use of Emerson's writing is evidentiary. His name recurrently appears in Wharton's letters and especially in her critical writings. During courtship, Edward (Teddy) Wharton endorsed the "original always" Emerson, and in 1898, Wharton expressed appreciation of his poem "Threnody."[25] Often cited is Wharton's 1907 invocation of Emerson's Sophoclean phrase at her first encounter with the journalist, Morton Fullerton, who became her lover: "'The moment my eyes fell upon him I was content.'"[26] Later, in 1912, Wharton enjoined Fullerton, "Read Emerson" (*L*, 281).

Emerson's essays, notably the *Essays: First Series* (1841), especially attracted Wharton, whose own critical writings claimed peer relation to his. She cited him in her attempt to explain the relative thinness of American literature: "It is because we have chosen to be what Emerson called 'mixed of middle clay' that we offer . . . so meagre a material to the imagination" (*UCW*, 154). In 1898, Wharton used that same phrase as a provisional book title.[27] Wharton admired Emerson's 1856 "reverent but lucid estimate of the Lake Poets" in *English Traits*, declaring that she knew "of nothing as honest and independent" (209). In an essay, "The Art of Henry James," she quoted James's own citation of Emerson's term, "the alien energy," in "The Over-Soul," glossed by Wharton as "personal inspiration" (314). She endorsed William Brownell's praise of Emerson in his essay on American literature[28] and listed "Emerson" in her library in Italy in 1910 (*L*, 238). Even toward the end of her life, in 1930, she sought in Emerson a title for her novel, *The Gods Arrive* (1932).[29]

As a reviewer-essayist herself, Wharton was in a position to self-identify with Emerson as a literary peer working in the same genre. And just as her own spiritual inquiry has seemed to be an assay of Emersonian transcendentalism, it might seem likely that any fictional expression would emphasize the divinity of nature and the human soul's participation in that divinity. Indeed, Carol Singley has recognized Wharton's eroticized (Walt) Whitmanesque transmutation of Emersonian transcendentalism in the novel *Summer* (1917).[30]

Yet *The Custom of the Country* exploits Emerson's texts in quite different ways. First, it employs Emersonian argumentive structures in congruence with the Darwinian binarism of lower versus higher natures. In Emerson, the fullest statement on binaries is found in the essay, "Compensation," which challenges a Chris-

tian doctrine that Emerson believed to be degraded in the contemporary moment, when spiritual compensation was reduced
to the mere deferred "bank-stock and doubloons, venison and
champagne" currently enjoyed by "unprincipled men." As a cor-
rective, Emerson set out to "record some facts that indicate the
path of the law of Compensation."[31]

The opening premise of his argument is that binary divisions
operate equally in nature and human nature, that "an inevitable
dualism bisects nature, so that each thing is a half." The essay
posits a "polarity . . . [which] we meet in every part of nature," and Emerson's examples include heat and cold, ebb and
flow, male and female, and "upper" and "under." The essay asserts binaries alike in nature and in humankind: "dualism under-
lies the nature and condition of man," so that "every excess
causes a defect; every defect, an excess."[32] More examples follow,
of loss and gain, wit and folly, pleasure and penalty. Within several paragraphs, "Compensation" will move to homology as the
structural fundament of nature ("the world globes itself in a
drop of dew").[33] Emerson goes on to argue that because "Nature
hates monopolies and exceptions," it achieves a leveling effect
and thus "keeps [its] balance true."[34] Emerson's polarities resolve
into wholeness.

It was not, however, Emersonian wholeness via homology or
balance that would serve *The Custom of the Country*, but rather his
binary divisions. Wharton, who wrote the novel over the span of
her own wrenching divorce from Teddy, was interested in antithesis, not complementary balance, and she deployed the
Emersonian polarity to stage and enforce her social Darwinian
schism. Emerson's own binarism, that is, provided Wharton a
model by which Ralph and Undine, as man and woman, could
represent the social disjuncture of identity as lower or higher and
do so in a strict, disjunctive, uncompromising gender polarity.

This move was far from simplistic. To understand its opera-
tion, one first presumes the authorial prerogative to excerpt from
Emerson aspects of argumentive design that serve the novelist in
the early years of the twentieth century. One acknowledges as
well Wharton's own personal "twisting" of sorts, a characteristic
she imputes to Undine but which she herself must undergo, for

gender reversal in *The Custom of the Country* is congruent with
Wharton's much-acknowledged self-identification with the masculine. Wharton, we know, "liked to think of herself as a 'self-
made man'," "preferred the company of men" (*UCW*, 15), and
"envisioned her creative self as masculine."[35] In large part, this
identification came from doubts about women's intellectual critical capacities. The editor of her *Uncollected Critical Writings* concludes that she was skeptical of "the critical capacities of women
generally" and notes that in Wharton's fiction, the outlets and fo-
rums in which women might venture into criticism (e.g., public
lectures and literary clubs) are "routinely and brutally satirized"
(*UCW*, 8, 11). In Wharton, "The figure of the critic, reviewer, or
scholar," concludes Frederick Wegener, "is predominantly and
conspicuously male" (*UCW*, 12). Maleness here means legitimate
authority and positional dominance: "the decidedly male direction of [Wharton's] philosophical and literary education allowed
her to link herself [with] . . . the dominant culture."[36] This
self-identification with critical-novelistic masculinity enabled and
justified Wharton's review-essays and her adoption of male nar-
rators or protagonists, such as the engineer of *Ethan Frome* or
Newland Archer of *The Age of Innocence* or Professor Linyard of
"The Descent of Man."

Wharton's "supple twist" (*N*, 680) of self-gendering doubtless
contributed to her fictional exercise of the systematic gender reversal which feminizes Ralph and masculinizes Undine. *The Custom of the Country* is, in fact, schematic in its gender role reversal.
As Ralph Marvell is shown to be the helpmate, the sensitive supporter of the spouse, the maternal figure who best nurtures his
child, the physically "small, well-knit, fair" figure whose skin, we
learn, "was as clear as a woman's" (*N*, 643, 667), so conversely is
the business-like Undine temperamentally and psychologically
masculinized. Physically, to be sure, Wharton follows the dictates
of conventional female beauty, which is Undine's capital: she
takes "joy" in "dramatizing her beauty" (*N*, 635) and a "larger
pleasure in the general homage to her beauty" (*N*, 683). Even in
times of constraint, she regards her mirrored reflection and
draws "fresh hope from the sight of her beauty" (*N*, 784).

Behaviorally, however, Undine's character is all utilitarian strategy, notably in its ties to male business practices. In Wharton's fiction, this marketplace transactional world was fully in play in *The House of Mirth*, as Wai Chee Dimock has shown.[37] In that novel, individual characters (e.g., the conniving Bertha Dorset) might be traced as proto-Undine figures but at most serve as preliminary sketches to the monumental protagonist of *The Custom of the Country*, whose readers have remarked on Undine's inheritance of her father's business acumen, a "business shrewdness which was never quite dormant" (*N*, 854). Martha Patterson, as noted earlier, argues that Wharton shapes Undine into "a well-managed corporate employee," while Elaine Showalter identifies "the art of the deal" as central to *The Custom of the Country*, her phrase the subtitle of a discussion featuring Undine as a major deal-maker.[38]

Gender inversion in the novel, however, enables an Emersonian-Darwinian binary scheme of the lower versus higher moral natures. Ralph Marvell, we find, is not only the representative of a moral nature committed to others' welfare but also is a would-be poet, whose "inner world" accords with Emerson's principles of correspondence between self and nature. Ralph's spiritual being is an internalized seaside cave, which corresponds to an actual cave discovered in his boyhood, "a secret inaccessible place with glaucous lights, mysterious murmurs, and a single shaft of communication with the sky" (*N*, 671). This cave is a barometer of Ralph's spiritual state, and prior to meeting Undine (and having lost his cousin, Clare, to marriage to Van Degen), Ralph reportedly felt an inner darkness and formed a new life plan: "to learn and to do—to know what the great people had thought, think about their thinking, and then launch his own boat: write some good verse if possible; if not, then critical prose" (*N*, 672). The literary career alludes to the injunctions of "The American Scholar," with Emerson's American "young men" responsibly seeking not only to understand intellectual predecessors but also to enter into the new age which "must write its own books."[39] Ralph's projected literary career echoes Emerson's own as poet and essayist.

Wharton further extends Ralph's Emersonian identity in his wedding voyage to Italy, where he lies on a hot, sultry afternoon with Undine in an ilex grove in Siena:

It was one of those moments when the accumulated impressions of life converge on heart and brain, elucidating, enlacing each other, in a mysterious confusion of beauty. He had had glimpses of such a state before, of such mergings of the personal with the general life that one felt one's self a mere wave on the wild stream of being, yet thrilled with a sharper sense of individuality than can be known within the mere bounds of the actual. But now he knew that sensation in its fulness, and with it came the releasing power of language. Words were flashing like brilliant birds through the boughs overhead. (*N*, 714)

Ralph's thought is expressed largely in terms compatible with those recurrent in Emerson. One could cite numerous instances of rhetorical apposition, for instance, this from "The Poet": "This hidden truth, that the fountains whence all this river of Time, and its creatures, floweth, are intrinsically ideal and beautiful, draws us to the consideration of nature and functions of the Poet, or the man of Beauty."[40] Or this from "The Over-Soul": "Within man is the soul of the whole; the wise silence; the universal beauty, to which every part and particle is equally related; the eternal ONE."[41]

Astute readers, of course, recognize cautionary terms in Wharton's portrayal of Ralph's transcendental experience, for instance, her use of the deconstructively anatomical "heart and *brain*," instead of the organic-spiritual "heart and mind" (italics added). The "mystic depths whence Ralph's passion spr[ings]," moreover, are sounded under Undine's influence, not that of Emersonian Nature. And the dilatory Ralph hardly seems like a confrere of the prolific Emerson, when he fails to summon and inscribe the beautiful flashing words which fly, birdlike, in the sky above him, thinking that for the moment, it is "pleasanter . . . to watch them" (*N*, 714).

We begin to see that in Ralph, Wharton gives us a version of Emerson, but deliberately an Emerson manqué. Her Ralph does not think or speak Emerson's rigorous transcendentalist thoughts, such as to be found in this statement, also from "Compensation": "Life invests itself with inevitable conditions, which the unwise seek to dodge. . . . He sees the mermaid's head, but not the dragon's tail."[42] Far too late in *The Custom of the Country* does Ralph learn how much he has dodged, how blind to that "dragon's tail," how fatally bereft of "compensation" is his life. Perceptive as he is, then, Ralph is shown to represent a lapsed, superannuated transcendentalism which is superficial, flaccid, feminized, effete. We see, in sum, Wharton's deliberate misreading of Emerson for fictional objectives that prove to serve a Darwinian scheme. Ralph's self-sacrifice for Undine is nothing less than self-defeat.

The Custom of the Country simultaneously develops Undine as the inverted Emersonian counterpart in this binary narrative design. Emerson's "Self-Reliance" is particularly useful in disclosing how Undine, absent Emerson's spiritual provisos, expresses a degraded self-reliance, which is to say an unbridled individualism of the kind that Alexis de Tocqueville had feared and deplored in American culture, and which appears in Darwin as a "low" moral nature. We note, first, that Emerson suffuses his essay with divine provisos, such as: "As soon as the man is at one with God, he will not beg. He will then see prayer in all action."[43] Or this: "The great man is he who in the midst of the crowd keeps with perfect sweetness the independence of solitude."[44]

Undine, however, is not such a "man." Wharton shows her to be a creature of the Emersonian binary—yet stripped of its proper divinity, as Ralph is deprived of intellectual-spiritual rigor. As self-reliance incarnate, Undine is monstrous. S/he is the tyrant standing in contempt of those others whom Emerson names as cowards, as minors and invalids in a protected corner, as beggars and sycophants.[45] She is self-assuredly superior to that love which, as Emerson says, odiously "pules and whines," and she is free of entanglements with friends, clients, children who "conspire" to importune one with "trifles."[46] Her every societal manipulation is sanctioned by pejorative terms which, in Emerson, cast society as "a conspiracy against the manhood of every one of its members," who are themselves an indifferentiated and perishable "wave" and an "intruding rabble."[47] Minus Emerson's remonstrative spiritual checks and balances, "Self-Reliance" seems to authorize Undine's divorces and cunning new directions: "Why drag about this corpse of your memory? . . . A foolish consistency is the hobgoblin of little minds."[48]

In self-referential terms, a self-reliant Undine is thus freed entirely to pursue her own self-interest. The mandate untethers her from fidelity to lineage, to social or familial tradition, or to custom. It severs her from deference to societal groupings or kinship networks. Emerson's words express the norm of her extreme self-interest: "I shun father and mother and wife and brother, when my genius calls me"; "Expect me not to show cause why I seek or why I exclude company"; "What I must do is all that concerns me, not what the people think."[49]

Emerson's own statements on nature's ontology, as his readers know, provide a counterbalance against such expression of self-interested egotism. When the essayist claims preference for genuineness in opposition to what is "glittering and unsteady," the binarism necessarily privileges the genuine and relegates all else to a realm of tawdry instability. In Emerson's world, we know where we ought to belong. Wharton does too, of course, but her plan for Undine requires a deliberate misreading as keen as that which abets her delineation of Ralph. "Self-Reliance" advises that the "cultivated man," when newly respectful of his "nature," is properly "ashamed of his property."[50] Undine, however, is not the "cultivated man." That identity is Ralph's, and it proves to be enfeebled. The self-reliant Undine, for her part, is brutally strong—the "brutes" Emerson identifies in the essay are creatures who conform to nobody.[51]

The reference to Undine as brute is not merely rhetorical here, considering Wharton's enmeshment of Emersonian binarism with Darwinism. The misreading or distortion of Emerson, that is, is but one part of the socially Darwinian design in *The Custom of the Country*. In fact, Wharton goes so far into Darwinian taxonomy as to class the Invaders among the lower vertebrates, the reptile-amphibians. Readers first encounter the ultra rich Peter Van Degen at a picture gallery, where Miss Undine Spragg returns the stare of this "unpleasant-looking" sportsman with an "odd physiognomy," which is specified as "this grotesque saurian head, with eye-lids as thick as lips and lips as thick as earlobes" (*N*, 653). The Invader era of Van Degenism is, in fact, named for this creature, the philanderer who has already invaded the Dagonet-Marvell family by marrying Ralph's intelligent and generous (yet sybaritically inclined) cousin, Clare, whom he virtually ignores, having installed her in his "lair" (*N,* 672). Repeatedly through the novel we hear of Peter Van Degen's "bulging stare" and his physical "bulk" (*N,* 746), his "bulging eyes and queer retreating face" (*N,* 653) and "batrachian sallowness" (*N,* 774). Elsewhere, writes Wharton, "shone the batrachian countenance of Peter Van Degen" (*N,* 665).

Readers may scurry for a dictionary to learn that Sauria are a suborder of reptiles, including the lizards, crocodiles, and alligators, while the Batrachia are amphibians that discard gills and a tail, notably frogs. It is possible that, in part, Wharton developed the frog-like countenance in recollection of passages early in William James's *The Principles of Psychology* (1890).[52] Ambivalent as she was about James (perhaps, as R. W. B. Lewis suggests, resentful of Henry James's "devotion" to his older brother [*L,* 10]), Wharton at some point was likely nonetheless to have perused *The Principles of Psychology*, in whose opening passages she would have found basic lessons in neurology instanced by frogs. The frog-like countenance of Van Degen may have been prompted by such a passage, in which James describes neural reflexes of male frogs: "A living frog . . . will restlessly explore the neighborhood [in a jar of water] until . . . he has discovered a path round its brim to the goal of its desires."[53] A few pages later, James turns to the subject of the frog's sexual desires: "he manifests sexual passion at the proper season, and . . . postpones this reflex act until a female of his own species is provided."[54] Primitive in neural reflex, the frog became one of Wharton's species of choice for her ur-Invader, who is appetite incarnate.

Though writers as recent as Rudyard Kipling might have drawn on the tradition of Aesop's and La Fontaine's animal fables for physical descriptions of characters, Wharton's fauna are Darwinian. The bulgy-eyed Peter Van Degen is a lower-order amphibian, a classification reinforced when, in a sitting-room, "in an attitude of easy intimacy, [he] stretched his lounging length" (*N,* 736). The man is literally a lounge lizard—and withal a predator, a "capriciously-treated animal" "with a large appetite for primitive satisfactions and a sturdy belief in his intrinsic right to them" (N, 812). Aroused, the "frock-coated gentleman [who] usually pined at Undine" metamorphoses into a flushed, sallow batrachian with the eyes of "primitive man" (N, 774).

Undine is herself less his prey than his primitive female double. Wharton never uses the same taxonomic descriptors for Undine as for Van Degen, for the protagonist's capital is the physical beauty of which she—and we—are ever mindful. Yet "there was more similarity of tastes [between Van Degen and Undine]" whose eyes meet in what seems to be "a quick exchange of understanding" (N, 748, 746). And Wharton relies on readers' mental images of the flexing vertebra of alligators and crocodiles, the saurians, to provide a species match-up with that Undine, who is early on described principally for her own tortuousness: "She was always doubling and twisting on herself, and every movement she made seemed to start at the nape of her neck, just below the lifted roll of reddish-gold hair, and flow without a break through her whole slim length to the tips of her fingers and the points of her slender restless feet" (N, 625). It is the twistiness of Undine that allies her with the saurian-batrachian Van Degen. As Ralph finds, "She would go on eluding and doubling" (N, 768).

Wharton exploits tortuousness as a salient component of Undine's temperament, which is to say that Undine displays the psychosocial forms of the Van Degen physiognomy. For instance, her "supple twist" when the manicurist-masseuse asks, "Ever been engaged before, Undine?" (N, 680), evades the question and shows her deftness at the serpentine movement. This is the supple twisting that signals Undine's adaptiveness to ever-changing situations that propel her through one affair and four marriages in a climb through American and French aristocracy and into the vast wealth of a business fortune.

Wharton further extends the identification of Undine with Sauria, the alligators and crocodiles, by assigning the protagonist a reflexive rage. Quite simply, her temper is to be read as primitive stimulus-response, though the origin of Undine's temper is sometimes mistaken solely for pediatric irresponsibility on the part of her parents, both of whom "had admired her [childhood] assertiveness" (N, 650), even though Undine would "scream" or "sulk" (*N*, 655) for toys or sweets. When thwarted, she shows "scorn and anger in every line of her arrogant young back" (*N*, 650), and in adulthood, Undine regularly reverts to "one of her little-girl rages" (*N*, 856). She weeps in "violence" (*N*, 742). At least one critic hypothesizes Undine's own (oxymoronically shallow) subjectivity as the result of the abdication of parental responsibility,[55] and it is true that Elmer and Leota Spragg exist to indulge their daughter, to gratify her every desire.

Regarded within the Darwinian classificatory system of Sauria, however, Undine is behaviorally sui generis, her rages characteristic of her suborder. Thus, her "passionate desire to obliterate, to 'get even'" with those who caused her "failures" (*N*, 687). Thus, also, her "blind desire to wound and destroy" (*N*, 970), her "primitive impulse to hurt and destroy" (*N*, 984). When blocked, "her eyes were like the eyes of an enemy" (*N*, 730). In these lines, the terms passion, blindness, and primitive impulse all signal circumvention of intellect and heart in neural reflexivity.

Cold-bloodedness, too, is a saurian-batrachian trait Wharton developed to emphasize Undine's cool nerve under duress, as when she works to manipulate an aroused and overwrought Van Degen: "Undine's heart was beating fast," but "a cool spirit within her seemed to watch over and regulate her sensations, and leave her capable of measuring the intensity of those she provoked" (*N*, 816). Darwin had described sexual selection in which males struggle for possession of females, and he used the example of "the males of polygamous animals," specifically male alligators, "fighting, bellowing, and whirling round,"[56] although he was silent on the female role within this "economy of nature."[57]

Wharton plausibly weighs in on the side of female sexual maneuvering among the cold-blooded fellow creatures, with Undine's "every nerve strung to the highest pitch of watchfulness" (*N*, 819) as she too plays a part in sexual selection. Undine's objective is to secure this new mate, having "found out that she had given herself to the exclusive and the dowdy [i.e., to Ralph] when the future belonged to the showy and the promiscuous" (*N*, 748). In Darwin's terms, this will be the future of the "polygamous animals." Undine only dissembles, in Darwin's term, as "an apparently unconcerned beholder of the struggle,"[58] but actually operates as the polygamous creature willing to abandon her deathly ill husband while battling for favor of a new mate, Van Degen. Temporarily she triumphs, reducing the besotted Van Degen to a "small and withered . . . old man's [face] . . . with a lower lip that trembled queerly" (*N*, 820), before losing him altogether when he realizes that he himself, in his moment of illness, that is, weakness, might in turn be abandoned by Undine, herself a serial polygamist.

While much is made of Undine as water sprite, we now need to recognize an important, quite different aquatic motive for her naming. Mistakenly, the bridegroom Ralph thinks his wife "Ariel-like" in her remoteness, but Undine's "coolness from the element from which she took her name" (*N*, 721, 714) radically changes meaning in context of the milieu of a saurian-batrachian Van Degenism. Ralph is correct, at least, in his perception that Undine is outside the human realm, but he mistakenly looks upward toward the spiritual-ineffable instead of downward into the muck, habitat of the frogs, alligators, and crocodiles. Undine is no Ariel but a lithe, cold-blooded amphibian camouflaged as a beauty. Her subsequent disregard for her offspring, Paul, a child who is more hatched than born, is but a continuation of this identity as a biologically cold-blooded lower vertebrate.

The imitativeness that Wharton asserts as a primary characteristic of Undine's pseudosociality is crucial here: "Undine was fiercely independent and yet passionately imitative." "Her mind was as destitute of beauty and mystery as the prairie school-house in which she had been educated" (*N*, 633, 718). Darwin had posited human evolution in which solitary animals perished while others "living in close association" and, taking "greatest pleasure in society," survived and "benefitted."[59] He thereby developed his theory of consocial sympathy and the evolution of emotional subjectivity, posited in *The Expression of the Emotions in Man and Animals* (1872).[60] Undine, of course, is incapable of such subjectivity. As Nancy Bentley says, Undine "turns her power for assimilation against the very social worlds that embrace her."[61] Disguised as a beautiful woman, she can only imitate higher human behavior.

In this portrayal of Undine, Wharton obviously travels a huge step beyond Darwin-Spencer, taking literary liberties as great as those she takes with Emerson's texts. In effect, she expels the Van Degens and their kind from the species homo sapiens. The societal incompatibility that proves fatal to Ralph is not that between different human racial groupings but between entirely different animal subclassifications in the Linnaean system. Darwin posited sympathy as the "foundation-stone" of "social instinct" in human beings and affirmed its strengthening by practice and habit.[62] Too late does Ralph learn that Undine is neither a virgin nor innocent, that she, like Van Degen, is the ur-Invader and literally no match for this superannuated Aborigine of Old New York. In sum, Ralph will finally recognize his own "hidden hereditary failing" (*N*, 911) but commit suicide (to which Undine has driven him) without full knowledge that the Invaders cannot biologically, let alone culturally, extend compensatory generosity. Biologically, they lack the traits of communitarian love and sympathy whose importance Darwin emphasized late-on in *Origin*, in *The Descent of Man*, and in *The Expression of the Emotions*.

Consistent with the evolutionary theories advanced in these texts, Wharton's readers may legitimately inquire into the process of natural selection as glimpsed in the generation to succeed Undine's. Surprisingly, we find in that projected lineage no saurian-batrachian but an authentic gentleman, represented in the figure of Paul Marvell, the reincarnation of Ralph (and the proper stepson of Raymond de Chelles, who is, like Ralph, a traditionalist, and whom Paul nostalgically calls his French father). At nine, Paul is a "big boy" (*N*, 1003) who, except for vacations, has grown up in isolation in a fashionable private school.

Wharton uses Paul's ignorance of his entitlement as a son qua son in large part to continue the critique of Undine. Arriving for Easter vacation at Undine Moffatt's new "big and strange" "*hôtel* overlooking one of the new quarters of Paris" (*N*, 1003), Paul spends the day awaiting the return of Undine and her new husband, Elmer Moffatt. The pathos of the boy's late-afternoon reunion with his mother is palpable, for Undine rebuffs his affection, and Paul overhears his new stepfather say, "Can't you ever give him a minute's time, Undine," to which she replies by "sail[ing] through the door with her head high, as she did when anything annoyed her" (*N*, 1010).

As much as the closing scenes reinforce the larger pattern of the novel, the presence of Paul Marvell suggests the limit of Wharton's Darwinian design and her provisional hope for the future. Through Paul, the novelist reintroduces the bearer of values supported in the figure of Ralph. Like his father, Paul has good taste and a reverent appreciation for heritage over many generations. The vulgarity of the new Moffatt hotel with its white fur rugs and brocade chairs embarrasses the boy. And he feels a righteous "rage of hate" (*N*, 1011) at Moffatt for the businessman-connoisseur's virtual theft of the cherished de Chelles ancient French family tapestries, which now hang as Invader trophies in the hotel.

Paul's taste and civility are compounded by his nascent literary sensibility, as Wharton writes that the boy's solitary life has engendered "a passion for the printed page" (*N*, 1005). We note as well Paul's effort to report to Undine his recent school prize in composition. In sum, in this young reader-writer, Wharton represents Ralph in the figure of Paul, and this move has important bearing for the future. Moffatt, it is true, fails to perceive in Paul the reincarnation of the Marvell sensibility, promising the boy a place in his business, a role for which Paul is doubtless as unsuited as was his father.

But in projecting Paul, in Moffatt's term, as potentially "the richest boy in America" (*N*, 1011), Wharton may express a guarded optimism for a "descent of man" beyond the Invader era. Before his death, Ralph had begun to write what *The Custom of the Country* supports as a creditable novel proceeding through steady application and craftsmanship honed through practice, which is to say something like Wharton's own work ethic as revealed in *The Writing of Fiction* (1925), in which she insists that inspiration must be "taught and guided," and authorial "time, meditation and patient labour [expended in] the process of extraction and representation" (*WF*, 20, 57). So, in turn, might Paul eventually reprise his father's aborted career as novelist and do so with financial undergirding from the fortune of an Invader, if not Moffatt, then another of Undine's husbands. For whosoever

Undine's spouse(s) may be in the future, he will certainly be rich, and Paul Marvell—indeed, all the Paul Marvells—will stand to inherit, wholly or in part, the fortunes of these saurians-batrachians. Their money might provide patronage for art and intellectual cultivation in generations to come. Through Paul, in fine, Wharton begins a new cycle that gives the Aborigines a possible second chance, a possible opportunity to live anew.

This futurist projection carries a historical critique of the bygone genteel caste which virtually conspired in its own extinction. Ralph dies of enervating despair, but Paul is fueled by a righteous rage that will motivate his socioliterary efforts. Energizing Paul in this way, Wharton casts forward a post-social Darwinian–Spencerian future to envision a new habitat for her own cohort, a regeneration and revitilization of her own species.

NOTES

1. See Katherine Joslin, "Architectonic or Episodic? Gender and *The Fruit of the Tree*," in *A Forward Glance: New Essays on Edith Wharton*, ed. Clare Colquitt, et al. (Newark: University of Delaware Press, 1999), 62–75.

2. Carol J. Singley, *Edith Wharton: Matters of Mind and Spirit* (New York: Cambridge University Press, 1995), 56.

3. See Candace Waid, *Edith Wharton's Letters from the Underworld* (Chapel Hill: University of North Carolina Press, 1991), 129–72.

4. See Maureen Honey, "Erotic Visual Tropes in the Fiction of Edith Wharton," in *A Forward Glance*, ed. Colquitt et al., 76–99, 82–91. See also Margot K. Louis, "Proserpine and Pessimism: Goddesses of Death, Life, and Language from Swinburne to Wharton," *Modern Philology* 96, no. 3 (February 1999): 312–46.

5. Martha A. Patterson, "Incorporating the New Woman in Wharton's *The Custom of the Country*," *Studies in American Fiction* 26 no. 2 (Autumn 1998): 213.

6. Cynthia Griffin Wolff, "Introduction," *The Custom of the Country*, by Edith Wharton (New York: Scribner's, 1997), 8.

7. Cynthia Griffin Wolff, *A Feast of Words* (New York: Oxford University Press, 1977), 232–33; Shari Benstock, *No Gifts from Chance: A Biography of Edith Wharton* (New York: Scribner's, 1994), 283.

8. Singley, *Matters of Mind and Spirit*, 4, 21.

9. Charles Darwin, *The Descent of Man, and Selection in Relation to Sex*, pts. I and II (1870–71; reprint, vols. 21 and 22 of *The Works of Charles Darwin*, ed. Paul H. Barrett and R. B. Freeman [New York: New York University Press, 1989]), 9.

10. Charles Darwin, *Origin of Species* (1859; reprint, vol. 16 of *The Works of Charles Darwin*, ed. Barrett and Freeman), 401–02.

11. Ibid., 428.

12. Carl Degler, *In Search of Human Nature: The Decline and Revival of Darwinism in American Social Thought* (New York: Oxford University Press, 1991), 11.

13. See Herbert Spencer, *The Principles of Biology* (New York: D. Appleton, 1886).

14. See Robert Heath Lock, *Recent Progression in the Study of Variation, Heredity, and Evolution* (1906; reprint, New York: Dutton, 1911), 47.

15. Spencer, *The Principles of Biology*, 41–42.

16. Jennie A. Kassanoff, "Extinction, Taxidermy, Tableaux Vivants: Staging Race and Class in *The House of Mirth*," *PMLA* 115, no. 1 (January 2000): 61.

17. Mike Hawkins, *Social Darwinism in European and American Thought, 1860–1945* (Cambridge: Cambridge University Press, 1997), 88.

18. George Brown Tindall and David E. Shi, *America: A Narrative History*, 3rd ed. (New York: W. W. Norton, 1984), 757.

19. Christopher Gair, "The Crumbling Structure of 'Appearances': Representation and Authenticity in *The House of Mirth* and *The Custom of the Country*," *Modern Fiction Studies* 43, no. 2 (1997): 355.

20. Quoted in Tindall and Shi, *America*, 762.

21. Quoted in Kassanoff, "Extinction, Taxidermy, Tableaux Vivants," 69–70.

22. Darwin, *Origin*, 401. See Patterson, "Incorporating the New Woman," 221.

23. Waid, *Letters from the Underworld*, 155–66.

24. Singley, *Matters of Mind and Spirit*, 209–10.

25. Benstock, *No Gifts from Chance*, 54, 171.

26. Ibid., 169.

27. Ibid., 92.

28. Ibid., 153.

29. Ibid., 421.

30. Singley, *Matters of Mind and Spirit*, 148–62.

31. Ralph Waldo Emerson, *Emerson: Essays and Poems*, ed. Joel Porte, et al. (New York: Library of America, 1996), 285–86.

32. Ibid.

33. Ibid., 289.

34. Ibid., 288.

35. Gloria Erlich, *The Sexual Education of Edith Wharton* (Berkeley and Los Angeles: University of California Press, 1992), 149.

36. Joslin, "Architectonic or Episodic?" 41.

37. Wai-Chee Dimock, "Debasing Exchange: Edith Wharton's *The House of Mirth*," *PMLA* 100, no. 5 (October 1985): 783–92; reprinted in *The House of Mirth*, ed. Shari Benstock (New York: Bedford St. Martin's, 1994), 375–90.

38. Elaine Showalter, "*The Custom of the Country* and the Art of the Deal," in *The Cambridge Companion to Edith Wharton*, ed. Millicent Bell (New York: Cambridge University Press, 1995), 87–97.

39. Emerson, *Essays and Poems*, 56.

40. Ibid., 447–48.

41. Ibid., 386.

42. Ibid., 291.

43. Ibid., 276.

44. Ibid., 263.

45. Ibid., 260, 268.

46. Ibid., 262, 273.

47. Ibid., 261, 281, 272.

48. Ibid., 265.

49. Ibid., 262, 263.

50· Ibid., 281.

51. Ibid., 260.

52. William James, *The Principles of Psychology*, vol. 1 (1890; reprint, New York: Dover, 1950).

53. Ibid., 7.

54. Ibid., 17.

55. See Susan Goodman, *Edith Wharton's Women: Friends and Rivals* (Hanover: University Press of New England, 1990), 62–64.

56. Darwin, *Origin*, 72, 73.

57. Ibid., 83.

58. Ibid., 72.

59· Darwin, *Descent*, 1, 109.

60. Charles Darwin, *The Expression of the Emotions in Man and Animals* (1872; reprint, vol. 23 of *The Works of Charles Darwin*, ed. Barrett and Freeman.

61. Nancy Bentley, "'Hunting for the Real': Wharton and the Science of Manners," in *The Cambridge Companion to Edith Wharton*, ed. Bell, 47–67, 63.

62. Darwin, *Descent*, 1, 103.

Wharton's "Others"

Addiction and Intimacy

Dale M. Bauer

Ever since the rise of Women's Studies and feminist theory, scholars have been continually revising their critical interests in Edith Wharton, one of the few twentieth-century female American authors canonized by the 1970s. Crucial to these reassessments has been the assumption that Wharton celebrated women's sexuality and power. R. W. B. Lewis's Pulitzer Prize–winning biography (1975) establishes Wharton as the consummate professional author, while Shari Benstock (1994) enshrines Wharton for her prominence as a female modernist. In 1977, Cynthia Griffin Wolff established Wharton as a self-fashioned ("anti-Romantic realist") artist, and Amy Kaplan (1988) cemented the interest in Wharton's "profession of authorship" by analyzing her major fictions as participating in the "construction of realism." In 1980, Elizabeth Ammons published her landmark study of Wharton's fiction. Other Wharton critics have followed through on the assumption that sexuality shapes the ground upon which the reader can find Edith Wharton's "argument with America" (Ammons), her "brave new politics" (Bauer), her "ethnography of manners" (Bentley), her "sexual education" (Erlich), her "inner circle" of friends (Goodman), her preoccupation with "shame" (Raphael), her "anxious power" (Singley and Sweeney), her exploration of women's social and sexual power

(Tichi), and her mythic "underworld" (Waid).[1] Yet in more than twenty years of focused study, Wharton's attitude toward sexuality has defied consensus because she seems to embrace passion, even while she distrusts its power. Wharton's fictive representations of sexuality frustrate contemporary critical assumptions about the efficacy of sexual power and agency.

Contemporary critical discourse has devoted itself to assessing modern sexuality, and such discussions often prize the experience of otherness and privilege its shadowy or marginalized proportions. This theorizing has led Wharton's critics to look toward her descriptions of racial, ethnic, or class "others" for signs of cultural anxiety. It has become commonplace to read sexual desire as "coded" or displaced or projected onto the taboo or primitive, the marginalized or the "other." According to its association with race and ethnicity, repressed sexuality can be analyzed for what Eric Lott calls the "racial unconscious."[2] That is, repressed desires get rechanneled and find expression as the opposite or "other" of the subject—a Jewish woman projects attitudes of superiority onto a gentile man, a white man fantasizes about the exoticism of an Asian woman, an African-American man redirects feelings of submission or domination onto a white woman, or any of a hundred similar scenarios. The object of sexual desire is really an inverted or distorted version of the way the subject sees herself or himself. Thus, sexuality becomes a primary way of understanding how the self *is* what it avows it is not. In this way, Wharton came to see sex expression, a phrase memorialized in V. F. Calverton's 1926 study, *Sex Expression in Literature*, as an experience of alienation rather than intimacy. Thus, while readers have come to see objectification in terms of racial and ethnic otherness, Wharton sees it in terms of sexual self-alienation.[3]

For Wharton, sex expression marks a struggle with her culture's promise of intimacy, and she offers her sense of that intimacy as an addiction, even literalizing the metaphor.[4] Wharton's ambivalence about modern sexuality surfaces in her social critique of alienation, which she understood not as repression or absence of passion, but as passion misdirected toward objects and ideas or, worse, as passion degraded to desire-driven consumerism.

For the most part, Wharton believed herself to be the other, identifying strongly with Milton's Samson, when she signs her letter to William Tyler on May 25, 1937, as "Edith Agonistes." Tricked by his own passion, Samson destroys the temple, the site of his own undoing.[5] Wharton's identification with Samson suggests how much she wanted to topple the temple of culture: the old Victorians, the new Freudians, the self-righteous Christian reformers. If, momentarily, she sees herself as the embattled Hebrew hero, throughout her career she trades a vision of Jewish otherness for one more central and more alive to her: her own. By focusing on the failed desires of one woman after another—first Lily Bart, then Justine Brent, Mattie Silver, and Zeena Frome; from Anna Leath to Undine Spragg to Charity Royall and Ellen Olenska—Wharton was able to show how women became estranged from themselves, their own other. She variously investigated this psychology of alienation, whereby women were forced to trade sex for social currency. Sexual power, for Wharton's heroines, gradually becomes the only way to protest the forces of cultural oblivion. In this scheme, as I will show, Wharton is highly attuned to the experience of otherness, though unresponsive as she was to the racial othering of Jews and African Americans. She yearned for women's freedom of sexual expression but saw it blighted by the cooptation of sexuality and intimacy as a form of business exchange.

For Wharton, the belief that sexual liberation could cure cultural alienation was wrongheaded. What she resisted in other American novelists was their celebration of sex as a release from malaise, even boredom. Wharton was not ambivalent about sex, as evinced from her passionate letters and poems about Morton Fullerton, but she protested against sexual liberation as an antidote to feelings of numbness or emotional paralysis. Ultimately, Wharton rejected women's sexual power because it results in personal as well as cultural alienation. Even more important, her novels, from *The House of Mirth* (1905), *The Fruit of the Tree* (1907), to *Ethan Frome* (1911), substitute the language of drugs for that of sexual liberation or women's freedom from Victorian mores. Drugs, not sex, take the place of her heroines' tragedies of alienation. Lily Bart takes chloral to sleep, perhaps to die; Bessy

Amherst dies of a morphine overdose; Zeena is addicted to patent medicines; Mattie becomes a lifelong invalid and, by extension in a culture devoted to painkillers, an addict. The trick with Wharton is to remember not her fear of drugs and drug-culture, but her view of these drugs as the endpoint of her heroines' failure to find sexual fulfillment. Drugs even literalize the metaphorical destruction of sexual intimacy.

Even as Wharton continually imagined sexual permissiveness as an addiction, her novels treat drug-taking as a central motif for the failure of intimacy. Drug-taking occupied Wharton's imagination: from her early references to the "drug-fiend" Ramy in "Bunner Sisters" to the recreational drugs of Lilla Gates and her set in *The Mother's Recompense*. "Bunner Sisters" takes us from sexual desire to drugs to death, a scheme similar to that in *The Fruit of the Tree*. Addiction serves as a powerful metaphor for Wharton's distrust of modern forms of passion. Intoxication, not intimacy, drives these modern romances. The "drug-fiend" and withdrawal symptoms become figures for Wharton's encounter with the other.[6]

The House of Mirth: Anti-Semitism and Addiction

Three examples from Wharton's writings illustrate her conflict with the promises of sexual liberation and the otherness that results from the failure of intimacy. Wharton's letters sometimes reveal her impatience with exploring the alienations of others. Although she often viewed the habits of her own kind as ironically tragic, Wharton could seldom sympathize with marginalized races, cultures, ethnicities, sexualities. For instance, in a letter about André Suarès's contribution to *The Book of the Homeless* (a collection of pieces by famous authors, edited to benefit Wharton's wartime charities), Wharton, writing to Minnie Cadwalader Jones, declares the piece "too Lesbian" for publication and expurgates those passages from the volume (October 26, 1915).[7] Nor did she sympathize with the mentally ill. A second example is from a 1934 letter, in which Wharton claims to be "a little weary of people who let themselves be bullied by neurasthenics. They (the N.s) have more than their share of fun in all the howling and screeching, and I do believe the old pre-Freudian way of dealing with them was better for them as well as for their victims!"[8] In short, Wharton doubted anything vaguely associated with modern expressions of self, whether sexual or therapeutic. No less prickly, and mostly more noxious, were her rejections of racial others, especially Jews and African Americans.

Finally, the best-known expression of Wharton's sexual and cultural antipathy concerns the characterization, in *The House of Mirth*, of Simon Rosedale, a Jew and foil to WASP gentleman Lawrence Selden. Rosedale is everything that Selden is not. Selden comes from an established family; Rosedale is an interloper. Selden enjoys a fineness of feeling and enjoins Lily Bart to be a citizen in the "republic of the spirit"; Rosedale is perceived as vulgar and materialistic, exhorting Lily to blackmail her way back into society. Selden cannot bear to acknowledge the presence of passion; Rosedale actually tells Lily how much he wants her. Lily first rebuffs Rosedale's proposal of marriage, then contemplates the prospect, but when her night thoughts turn to an image of herself with Rosedale, she finds the idea of sex with him too revolting. Lily's principal objection to Simon Rosedale is not that he is materialistic or vulgar or sexually aggressive, but that he is all those things, a Jew.[9] His Jewishness marks, in the context of the reigning prejudices, just how steeply Lily's status has declined. If everything were right in Lily's world, a Jew could never even hope to approach her. Perhaps the most inadvertently touching scenes in the novel occur when Lily momentarily forgets that Rosedale is a pariah and sees him in his human proportions, playing with Carry Fisher's child or offering her a cup of tea. Such scenes work because Lily's kindly feelings surprise her (and perhaps also Wharton), since they violate her conception of Jewishness. As a repository of everything degenerate in Lily's world, Rosedale keeps Lily from acknowledging her connection to the material reality she must face and, by contrast, the compelling appeal of the vision of spiritual freedom Selden trades in. Wharton suppresses Rosedale so effectively that he disappears from the novel. Thus, Selden's cultural alienation—expressed in

his hopelessly romantic idealism of the "republic of the spirit"—
looks like a responsible, conscious choice. The novel ends tear-
fully with Selden's bedside visit to the scene of Lily's suicide and
the word that he might have spoken.[10]

Yet without extenuating the circumstances of her racism, we
can still see how Wharton was a social critic and, in her fashion, a
voice of the other. Never to be understood as a novelist of "the
people," Wharton nevertheless represents alienation from an
outcast's perspective, particularly in her early fiction. For example, as Jennifer Travis argues about *Ethan Frome*, rather than "a
voice of labor," Wharton expresses a "concern with the suffocation of the small farmer, a suffocation not only by rural poverty,
but by the increasing anonymity of the industrial United
States."[11] Yet it is not only the anonymity but also the alienation
that strikes Wharton as symptomatic of a desire-driven com-
modity culture. Consider how social mistress Carry Fisher in *The
House of Mirth* reveals Wharton's true sense of otherness: "It
was, in fact, characteristic of Carry that, while she actively
gleaned her own stores from the fields of affluence, her real sym-
pathies were on the other side—with the unlucky, the unpopular,
the unsuccessful, with all her hungry fellow-toilers in the shorn
stubble of success" (*N*, 261). Carry's sympathy is saved for the unfortunate class, but Wharton's description reveals her limits. To
be "unlucky, unpopular, or unsuccessful" is not to be racially, eth-
nically, or sexually marked, but to fail, as a quirk of fate, personality, or social circumstance, generally to fit in. Luck, popularity,
success: none of Carry's objects of compassion are sympathetic
because of their spiritual or ethical qualities; their appeal lies in
their social failures and economic deficiencies. In fact, as I will
show, Wharton's earlier heroines emerge as they do because, like
Wharton, they reject—unluckily and unpopularly—impractical
idealism and hopeless cynicism, embracing more modern forms
of alienation like drug-taking. They are ultimately pitted, on the
one hand, against the alienated cultural heroes, a Lawrence
Selden or an Ethan Frome; or, on the other, against the repressed
figures of the culture—the working class, the Jews, and an assort-
ment of social failures. Wharton constructs her social critique
through the figure of women: her later heroines' repressed pas-

sions return to destroy them. This is the logic by which Wharton's women are transformed into sexual others, out of sync with the culture's ideals or habits of intimacy.

No one is more out of sync than Wharton's most famous heroine, Lily Bart. Her refusals of culture's promises lead her to ingest an overdose of chloral. Chloral—once prescribed for sleep and anxiety—gives Lily rest from the anxieties of living as the outsider.[12] Wharton designates chloral as the antidote to the failure of idealism and intimacy, both of which Lily experiences with Selden. As the reigning value of the culture, intimacy exerts its own kind of tyranny, since it can be achieved as easily by blackmail or adultery. The failure of reciprocal relations, in Wharton's fiction, leads to alienation and othering. In Wharton's 1905 novel, cultivating a social life makes Lily unfit for the private, intimate one she yearns for. While Lily is attracted to idealism and intimacy, she prefers to keep at arm's length the social inferiors with whom she might be confidential (on their terms): Mrs. Haffen, the blackmailer; Rosedale, the Jew; Gerty Farish, the poor cousin; Netty Struther, the working girl; and even Selden, the alienated lover. Tricked by the illusion of choice between success and intimacy, Lily achieves neither, failing at the new imperative of American culture. What else is Selden's "republic of the spirit" but the idealization of intimacy? What else is Mrs. Peniston's bond with Grace Stepney than the tyranny of intimacy, whereby the two exchange gossip as a form of affection? At once devoted to the ideal of intimacy and repulsed by its demands, Lily convinces herself that she is really someone other than she believes and hence is self-alienated; her distress is alleviated only by the drug she takes to sleep and to dream of an intimate life with a fantasy child she hallucinates before she dies. Other forms of "relief" were being offered in Wharton's day as an antidote to intimacy—whether in social reform or psychological renewal—but she rejected them, along with younger women writers' response to malaise, such as in Gertrude Atherton's 1895 novel *Patience Sparhawk and Her Times* (her heroine successfully uses her sexual magnetism to get out of jail). Wharton's fictional "failures" are the means by which she registers her protest against the cultural norms of legislated affection.

Wharton and Freudianism in Her Time

Wharton's rejection of anything too "lesbian" or Freudian, along with her complex treatment of Rosedale or such self-ironizing claims to be a Samson, makes even clearer sense if we read them in the reform context of sexual and social psychology with which she contended. During the years of Wharton's ascendancy, reform of all sorts was everywhere: sexual control was the necessary corollary of Christian benevolence and social melioration, while sexology and later Freudianism became popular, partly as a response to the American exceptionalism that dominated such Social Gospel literature. Ultimately, three kinds of reform—industrial, Christian, psychosexual—touched almost everyone of the middle and upper classes. These reformists clashed in the first decade of the twentieth century, thereby leaving writers like Wharton to devise their own moral compass. Such reformers identify the "other" as the object of reform, but Wharton's innovation was to focus on the alienation of the "other" from reform.

Ideas about the unconscious competed with those of the Social Gospelers—heralded by Walter Rauschenbusch, Josiah Strong, and the preeminent novelist of this movement, Charles Sheldon—for the hearts and minds of Americans in the first decade of the twentieth century. These leaders of the Social Gospel movement enlisted Christian ethics into a national program to eliminate social ills through Christian principles of justice. Like socialism, Social Gospel writings—part theology, part social engineering—promoted the idea of self-control over impulsive greed. Christian discipline would institute a new world order, in which individuals would willingly and consciously submit to sacrifice for the greater good. A best-seller like Sheldon's 1895 novel, *In His Steps,* reveals just how much Americans wanted to believe in the power of consciousness (over unconscious resistance or psychological ambivalence) to change their social circumstances and to overcome the very alienation that plagued the middle classes. Sheldon's novel is especially instructive, for he delivers a model of reform based on the question: "What Would

Jesus Do?" Sheldon's characters answer that question for themselves and, in the process, create social change through personal, profoundly deliberate decision. They ask themselves Jesus' intentions, then commit themselves and their resources to following that lesson through. Through concentration alone, Sheldon believed, people could intuit, interpret, and implement Jesus' will. No complex motivation ever troubled them; there was never an unconscious backlash against such altruistic sacrifice or such a traumatic call to "come and suffer."[13] Sheldon's capitalist hero and his family suffer the social shame of rejecting middle-class individualist values: "his family and social relations have become so changed that he and his family no longer appear in public."[14] Later, as a result of his pledge to Jesus, the capitalist disciple even suffers "the estrangement of wife and friends," a paltry estrangement in the face of the greater commitment to doing as Jesus would. In keeping with the sentimentalist tradition, social reformers—as Lauren Berlant writes—banish conflictedness, only to have it resurface in women's ambivalence toward intimate relations, which is the locus of conflict for Wharton's heroines.[15]

Wharton's ambivalence about modernity included both a profound distrust of Christian self-righteousness *and* a rejection of what she saw as unconscious motivations promoted—or excused—by sexual psychologies. The Social Gospelers, according to the Protestant perspective, developed a reform platform that brought working classes into the fold of Christian oversight. The "Jewish science," as Freudian psychoanalysis was pejoratively called, negated the idea of social reform in favor of intense inward focus. Freudians attacked the self-certainty of reformers by calling into question their own motives and repressed desires that informed their meliorating efforts. Social Gospelers believed that the mind could curb sexual impulses. Freud's followers, on the contrary, saw this repression as inviting neurosis. For her part, Wharton saw sexual display as revealing the faultlines between the old Protestant order and the multifold new cultures appearing in America. The underside of this sentimentality, as Jonathan Elmer among others has put it, is sensationalism: "the sensational—the moment of shock, or horror, or revulsion—

erupts from within the sentimental."[16] Wharton negotiates the sentimental-sensational divide by focusing, instead, on the unspoken term between them: the sexualization of American culture that, for her, produces her horror of and revulsion from modern culture.

Wharton's contemporary, Mary Austin, expresses this conventionally held entanglement of sentimentalism, sensationalism, and sexuality in announcing that

> neither the Russian nor the Jew has ever been able to understand that Puritanism may have been a way of escape; or that not to have had any seriously upsetting sex adventures may be the end of an intelligently achieved life standard. The avidity with which the Jewish intellectual in particular has seized upon psychoanalysis emphasizes a need of proving that everybody is as full of secret troubling as himself, a need which could arise out of a lack of that intensity of experience it undertakes to demonstrate.[17]

By 1923, Austin can confidently declare that Jewish intellectuals have been obsessed by too much sexual avidity. Like Austin, Wharton feared the disintegration of culture that Freudian intellectualism and sex expression heralded; in short, the rejection of normative sexuality, which she hated as part of a repressive Victorian America and as part of her WASP birthright. This has been true ever since middle-class reformers, from Helen Campbell to Jane Addams, visited the tenements to institute reform and clean up the sexuality of the tenements.

Yet even though Wharton derogates sexology and rejects Social Gospelism, she is remarkably engaged with them. Fighting the cultural influences of Freudianism and socialism leads her, I believe, to grapple with some of its major popular influences in American culture. Wharton's fictions address the crisis of a "deadening of feeling" she saw as symptomatic of modern America's increasingly capitalist—even Taylorized—work ethic and habits of consumption. She wanted to resuscitate feeling by reinvesting meaning into work and into intimacy while divesting the new cultural preoccupations of their glamor. In short, Wharton took up alienation in all its guises: on the labor force, in social circles, in sexual intimacy itself. Against the new psychosexual movements, Wharton argued that the deadening of feeling could not be relieved by the drug of sex. Whereas younger women writers embraced sexual freedom as liberating, Wharton asserted its moral terms: first, she hated how women used sexuality as a way to mitigate their social alienation, just as she despised how they used sexual power to distance themselves from the racial and ethnic others that people her fiction. Second, Wharton hated the sexual power associated with the new idea of sex expression just at the time that a host of modern American women writers had celebrated this sex power.

What sets Wharton apart from later modern American women writers is her insistence on negotiating American culture on terms set by Howells, James, and even Dreiser.[18] She investigated contemporary motives through what William Dean Howells termed the "economy of pain" that accompanied modern American culture. Wharton qua "realist" became obsessed with weighing the modern pursuit of pleasure against the Howellsian ethic of managing pain. The realists, and naturalists that followed them, formulated a logic by which cause-and-effect resulted from the acting out of desire (i.e., Carrie Meeber wants celebrity, so she must lose her virginity to gain it). By rejecting the "economy of pain" and devoting themselves to the value of pleasure, women writers after Wharton abandoned the idea of "paying for" their happiness or pleasure. Afraid to be surpassed by writers who no longer followed such Victorian precepts, Wharton challenged them by attacking their endorsement of women's sexual agency.[19] As much as she criticizes passion gone awry, her most memorable characters (Undine Spragg, for example)—not necessarily her most sympathetic ones—live by the rule of a single passion. For as soon as desire became plural, Wharton saw it as defused, no longer the centrifugal force she expected it to be. Modern culture brought all desires and impulses too promiscuously together, balking her preference for classical values of symmetry and balance.

The Fruit of the Tree: Impulse and Addiction

The relations among psychoanalysis, reform, and sexual license, along with the lingering influence of Christian Social Gospel, give us a key to Wharton's 1907 labor novel, the elusive *The Fruit of the Tree*, published one year after Upton Sinclair's muckraking best-seller *The Jungle*.[20] The novels bear surprising resemblances: like Sinclair, Wharton focuses on the rising tide of drugs in her culture: his heroine Ona's patent medicines are self-medications to drown pain through alcohol and opium. Just as Jurgis's only son dies, so too the son in *Fruit* dies. Wharton not only comments on industrial reform but her close observation of class organization also results in a narrative theme that, earlier, had been generally urged in the name of Christian amelioration.

Wharton's specific province in this work of reform fiction, however, is the theme of sexual conduct—the complex entanglement of sexual craving and social reform. In fact, Wharton's complex attitudes toward sexuality are not so much projected onto another character as they are emplotted in a text. The "other" in Wharton's writing may be less a figure in its own right than an uncanny scene or a recognition of oneself as other. As Barbara Johnson argues, Freud saw signs of and recognized the uncanny in "dismembered limbs, a severed head, a hand cut off at the wrist . . . feet which dance by themselves."[21] Wharton plays out the uncanny as her character's shock of recognition of the other as *like* the self, but different, a scene of identification that does not provoke sympathy or empathy, but fear. Wharton's habit of repeating certain stock scenes or plot devices are her "tell." They suggest her procedures for finding the identity of the other, in exaggerated or distorted scenes as well as images to which the novelist seems compulsively to return: in *Fruit of the Tree* and *Ethan Frome*, there are sled rides that precipitate disasters; in many short stories, ghosts operate to articulate selves that cannot otherwise be spoken; and in novels ranging from *Summer* (1917) to *Twilight Sleep* (1927), scenes of symbolic incest disclose the fraught sexuality lurking in Wharton's metaphors of othering. These repetitions revisit the acts—accidents, addictions, sexual transgressions—which formulate female subjectivity.

Wharton introduces the considerable repressions of reform, specifically women's cultural alienation. Unwilling to embrace popular sexology, which attributed so much to the unconscious, Wharton nevertheless rejected the belief that human beings could act by conscious will alone. She propelled her narrative with this conscious/unconscious split: not only to reject the conventional WASP control over desire but also to refuse the Freudian (and for Wharton, the essentially Jewish) notion of uncontrollable urges and impulses. These cultural fantasies of Jewish avidity were driven by nativistic projections onto immigrants, who most often embodied, for sociologists like E. A. Ross, the dystopic fears of passion run amok. Wharton finds herself straddling all sorts of splits: the one between male alienation from work and female alienation from consumption; passion and sacrifice; sexuality and celibacy.

The Fruit of the Tree expresses Wharton's vision of America as a drama of dismemberment and death; her road to reform is paved with corpses and mangled bodies, so many sacrifices to the greater good of industrial reform and modern consumer culture. The novel begins with an account of Dillon, whose arm has been mangled at work, and his consumptive wife, whose lungs have been ruined by the mill's cotton dust. The nurse in charge of his case, Justine Brent, brings these dire conditions to the attention of the assistant manager John Amherst. Following the Social Gospel doctrines of his day, Amherst harnesses his intellectual passion for social melioration. Dedicated as Amherst is to improving the lives of the workers by eschewing "baneful paternalism," he prefers a new industrial system based on collaboration, not antagonism (*FT*, 194). He mistakes Bessy's (the owner of the mills) interest in him, however, for devotion to the project, and he marries her in the hope of converting her exploitation of her "work-people" to a religious devotion to them (*FT*, 74). After their infant son dies, Amherst throws himself into ever-more expensive reforms, while the neurasthenic Bessy pursues ever-more expensive tastes, like collecting Ming vases and building a private gymnasium on her estate. Their estrangement escalates until Bessy suffers permanent and excruciating spinal damage in a reckless riding accident.

The accident suggests that her life of reaction—her oppositional desire and her life's only informing passion—can never be disciplined and therefore must destroy her. Bessy's life of patriarchal indulgence and disregard is a version of Perley Kelso's, but without the change of heart at the crux of Elizabeth Stuart Phelps's 1871 novel *The Silent Partner*. In her animal pain, Bessy begs her nurse—the same Justine Brent who worked at the mill hospital—for morphine, but the request is not necessarily for the overdose Justine actually administers. Is Bessy asking for assisted suicide? Or is Justine committing a mercy killing? The novel doesn't say. Two years after Bessy's death, Amherst marries Justine, whose interest in social work more closely matches his own. Yet once he discovers that his new wife administered his first wife's fatal dose, Amherst commits himself to the *memory* of his first wife Bessy: "it was as though her small malicious ghost had devised this way of punishing the wife who had taken her place!" (*FT*, 628).

Wharton's three metaphors for this displaced passion—impulse, addiction, and reform—are partly inherited from her culture: an impulsive and desire-driven culture, a growing obsession with a drug culture, and finally the Protestant passion for reform. In their social dimension, these three themes concatenate such major engines of reform as the Freudianism, Christian socialism, and muckraking movements of Wharton's day.

Wharton's least subtle moment comes when she assigns the name "Impulse" to Bessy Westmore's horse and thus signals the means of her destruction. Bessy Westmore's marriage to Amherst is rash; she decides to marry him after an impetuous sled ride down a snowy mountain, a precursor of *Ethan Frome*'s more overtly tragic move. (Here is another example of Wharton's compulsion to repeat: she refurbishes the same plot devices and figures, until she gives them the right turn of the screw, to disclose her characters' most central anxieties.) During his estrangement from Bessy, John writes to Justine, "Please don't let my wife ride Impulse" (*FT*, 372). Pages later, Wharton describes Bessy's impulsive nature "as the seeds of disaster": her "escaping impulses" compel her to ride Impulse (*FT*, 383). The horse is, as

Wharton describes him, "under-exercised and over-fed," wild, defiant, hot (*FT*, 307).

What else is "Impulse" but the repressed passion Bessy indulges when her husband tries to reform her, to rein her in? The one animating emotional commitment she has, after she spends her money, is to oppose him. She mirrors other people's desires; Wharton even depicts her quivering, "like the horse," under Amherst's authoritative gaze (*FT*, 307). Bessy represents "animal" pain and pleasure, a passion emerging from the basic impulsive needs of the body. Moreover, her oppositional desire proves that she is not his pawn in a reform gambit. Through a series of symbolic substitutions, Wharton shows how the passion of the Protestant reformer is attenuated by the stages of his distance from the body, especially his wife's. The impulse for reform is underwritten by a powerful sexual investment that Amherst cannot sustain.

Disastrous as impulse proves, addiction is even worse. The addict—or what Wharton calls the "drug-fiend" (*CS*, 2:227) in the early novella "Bunner Sisters" (a story published in 1916 but drafted as early as 1891 or 1892, according to James Tuttleton)[22]—recurs throughout Wharton's oeuvre as a figure of scorn, solipsism, and degradation, never pity (even the medically induced "twilight sleep" in Wharton's novel by that name is held in contempt). In *Fruit*, one of Bessy Westmore's country doctors suffers morphine addiction. Early in the novel, he is introduced as Dr. Wyant, an ambitious if bored country doctor, "grumbling" and "discontented"—"not strong" (*FT*, 158): "while in the early days of the habit he had probably mixed his drugs, so that the conflicting symptoms neutralized each other, he had now sunk into open morphia-taking" (*FT*, 497). A "tremulous degraded hand" gives his addiction away (*FT*, 510). Justine finds him whining and unfit but quails before his threat to reveal that she had "shortened the term of Bessy Amherst's sufferings" (*FT*, 482). Wharton's is an odd euphemism, since "shortened the term" sounds businesslike, while "overdose" has more criminal resonances. Succumbing to the "fatal habit" (*FT*, 479), he blackmails Justine with his suspicion that she killed Bessy, and he tricks Amherst into recommending him for a post at the new wing of the mill hospital. Amherst writes the letter before he knows about the blackmail or about Wyant's addiction.[23] Following in the tradition of the gothic, Wharton has Wyant hover over Justine's marriage like the ghost of Bessy herself.

Wharton focuses on Justine's "physical repulsion" from Wyant, even as Justine similarly recoiled from Bessy's pain after the accident. The nurse hates both the addiction and the "secretiveness of the drug-taker" (*FT*, 499). In confronting Justine, who had once rejected his proposal, Wyant bemoans his failed career now that she has killed off his most illustrious patient, Bessy Westmore Amherst. According to Wyant's logic, the nurse owes him something. For Wyant had planned to make Bessy Westmore's "case" a beautiful one, creating his success by prolonging her life: "But what [Justine] shrank from was his resolve to save Bessy's life—a resolve fortified to the point of exasperation by the scepticism of the consulting surgeons, who saw in it only the youngster's natural desire to distinguish himself by performing a feat which his elders deemed impossible" (*FT*, 419). His naked ambition is as repulsive as his clandestine drug-taking; his "natural desire" for distinction as troubling as Bessy's impulsive desire. In fact, his drug habit has also instigated his bad marriage to the young country girl who nursed him back to health after his withdrawal. His addiction points to the radical self-*in*sufficiency that leads to a series of sexual and criminal mistakes.

Drug abuse is not the only form that addiction takes in Wharton's novel. When Wharton likens Justine's sexual power to addiction, that sexuality is intertwined with the plot logics of reform, addiction, euthanasia. Perhaps the most telling moment comes in the renewed passion that Amherst and Justine share after the truth of the administered overdose is revealed. For Wharton, that passion is the most suspect, since it marked "the ascendancy of youth and sex over [Amherst's] subjugated judgment" (*FT*, 533). Indeed, Justine "began to hate the power by which she held him" (*FT*, 534). This is the same language that Charity Royall uses in a later novel, *Summer* (1917), to describe her sexual dominion over Royall: "Charity ruled in lawyer Royall's house. She had never put it to herself in those terms; but she knew her power, knew what it was made of, and hated it"

(*NW*, 167). Wharton's heroines hate their sexual power, especially when it is associated with youth and beauty, because that power cannot be rationalized. Sex expression as the source of that power is thus made to seem temporary or merely conditional, since such power is circumstantial rather than intrinsic. Sex "subjugates" judgment, a power that comes too close to addiction and evasion; these women despise that power too since it seems to undermine any purer basis for intimacy. Wharton likens sex expression to a drug addiction that erases or ends feeling: she celebrates the time "when their love was not a deadening drug but a vivifying element that cleared thought instead of stifling it" (*FT*, 534). In this complex formulation, middle-class sexuality is distinguished from "impulse" by its clarifying—"unsubjugated"—judgment.[24]

Wharton's women prefer abstinence to any sexuality that isn't pure, voluntary, uncompromised. Most of the men peopling the novel, as Bessy and Justine agree, "'enhance the charms of celibacy'" (*FT*, 349). In a novel about passions—impulse, addiction, reform (all as means of achieving sexual intimacy)—claiming celibacy as a "charm" is especially telling. Both Bessy's and Justine's belief in celibacy reveals their ambivalence about sexual power, long held as the only power available to women. The two women share this view just as they also share the same husband.

If impulse and addiction literally and figuratively kill love, what hope is there for reform? The hero's passion is reform, and reform mediates his love of women: "He loved the work itself as much as he hated the conditions under which it was done; and he longed to see on the operatives' faces something of the ardour that lit up his own when he entered the work-rooms." Amherst loves the work, not the workers. But he wants his wife to love them so that they may love her back and, by extension, adore him. This typical division of labor—work versus caregiving—perpetuates the tradition of the Social Gospel, where men give money and women give love. Further descriptions of Amherst's "passion for machinery" are all linked to a galvanizing power "that thrilled him": the "throb of the great engines . . . produced in Amherst a responsive rush of life" (*FT*, 56–57). Like the horse's name, Impulse, this description seems too contrived: machine power far too closely imitates the phallic dynamic of thrust and throb. As heavy-handed as these descriptions are, Wharton makes it clear that Amherst excites Bessy's "responsive rush of life," her animal passion. Wharton, however, seems to hate the exchange value of Amherst's sexuality almost as much as she derogates Justine's sexual power. His is the less conventional exchange of Bessy's money for his body, and when he doesn't get what he wants in terms of support for his mill project, he disappears: first to a new mill job in the South and eventually to South America. Thus, Amherst uses his sexual power to keep Bessy in line: "he had known, when he exacted the sacrifice [of her income], that she made it only to please him, on an impulse of reawakened feeling" (*FT*, 289). Amherst plays upon her impulses; when she rides her horse in opposition, the displacement Bessy enacts in choosing to exercise her animal passions on Impulse seems overwritten.

In order to win her support, however, Amherst must believe that passion can be easily transacted between bodies and reform: "I would rather talk of my wife's interest in the mills than of her interests there," Amherst declares over dinner, by which he means he prefers her social concerns over her financial ones. In doing so, he confuses the difference between the individuating interest he has imparted and the multiple, decidedly pecuniary investments she represents. In addition, the transition from singular to plural interests also captures the spirit of the day: the move from single passion to multiple, diffuse passions, from "its welfare as a social body"—conceived as a unit—*to* the rise of the private individual and aggregates of individuals alienated from each other or "as a commercial enterprise" (*FT*, 189). Amherst wants to manage Bessy's desire. Although he had once been heartened by Bessy's earlier "bond of blood between herself and these dim creatures of the underworld," Bessy's interest in her workers dissipates with her growing sense that her husband plans to reform her (*FT*, 64). Yet his wife proves intractable in her self-interest. She refuses this sympathetic identification with the workers: to recognize them as like her is to see herself as much an object of reform as Amherst sees the workers.

In short, as Wharton probably understood from her own marital troubles at this time (Teddy's earlier "collapse" of 1903, coupled with his financial dependence on her), one can't make a spouse into a reform project.[25] Amherst, like Newland Archer in *The Age of Innocence* (1920) after him, sees his wife as an extension, thereby negating her sexual impulses:

> Bessy was too much the wife—and the wife in love—to consent that her husband's views on the management of the mills should be totally disregarded. Precisely because her advisers looked unfavourably on his intervention, she felt bound— if only in defense of her illusions—to maintain and emphasize it. The mills were, in fact, the official "platform" on which she had married: Amherst's devoted *rôle* at Westmore had justified the unconventionality of the step. And so she was committed—the more helplessly for her dense misintelligence of both sides of the question—to the policy of conciliating the opposing influences which had so uncomfortably chosen to fight out their case on the field of her poor little existence. (*FT*, 183)

Reform in itself might be possible, but not reform of the other— either a wife or an operative. Bessy's body is the "field" on which Amherst's platform is erected, the body ultimately broken by impulse. Consider the modifiers Wharton uses about Bessy: defensive, unconventional, helpless, misinformed, conciliating, uncomfortable, dense. With whom does Wharton sympathize? The misunderstanding wife, the misunderstood husband, or the pained second wife? Even more so than in *The House of Mirth*, Wharton leaves us with no secure moral hold, no firm object of identification.

Amherst's final reform plan—to build the gymnasium at the Westmore mills that he makes himself believe his first wife was going to build for the workers instead of for herself—is another vain attempt to exorcise her ghost. He is not left impotent or paralyzed, just deluded: that Bessy had created the blueprints as an act of their shared passion. As in most of Wharton's tales about othering, the repressed other—in this case Bessy's dead body—comes back in symbolic form: the blueprints. Amherst seizes upon them as sentimental justification for his ongoing work, while Justine is revolted by his delusion and by the uncanniness of Bessy's return into her life. In order to repress her complicity with Bessy's death, she must accept the enshrining of Bessy's memory.[26]

Wharton replaces the Social Gospel narrative of sexual control with a plot that demonstrates how sexual "subjugation" leads to unchecked impulses, unmanageable addictions, and repression that is barely disguised as reform. As Justine herself says: "Must one be content to think for the race, and to feel only—feel blindly and incoherently—for one's self?" (*FT*, 526). In short, the Protestant self thinks in the aggregate, of the "race" and its preservation; the narcissistic self, of itself and its own passions. Wharton wants to negotiate this divide without endorsing either side. Moreover, Wharton refuses in *The Fruit of the Tree* to accept the blighted signs of passion in her culture: the youth and sex that bind Bessy and Amherst as she would later in Kate Clephane's frank, middle-aged desire for Chris Fenno in *The Mother's Recompense* (1925) or in the specter of incest between Lita and Dexter Manford in *Twilight Sleep* (1927). The propinquity of sex and power unsettles Wharton's vision of a world of tempered desire. She wants her intellectual pleasures to remain distinct, the unalienated wish for unalloyed passion or unalloyed intellect.

Ethan Frome: Sex Expression as Sex Addiction

The changing forms of passion disturbed Wharton's sensibility. If she viewed sex in turn-of-the-century America as an amalgam of the older Protestant ethic of repression with mass cultural images, psychosexual impulses, and new urban mores, Wharton introduced in the teens and the twenties even more improbable, tortured metaphors for the condition of American sex. She worried that sex seemed too much like recreation and, worse, addiction, that sex was becoming not a means to pain or pleasure (she experienced the possibilities for both) but an avoidance of intimacy. Consider Wharton's resolutions for disclosing the consequences of passion: suicide in *The House of Mirth*, euthanasia in *The Fruit of the Tree*, paralysis and disfigurement in *Ethan Frome*. Starting with *Summer* in 1917, symbolic incest figures in and contorts novel after novel, including *The Mother's Recompense* and *Twilight Sleep*, and the actual incest of "Beatrice Palmato."

In *Ethan Frome*, Wharton turns more forcefully to criticizing sex expression as an addiction, whereas in *Fruit* both themes were present but not so explicitly connected. Bringing the terms of sexual passion and drug addiction into direct relation, *Ethan Frome* is *Fruit of the Tree* writ small, a compact narrative of passion gone awry. The novel employs the same motives and plot devices: a woman controlled by her nerves and impulses (Bessy, Zeena); a poor relation or friend, forced to be nursemaid to the other woman (Justine, Mattie); a man caught between two women, the one he misapprehends and marries and the other whose dreams he shares (Amherst, Ethan). Between 1907 and 1911, Wharton changes the circumstances slightly: while Bessy dies, Mattie survives, only to have Zeena nurse Mattie's and Ethan's "crippled lives" (*NW*, 136).

This very set of linked terms—addiction and passion—is at the heart of the book for which Wharton was once best known, *Ethan Frome*. Throughout the novella, drugtaking is central: Zeena chugs patent-medicine, and her cousin Mattie is her drug connection. Mattie's father was himself in the "drug" business, and when that business fails, "his wife died of the disclosure" (*NW*, 92). The taint of the drug business attaches to Mattie, whose health fails when she is required to work at a department store.

Like *Fruit of the Tree* before it, *Ethan Frome* employs the context of labor reform to enact a drama of sexual impulse. As Jennie Kassanoff notes about the former novel, Wharton links the dilemmas of labor reform to those of social engineering, specifically eugenics and euthanasia.[27] Both novels use the scene of alienated labor to work through the urges of sex expression: Frome's Starkfield illustrates the desolating effect of New England industrialization on rural farms. Such modern consequences of industrialization also reflect the hero's sexual alienation. It is not simply a coincidence that both *Fruit of the Tree* and

Ethan Frome turn on a sledding scene: Wharton famously refines the act as a scene of self-destruction, one tragically akin to Bessy's ride on Impulse. Ethan becomes defined by the "impulses near the surface" of his conscious responses. That sledding is also a "suicide pact" in the latter novel perhaps suggests how Wharton was following through on Lily's suicide in these successive novels: Bessy's suicide on her horse, Ethan's and Mattie's intended romantic death. The literary suicide, as Margaret Higonnet analyzes, is a metaphor for "speaking silences"—a passion unexplored or unspoken, a mute and muted critique of the sexual possibilities in an alienated culture.[28] In both cases, what begins as (quasi-)sexual impulses ends as "crippling" accidents, by which Wharton means—I would argue—metaphors of failed sexual drives. Riding horses and sledding down hills, in Wharton's fiction, displace heterosexual intercourse and lead to destruction. Wharton literalizes the metaphors of passion that many of her contemporaries only used figuratively: the break-up, the killing of a rival, a crime of passion. These are all psychological states that Wharton figures as effects upon the body.

The reworking of the plot from *Fruit of the Tree* to *Ethan Frome* is not as remarkable, however, as Wharton's repetition of the tropes of desire. Mattie and Ethan measure time by their decision to "go coasting" down the snow-covered hills. Mattie survives the spinal injury: "Under her shapeless dress her body kept its limp immobility, and her dark eyes had the bright witch-like stare that disease of the spine sometimes gives" (*NW*, 152). The spinal injury distortingly represents a failure of will, just as cultural alienation breaks the will and compels its sufferers to embrace pain rather than pleasure; both Bessy and Mattie become possessed or "witch-like" in their pain, so focused are they on physical response rather than emotional loss. Here, as elsewhere, Wharton substitutes the language of physical pain for the language of unfulfilled passion. The fatal or paralyzing spine injury is the overdetermination of the crushing effects that Wharton assumes failed passion wreaks upon women. What is alienation but a blow to the primary narcissism—or ego-ideal—of the individual, an ego-destroying trauma that has two effects, crippling or death?

Ethan Frome's power comes from its narrative of sexual repres-

sion and misdirection, from the breaking of Zeena's famous red
pickle-dish to the smash-up on the sled. When Zeena calls Mattie
a "bad girl," she does not mean sexual wantonness but something more generally destructive: Mattie has ruined Zeena's one
claim to material pleasure. Like Bessy, Mattie touches the one
thing she was told not to touch (like Bessy's riding the horse her
husband has told her not to ride); Mattie's sexuality trumps
Zeena's domestic order. She aggrandizes one woman's domestic
pleasure for her own sexual advancement. Zeena's outrage
marks her fury over Mattie's narcissism, the fury of displaced
domesticity over individual yearning.

Wharton provides no alternatives to the cultural conflicts between Victorian domesticity and modern sexuality. She can point
to this conflict, dramatize it, but not quite resolve the ambivalence it stimulates. In *Ethan Frome*, she sees women's illnesses as
part of the country's "pathology," a word she uses twice in describing Zeena's connection to other women who had turned
"queer" (*NW*, 98). Mattie's spinal injury is even culturally symbolic: it is a broken will, a fate for women who oppose the patriarchal script but fail to rewrite it. Whether or not Zeena's
maladies are "implicitly sexual" ones, as Maria Farland argues,
they do express Wharton's ambivalence toward women's impossible choices: to die, to disappear, or to turn "queer."[29] These
pathologies demand ever-more impulsive acts to counter their
deadening effects. As Wharton explains, "complications" such as
Zeena's lead to a "death-warrant" (*NW*, 118). Wharton's fictions
ask, how do heroic individuals stave off these death sentences,
the pathologies that result from the increasing alienation that industrial and consumer cultures wreak? Ethan's mother, too,
heard voices (perhaps the consequence of a long-term opium addiction). Zeena is transformed into Ethan's mother, the invalid,
just as Mattie is transformed into Zeena.[30] In *Fruit*, Justine becomes Bessy to Amherst. In this unexpected way, Wharton's
women come to be indistinguishable from each other.

The narrative effect of Wharton's early fictions is to erase all
differences between women so that they seem the same, even to
the men who arguably love them the most. It is significant that
Wharton abandons this plot device after her successful *Ethan*

Frome. We can only assume that in the 1911 novel, unlike her earlier fictions, she had worked through the sexual ambivalence that had fueled her fictions since "Bunner Sisters." From *The Reef* (1912) and *The Custom of the Country* (1913) to *The Age of Innocence* (1920), Wharton turns to less ambivalent, though no less troubling, endings to women's quests for sex expression.

For better or worse, these early novels level Wharton's critique against the democratizing effects of liberating sexuality and, in a larger vein, the commodification of American culture. At the time when the flapper was being invented as the figure of misdirected or wanton passion,[31] Wharton's preoccupation with the life of passion led her to invent the frightening (at least, for twenties culture) figure of middle-aged desire. These plots include Lawyer Royall's attachment to Charity Royall of *Summer*, Kate Clephane's interest in a younger man in *The Mother's Recompense*, and Martin Boyne's fascination with Judith Wheater of *The Children*. Unlike the new celebrants of sexual liberation, Wharton was willing to see passion in the lives of her characters supposedly beyond the pale of sexual experience: middle-aged men and women, mothers, and their postadolescent children.

The new generation of American women writers—Dorothy Parker, Julia Peterkin, Gertrude Atherton, Anzia Yezierska— more freely explored female sex expression, the latter going so far as to declare a "democracy" of sex expression for immigrant women. Wharton resisted the new permissiveness that gave other women writers their claim to fame; for example, while she lauded Anita Loos's *Gentlemen Prefer Blondes* (1925), she distrusted the sentiments that made Loos's work so popular. *Blondes* is based on the same erotic model as Wharton's fictions, but with a twist: the Aryan bombshell, Lorelei Lee, uses her sexuality as a strategy for social power. As a way to escape otherness or alienation, sexuality proves futile for Wharton; such feelings end in addiction, despair, or death. Wharton reluctantly concluded that such expression would only lead to more pain and less pleasure, as well as otherness and alienation. In hindsight, it is hard to agree with Wharton's resistance to sex expression, but she was one of the few to question whether sex subjugated more than it liberated.

NOTES

I want to thank, as always, Priscilla Wald and Gordon Hutner for their great help. Without Susan Griffin, Dana Nelson, Ellen Rosenman, and Carol Singley, this essay would not have materialized. My thanks also go to Tom Byers at the University of Louisville's Twentieth-Century Literature Conference and to Joel Pfister and Wesleyan University's Department of English.

1. See, for instance, Cynthia Griffin Wolff, *A Feast of Words: The Triumph of Edith Wharton* (New York: Oxford University Press, 1977); Amy Kaplan, *The Social Construction of American Realism* (Chicago: University of Chicago Press, 1988); R. W. B. Lewis, *Edith Wharton: A Biography* (New York: Harper & Row, 1975); Elizabeth Ammons, *Edith Wharton's Argument with America* (Athens: University of Georgia Press, 1980); Dale M. Bauer, *Edith Wharton's Brave New Politics* (Madison: University of Wisconsin Press, 1994); Nancy Bentley, *The Ethnography of Manners: Hawthorne, James, Wharton* (Cambridge: Cambridge University Press, 1995); Gloria C. Erlich, *The Sexual Education of Edith Wharton* (Berkeley: University of California Press, 1992); Susan Goodman, *Edith Wharton's Inner Circle* (Austin: University of Texas Press, 1994); Lev Raphael, *Edith Wharton's Prisoners of Shame* (New York: St. Martin's Press, 1991); Carol J. Singley and Susan Elizabeth Sweeney, "Forbidden Reading and Ghostly Writing: Anxious Power in Wharton's 'Pomegranate Seed,'" in *Anxious Power: Reading, Writing, and Ambivalence in Narrative by Women* (Albany: State University of New York Press, 1993), 198–217; Cecelia Tichi, "Women Writers and the New Woman," in *Columbia Literary History of the United States*, ed. Emory Elliott (New York: Columbia University Press, 1988), 589–606; and Candace Waid, *Edith Wharton's Letters from the Underworld* (Chapel Hill: University of North Carolina Press, 1991).

2. See Eric Lott, "The Whiteness of Film Noir," in *American Literary History* 9, no. 3 (Fall 1997): 542–66. Social engineers and scientists interpreted such repressed passion as a residual racial trait, viewing sexual propensities as signs of the "degeneration" of one ethnic group or another. For example, in "Parasitism and Civilised Vice," Charlotte Perkins Gilman saw sex expression as a vestige of women's "civilised vice" and parasitism (*The Yellow Wallpaper*, ed. Dale M. Bauer [Boston: Bedford, 1998], 259–77). Women's sexuality

was thus deployed as a category for establishing hierarchy among racial groups.

How did "othering" become a category of analysis in fiction? The rise of race, class, and gender studies, as well as postcolonial cultural theory, inaugurated a critical interest in normative power and those it marginalizes. Toni Morrison's landmark essays in *Playing in the Dark* (New York: Vintage, 1992) on the racial unconscious of white writers has been the starting point for many Americanist critics arguing for the meanings of whiteness. Wharton was no stranger to the phrase, "That's white of you," and its less-than-subtle racial hierarchizing, which "others" anyone who does not look like—or act like—the powerful white models that Wharton holds up as mirrors for her readers.

3. V. F. Calverton, *Sex Expression in Literature* (New York: Boni & Liveright, 1926).

4. In a letter to Gaillard Lapsley dated May 21, 1920, for example, she compares her "addiction" to conversation to a cocaine habit: "Poor Billy Carleton's taste for cocaine was as nothing to mine for your conversation" (Wharton Collection, Beinecke Library, Yale University, New Haven, Conn.).

5. As Nancy Bentley explains, Wharton and her contemporaries clung to their roles as the "custodians of culture." Bentley quotes a 1918 notebook entry: "I want the idols broken, but I want them broken by people who understand why they were made, and do not ascribe them to the deliberate malice of the augurs who may afterwards profit from them" (64). In other words, Wharton wants to control the destruction herself. See "'Hunting for the Real': Edith Wharton and the Science of Manners," in *The Cambridge Companion to Edith Wharton*, ed. Millicent Bell (New York: Cambridge University Press, 1995), 47–67.

6. This repression operates in one famously sentimental example, focused on the trope of the dead baby. The fantasy baby in *The House of Mirth* ostensibly shows Lily's maternal instinct, never to be fulfilled. Or is it the inner child, which Lily can only embrace when she gives up the facade of her other life?

Two plot details link "Bunner Sisters" and *The Fruit of the Tree* (written within nine years of each other): the dead baby and drug addiction. As Karen Sánchez-Eppler writes about the nineteenth century, "the repetitive portrayals of a dead or dying child work to articulate anxieties over the commodification of affect in an increasingly urbanized, industrialized, and impersonal America" (64). In Wharton, as in James, the dead baby signals something different: the failure of intimacy, the disjunction between the old Victorian order and the new permissive America. The lost child is key to the grief of the present. That Wharton could never "do" children is a critical commonplace, but a deceptive one: she did them, but as images of passion and grief rechanneled into psychic wounds. These wounds need healing, and in the absence of old rituals, the survivors turn toward new means of forgetting: addiction and sex. See Karen Sánchez-Eppler, "Then When We Clutch Hardest: On the Death of a Child and the Replication of an Image," in *Sentimental Men: Masculinity and the Politics of Affect in American Culture,* ed. Mary Chapman and Glenn Hendler (Berkeley: University of California Press, 1999), 64–85.

7. See André Suarès's "Song of the Welsh Women," in *The Book of the Homeless,* ed. Edith Wharton (New York: Scribner's, 1916), 143–50. See also Wharton's letter to Jones, October 26, 1915, Wharton Collection, Beinecke Library.

8. Wharton Collection, Beinecke Library.

9. As many critics have noted, Wharton's fiction and letters were often concerned with Jews and their status in her culture. For Wharton, Jewish otherness—like Freudian psychology—brought sexual passion too close to the surface of culture. Her references seem uncomfortably compromising: from the "glossy" Rosedale in *The House of Mirth* to the Hollywood mogul Klawhammer in *Twilight Sleep,* who has a "glossy shirtfront" and a "voice like melted butter" (*TS,* 90); from the "Levantine" Palmato in the pornographic fragment of father-daughter incest in "Beatrice Palmato" (ca. 1918) (Lewis, appendix C, 544–48); to the grubbing portrait-seller Shepson in the story "The Pot-Boiler" (1904, 1908). Shepson's portrayal anchors her case against the Jew's social and sexual avidity: wanting to attract buyers, Shepson also wants to associate with them, a social proximity Wharton feared would lead to sexual commerce (*Scribner's Magazine* 36 [December 1904]: 696–712; rpt. in *The Hermit and the Wild Woman* [New York: Scribner's, 1908], 213–59). Her malicious stereotypes have stymied critics in their efforts to vitiate or explain her racism, although many now agree that Wharton's views echoed dominant WASP-establishment attitudes about racial superiority.

Myriad studies have pointed to Wharton's exclusionary politics, whether she unconsciously or consciously endorsed that "othering." As Elizabeth Ammons has argued in "Edith Wharton and Race" (*The Cambridge Companion to Edith Wharton*, ed. Bell, 68–86), *The House of Mirth*, the exemplary text in elaborating Wharton's racial politics, identifies the heroine as *"very* white—the apex of white, which is to say, in turn-of-the-century U.S. racial theory: Anglo-Saxon" (77). Remarking upon the colonial subtext of Wharton's 1905 novel, Ammons demonstrates how the book's "global" "stage" sets the scene for the drama of privilege; moreover, the local environs of New York witness the "terrible fate escaped in this book . . . not marriage, but marriage to a Jew: the union of beautiful, pure, upper-class, Anglo-Saxon Lily Bart to the shiny, Semitic invader [Simon Rosedale]" (78, 79). See also Annette Zilversmit, "Edith Wharton, Jews, and Capitalism" (paper delivered at the annual meeting of the Modern Language Association, Chicago, December 1985), and Irene Goldman-Price, "The Perfect Jew and *The House of Mirth*: A Study in Point of View," *Edith Wharton Review* 16, no. 1 (Spring 2000): 3–9.

10. The psychology of reform fiction in Wharton's day, particularly its obsession with the other, postulates a psychology of conscious will, that is, a strict cause-and-effect relation between the raising of consciousness and effecting national change. As Keith Gandal explains about Stephen Crane in *The Virtues of the Vicious* (New York: Oxford University Press, 1997), "the traditional moral concept of the will is fantastical"; authors like Crane introduce the notion of the unconscious in reform fiction. "Crane's work contains no concept of will, conscience, moral character, eternal soul, or reason as a higher faulty or supreme arbiter" (9). Crane rejects Christian or spiritual transcendence, where one's passion is held in check and is replaced by a therapeutic model of culture. Like Crane, Wharton marked the change in social psychologies, from the Protestant reform culture to the culture of abundance, represented first by the fulfillment of passions and second by charity. Wharton attacks the idea of a disinterested reformist gaze, showing that "her kind" sees the poor with disgust, not sympathy, particularly so in Wharton's 1899 story, "A Cup of Cold Water" (*CSS*, 1:151–72).

As analysts of sentimentalism have now expounded, the logic of social reform depends on audience identification and change of heart as a prelude to changes in politics. The cultural fascination of reform fiction comes in its marshaling of sympathy. Reform fiction—whether Christian or socialist—seeks to banish ambivalence. But banishing ambivalence in one place displaces it onto the "other." Wharton shows the inherent paradox or conflict in reform: reform seeks to meliorate the condition of others, even as it forces or compels an internalization of the other in order to work. As Lauren Berlant argues, sentimental texts usually repress sexuality, the former by conscious will and the latter by unconscious associations and disruptions.

This ambivalence and its displacement make postsentimental novels less satisfying as reading experiences, so immobilizing are they in contrast to the sentimental texts that "change" one's experience or change one's life. This is why Wharton's *Fruit of the Tree* seems (but is it?) a failure in comparison to Upton Sinclair's *The Jungle* and Charles Sheldon's *In His Steps*. The latter still cling to the unconflictedness of sentiment. Wharton's novel, on the contrary, gives no consolations of sympathy or satisfactions of change. See Lauren Berlant, "Poor Eliza," *American Literature* 70, no. 3 (September 1990): 635–68.

11. Jennifer Travis, "Pain and Recompense in *Ethan Frome*," *Arizona Quarterly* 53, no. 3 (Autumn 1997): 53. See also Gandal's analysis of the reform novel at the turn of the century in *The Virtues of the Vicious*, 98.

12. See Bonnie Lynn Gerard's "From Tea to Chloral: Raising the Dead Lily Bart," *Twentieth Century Literature* (Winter 1998): 409–27.

13. Charles Sheldon, *In His Steps* (New York: Odyssey, 1895), 110.

14. Ibid., 188.

15. Berlant, "Poor Eliza," 635–68.

16. Jonathan Elmer, *Reading at the Social Limit: Affect, Mass Culture, and Edgar Allan Poe* (Stanford: Stanford University Press, 1995), 93.

17. Mary Austin, "Sex in American Literature," *The Bookman* 57, no. 4 (June 1923): 390.

18. As Gloria Erlich writes, "In matters of sexual choice, she frequently echoes Howells's economy of pain principle, that is, her texts repudiate the useless sacrifice of one woman's love opportunities for the benefit of another" (103). Erlich cites "Bunner Sisters," *The Mother's Recompense*, and "Afterward" as examples of Wharton's Howellsian mode ("The Female Conscience in Wharton's Shorter

Fiction," in *The Cambridge Companion to Edith Wharton*, ed. Bell, 98–116).

19. Wharton harbored a theory of ruling passion, a compelling desire that she believed would neatly organize thought and intimacy. That defining principle—whether love or reform—would purify an alienated, overly avid culture. As Lori Merish argues in *Sentimental Materialism* (Durham: Duke University Press, 2000), sentimental consumption "produced an increasingly sexualized female body— one riddled with desires—while simultaneously promoting norms of taste, 'proper' affect, and political and economic discipline" (13). For the meaning of this cultural change, see especially page 99.

20. See James Tuttleton on the relation of this novel to the "industrial mill" fiction and to Wharton's labor politics. Reform— conventionally linked with female judgment and taste—sentimen- talizes or sensationalizes sexuality (*"The Fruit of the Tree*: Justine and the Perils of Abstract Idealism," in *The Cambridge Companion to Edith Wharton*, ed. Bell, 157–68).

21. Barbara Johnson, *The Feminist Difference: Literature, Psycho- analysis, Race, and Gender* (Cambridge: Harvard University Press, 1998), 77.

22. Tuttleton, "Justine and the Perils," 158.

23. Chloral, one of the first sedatives developed for sleep disor- ders, was addictive. In *Fruit*, morphine follows the pattern associ- ated with the 1870s and 1880s: physicians were some of its most fre- quent users. In *Twilight Sleep*, the drug scopolomine completes the very circuit Wharton fears—it induces amnesia so that people forget the very lesson of pain they are supposed to remember and, after Howells, economize.

24. Later in the novel, when Amherst runs into the doctor and beats him up in defense of Justine's honor, "the primitive woman in her glowed at contact with the primitive man" (*FT*, 531). The "primi- tive" is Wharton's code for the atavistic bond they share. As Nancy Bentley explains, Wharton's "ethnographic turn" signals her "para- doxical modernity," demonstrated in looking backward to a less at- tenuated, more authentic culture and emotions. Modern culture is too attenuated, too mediated for her characters ("'Hunting for the Real,'" 58–59). In this culture, no passion except the primitive kind can be pure enough.

25. See Lewis, *Edith Wharton: A Biography*, 192.

26. At the end of the novel, when Amherst and Justine can never be "where [they] were before" (*FT*, 617), only Bessy's daughter, Cicely Westmore, is left. With both of her parents dead, she represents the ambivalent product of her biological parents' unchecked materialism versus her step-parents' equally unchecked sentimental reform. Cicely is Wharton's Maisie, the vessel in whose name the fight over the mills has been waged: "Cicely was the argument most effectually used by Mr. Langhope and Mr. Tredegar in their efforts to check the triumph of Amherst's ideas." Bessy treats her daughter sometimes as "an innocent victim," and sometimes "the chief cause of the dissensions which had soon clouded the skies of her second marriage" (*FT*, 258). Cicely exacts her own revenge on her mother, claiming that "Mother's prettiest—but I do like Justine [her governess] the best" (*FT*, 261). The novel ends on her tenth birthday celebration at the mills. She is there to survey her mills, now reformed and under the control of her step-parents. The daughter's role is the culmination of her mother's estrangement and her step-mother's guilt, with Cicely reproducing but not surpassing her mothers. She will be indistinguishable from them, in a long line of frustrated women, who seem to have the world before them. The daughter's story is really the step-parents' struggle since the (m)other returned again, this time not in Wyant's blackmail but in her own private blueprints.

27. Jennie A. Kassanoff, "Corporate Thinking: Edith Wharton's *Fruit of the Tree*," *Arizona Quarterly* 53, no. 1 (Spring: 1997): 25–59.

28. Margaret Higonnet, "Speaking Silences: Women's Suicide," in *The Female Body in Western Culture* ed. Susan Rubin Suleiman (Cambridge: Harvard University Press, 1986), 68.

29. Maria Magdalena Farland, "*Ethan Frome* and the 'Springs' of Masculinity," *Modern Fiction Studies* 42, no. 4 (Winter 1996): 717.

30. See ibid., 725.

31. As Elizabeth Lunbeck concludes in *The Psychiatric Persuasion* (Princeton: Princeton University Press, 1994), "the hypersexual was normalized as the flapper. The hysteric, harking back to a Victorianism that nearly everyone agreed was dead, largely faded from psychiatrists' view" (308).

Wharton, Travel, and Modernity

Nancy Bentley

Edith Wharton loved the sensation of speed. In *The Custom of the Country* (1913), when Wharton writes of the "rush of physical joy" that comes from flying in an open car at twilight through the wintry boulevards of Central Park, the passage bespeaks her own infatuation with motor cars and their mechanical power (*N*, 754). For Wharton, local motor-flights and transatlantic travel were fundamental conditions of living. Henry James always pictured her "wound up and going"; in alarm and bemusement his letters define her through "her dazzling, her incessant braveries of far excursionism."[1] Edith Wharton loved speed, almost as much as she loved stillness—the contemplative space of gardens, the quiet stimulation of indoor conversation, the nearly motionless concentration necessary for the work of writing. These contraries—mobility and reflective stillness—inform Wharton's complex stance as an observer of modern life. Her taste for speed and travel on the one hand, and the rooted critical focus she achieved in her writing on the other, reflect Wharton's divided disposition about the kind of world she saw emerging in the first two decades of the twentieth century.

Though Wharton is frequently associated with the Old New York of some of her best-known fiction, this essay explores her relation to what she called the "perpetual modern agitation" of her times, the radical mobility that characterized the twentieth-century world in which she lived and wrote (*TS*, 126). Critics generally agree that Wharton possessed an "antimodernist" outlook, a skeptical and largely disapproving perspective on the changing mores of her time. In Wharton's eyes, the erosion of traditional social orders and the rise of mass culture threatened to damage beyond repair the kind of rich interior life she prized most. But whereas some scholars see these sentiments as the fears of an entrenched conservative, others see Wharton's antimodernism as part of her forward-looking analysis of misogynist and totalitarian impulses that came to fruition in the 1930s.

Was Wharton reactionary or was she politically prescient? Dale Bauer is probably right to say that the divided scholarly view comes less from the critics than from Wharton herself. As a cultural observer, Wharton exhibited neither blind nostalgia nor a consistent progressivism. Instead she wrote with a profound ambivalence about what Bauer calls "the increasing speed of cultural production" in the twentieth century.[2] Wharton was fascinated as well as alarmed by the rapid changes in customs, family life, and material culture—the buildings, landscapes, and polyglot populations—she confronted in modernity. Wharton's own day-to-day living could be as divided as her views. Writing in the morning quiet of her bedroom, Wharton would satirically dissect the modern "goddess[es] of Velocity," who traveled on yachts and high-speed automobiles and the men of wealth they pursued, married, and divorced (*TS*, 297). She then emerged in the afternoons to instruct her driver to prepare the Panhard motor for the swooping journeys that prompted friends to dub her the "Angel of Devastation."[3]

Modernity, then, was not only an object or topic for Wharton but also a formative context that shaped her work from within. The energies of modernity animate her novels with a sense of risk just below the surface of social routine. Featuring rapid shifts in location and increasingly curious, deracinated (anti)-marriage plots, Wharton's fiction transforms the novel of manners, the genre she inherited from nineteenth-century fiction. Combining sympathy with mordant satire, her novels depict a startling reinvention of family and erotic relationships. As reimagined by

Wharton, the novel of manners is less about local social patterns than about the disruption and global dispersion of those patterns. These features, I want to suggest, represent an internalized modernity that Wharton otherwise views at a critical distance as she explores modern Anglo-European manners. In this chapter, I analyze those features and their implications by tracing Wharton's central preoccupation with high-speed travel—the journeys that structure her plots, the travel-related tropes that are keynotes for her characters, and the specific forces of travel (mechanical speed, imperial reach, intercontinental communication) that were the very conditions for Wharton's writing.

Manners and Machines

As defined by social theorists, modernity is less an epoch than a tempo.[4] The modern life confronting Wharton and her contemporaries was the result of specific accelerations, velocities of change fueled by wealth and new technologies. Faster steamships, telegraph cables, the expansion of European empires and of U.S. territorial reach, the rapidly growing volume of print and consumer goods that spanned these global territories: these and other innovations created a global geography of rapid transit, a new alignment of space that resulted from technologies of speed. Between 1875 and 1925 (a period roughly matching the span of Wharton's lifetime), the global travel and contact that had been underway for several centuries entered what historian Roland Robertson terms a "take-off phase."[5] The exponential change meant that the category of place was increasingly transformed by new modalities of time. Living in Rome or Bombay, traveling to North Africa or New York, all became very different enterprises when cables, phones, and motor cars made these places of local dwelling into sites of instant relay. Social theorist Anthony Giddens describes this transformation as "a 'lifting out' of social relations from local contexts of interaction and their restructuring across time and space."[6]

It is impossible to conceive of either Wharton or her writings outside of this modern world of transit. Her own addiction to travel—she may have crossed the Atlantic as many as seventy times—meant that Wharton lived a good portion of her life in the mobile space of travel routes.[7] But, more fundamental, her career and the novels themselves are the product of this modern mobility. Because she spent her adult life largely in Europe but published her work in the United States, Wharton's literary production was quite materially transatlantic. The same betweenness of travel frequently serves as the connecting ties in the plots of her novels. Trains, steamships, and yachts are the settings for dramatic discoveries or crucial evasions, as movement through space intensifies or resolves the particular human problems under view. Even the works that present a single locale—the precincts of wealthy Manhattan or her rural New England enclaves—are described with an ethnographic cast that presumes the gaze of a traveled observer.

To take up the question of Wharton's relation to modern travel, however, is to confront a certain paradox. Wharton's affinity for intercontinental travel is an index to her class privilege, her membership in the moneyed elite. Only the wealthy few could make globalization a means for pursuing personal aspirations; for the vast majority, the increasing connectedness of the world's cities and regions was experienced largely as impositions of imperialist domination and global trade. Wharton was one for whom these developments in travel offered a number of rare freedoms—the liberty to leave a stifling marriage, for instance, and the opportunity to cultivate close friendships with European and expatriate American writers, not to mention the chance to write successful travel books on France, Italy, and Morocco. Yet while Wharton embraced her own freedom of movement, in her writing travel also became one of her most charged objects of satire. In her later novels, in particular, Wharton savages the class of rich travelers who "inter-married, inter-loved and inter-divorced each other over the whole face of Europe" and beyond (*GM*, 47).

There is an apparent irony, then, in the fact that Wharton, a wealthy, divorced expatriate and inveterate traveler, cast such a critical eye on the jet set of her age. Yet the irony gives way when we recognize that both Wharton's life and her satirical portraits show us two sides of the same phenomenon. Wharton can be said to critically explore in her writings the very conditions she negotiated more warily, at times more blindly, in her own life. The fictional velocities in Wharton's work, the many continental and marital crossings that structure her plots, can serve as a kind of index to the global powers that are otherwise absent from her novels of manners. These mechanical, commercial, and imperial forces supply to Wharton's stories particular narrative texture, a record of "modernity as embodied sensation" and lived experience, to borrow from theorist Arjun Appadurai.[8] The novels' evocations of rapid change and dislocation are sensations her characters find variously thrilling, reckless, and disastrous, while only vaguely recognizing any connection between these sensations and their underlying conditions.

Ships, cars, and trains are machines that transform manners in Wharton's fiction. In *The House of Mirth* (1905), for instance, Lily Bart is saved by a yacht. An invitation from her friend Bertha Dorset to travel the Mediterranean on the Dorsets' steam-yacht allows Lily to escape the threat of ruinous gossip in her Manhattan circle. Though she knows Bertha's social world is ignoble, it is the only world in which Lily can imagine finding security and pleasure. Carrying her away from the danger of social ruin, the transatlantic cruise seems to embody both safety and luxury— indeed, safety is for Lily the ultimate luxury. Yet at the moment she believes herself most secure, Lily is headed for a fall. An episode in Monte Carlo is marked, in no less than four passages, by the metaphor of a disastrous crash. When Lawrence Selden gets his first glimpse of Lily, for instance, he sees a young woman "on the verge of disaster" and thinks of her as someone about to be "fatally involved" in a "possible crash" (*N*, 222). The yachting trip, promising safety, instead delivers Lily into a danger that Wharton expresses through the trope of a violent accident.

The theme of the disastrous wreck or car crash would become a major focus for modernist and postmodernist fiction, from F. Scott Fitzgerald's *The Great Gatsby* with its fatal auto accident, to the work of present-day writers like J. G. Ballard, whose novel *Crash* features characters who violently desire the ironic star status of car accident victims. As a theme or trope, the travel accident signifies the tremendous powers and desires, seductive as well as menacing, generated by the velocities of twentieth-century life. In most respects, these impersonal forces are not directly visible in *The House of Mirth*. The novel's dramatic action is supplied not by modern forms of mechanical power but by the more compressed and coded field of manners—the drama of subtle gestures, allusive speech, the covert glance. Lily's is still a world governed by the reign of social appearances, overseen through the mutual surveillance of a community of recognized insiders. But the modernist poetics of disaster figure at the margins of Wharton's fiction and mark her use of the dynamic energies of an industrialized mass culture. In *The House of Mirth*, for instance, Lily's "crash" in Monte Carlo, a public humiliation in a fashionable restaurant, precipitates her descent to the less illustrious society of the "Gormer set," whose social life is organized around "motors and steam-launches." The members of the Gormer circle imitate the cosmopolitan mobility of the established elite, but in doing so they reproduce cultivated travel as merely frantic, heedless movement, a social life in a constant state of near violent transit. In this world a crash seems just a matter of time: Lily experiences the "sense of having been caught up into the crowd as carelessly as a passenger is gathered in by an express train" (*N*, 244).

It is instructive that Wharton here stylizes the heedlessness of the Gormer set not merely through the figure of the speeding train, but more specifically through Lily's internal "sense" of train travel, the remembered sensation of being hustled impersonally into a powerful mechanical vehicle. Evoking kinetic excitement as well as foreboding, the figure identifies with surprising precision a species of human consciousness that is born of modern travel. Wharton places a good deal of weight on this figure. Lily's "sense" of being caught up in an express train echoes an earlier description of her anxious foreboding in Monte Carlo. When Bertha Dorset and a male guest one night fail to return to the Dorsets' yacht, Lily feels an immediate sense of alarm—as well she should, since she will become the scapegoat for the lovers' exposed affair and will be expelled from both the yacht and the Dorsets' social circle. Lily first expresses her alarm as the fear of a train wreck: "What happened—an accident to the train?" (*N*, 210). What the narrator calls "the peril of the moment" is a marital and social peril, but the sense of danger reverberates through the chapter and indeed the whole novel as the physical danger of an accident (*N*, 211). The trope returns, for instance, in Lily's subsequent "sense of being involved in the crash, instead of merely witnessing it from the road" (*N*, 212). And the same figure governs Lawrence Selden's internal thoughts. His musing likewise derives a distinct "sense" from the anticipation of a violent accident: Selden wonders "to what degree was [Lily's] dread of a catastrophe intensified by the sense of being fatally involved in it?" and concludes that whatever "her . . . personal connection" with the "disaster" to come, she "would be better out of the way of a possible crash" (*N*, 222).

Through tropes of disaster and speed, Wharton revises the ancient meaning of dread. Instead of the fear of an absent or invisible power like a god, dread in *House of Mirth* is expressed through the anticipation of a distinctive kind of modern event, the high-speed accident. The travel accident, though befalling relatively few, carried a far broader mass meaning. The fear of a "possible crash" shared by the characters in *House of Mirth*, that is, had become a "sense" shared by millions. In 1905, when *Mirth* appeared in print, passenger travel had been recently revolutionized. Though train travel, in particular, had introduced a new order of speed early in the nineteenth century, it was only in the 1880s and 1890s that inland and intercontinental travel had become a phenomenon involving massive numbers of passengers and far higher rates of speed than ever before. Through her tropes of travel and its risk, Wharton inscribed both a history of modern travel and a record of modernity as "embodied sensation," in Appadurai's terms, that history had brought into existence.

The increasing coordination of railway and ocean steamer lines in the later half of the nineteenth century produced significant new levels of international trade, but it was ultimately passenger travel, the transport of humans, that had the most profound effects. British railway travel increased twentyfold the number of passengers during the period from 1840 to 1870, with a comparable rate of increase taking place in America during a somewhat later period.[9] Oceanic travel surged with the mass emigration from Europe to America and the British dominions, with spectacular increases in 1880–1883 and 1900–1913.[10] Ocean liners grew rapidly in size and, more important, grew more diversified in accommodations: the most successful companies learned to combine a large capacity for steerage bookings with luxuriously appointed cabins for wealthy tourists and businessmen. Eventually, the famous Cunard Company innovated the tourist class accommodations to reach middle-income shipboard travelers. As other steamship companies followed suit, transatlantic leisure travel became so widespread as to verge on the commonplace.

A "rediscovery of America" by elite Europeans meant that tourist traffic flowed both ways across the Atlantic. In 1895, for instance, a total of 96,558 cabin-class and 258,560 steerage passengers arrived in New York alone.[11] Though emigration and tourism made North Atlantic routes the most heavily traveled, in the wake of imperial expansion, steamship lines were increasingly adding passenger routes in the Pacific, to South and Central America, and to the Caribbean. Just how closely passenger travel was related to commerce and military ventures is illustrated in 1899 in the wildly successful effort by the American Line to book its luxury liner *Paris* for a West Indies cruise to the sites of the Spanish-American War. After stopping in Haiti, Puerto Rico, Trinidad, and Jamaica, the *Paris*, which only a year before had served the U.S. navy as the auxiliary cruiser USS *Yale*, took its 400 passengers to excursions of famous war sites along the Cuban coast. The highlight of the March cruise was the formal ball aboard the *Paris*, anchored in Santiago Harbor, with music supplied by a Cuban band and the Fifth United States Infantry band.[12] *Mirth*'s Lawrence Selden, in response to his ambivalent feelings for Lily Bart, flees to this newly reopened Caribbean travel route, something Lily learns when she reads a newspaper announcement that Selden was one of the passengers to set sail "for Havana and the West Indies on the Windward Liner *Antilles*" (*N*, 188).

Lily's own escape—hers across the Atlantic to the Mediterranean—is never described in the narrative, but its very omission can be read as an indicator of the revolutionary speed that distinguished modern travel. No sooner does Lily receive the yachting invitation than we turn the page to find her in Monte Carlo. The wax seal Lily uses for personal letters, "a grey seal with *Beyond!* beneath a flying ship" could have served as equally well as a travel industry logo as it does a signature for Lily's personal yearnings (*N*, 163). Steamship lines vied for the "Blue Riband" for fastest transatlantic trip, an industry competition that eventually reduced an Atlantic crossing to four and a half days.[13] At times, steamers found themselves in head-to-head races, with passengers on deck doubling as spectators for their own competitive journey, though on more than one occasion such races ended with a ship run aground during the final race to port.[14]

It was the motor car, however, that gave the new speed of travel its greatest immediacy. The ability of personal motors to supply close-up sensations of speed and daring gave the car both a glamour and class hauteur. Critics complained that "automobilism" in its early stages was "a pastime for the rich." The resentment was captured in Kenneth Grahame's lightly satiric juvenilia, *The Wind and the Willows*, when Badger charges the gentleman Toad with causing disruption "by your furious driving and by your smashes."[15] Nevertheless, the "breath-snatching" beauty of the machines was widely praised.[16]

The speed and power visible in these modern forms of transport gave travel a new charisma. An appeal formerly reserved for celebrities was transferred to specific ships and makes of automobile. The Panhard motor car and the Lucitania ocean liner were names as famous as Houdini and Edison. This mechanical glamour had as its inverse a public apprehension about the potential for mechanical havoc. Both elements, the fascination and the fear, made the 1912 sinking of the *Titanic* into what may still be the most famous travel accident in history. The symbolic capacity of high-speed travel transformed the *Titanic* into an international icon of modernity with its risks.

By evoking Lily's social risk through the dangers of high-speed transport, Wharton makes us aware of what otherwise remains largely invisible in this novel. As in most Wharton novels, the actual sources of wealth for the rich—the economic markets and the era's rapid imperial expansion—are nowhere depicted. But in the "motors and steam-launches" that propel the plot, the novel locates the mechanical power, speed, and economic expansion that were transforming the globe. As a result, Wharton's fiction is structured around a tension between closely observed communities, with their local rituals and inherited gender roles, and the sweeping forces of a new economic world seen only obliquely but felt on every side. The latent power in these forces, their significance for her characters as well as for Wharton herself, was a persistent anxiety and an enduring interest, and the figure of the anticipated crash pinpoints a convergence of impersonal powers and anxiety about those powers.

Lily's "sense" of an impending wreck, then, can be seen as an internalized register of powers that remain out of sight. The crash that eventually ruins her is precipitated by gossip and social intrigue, old-fashioned harms to be sure. But whereas Wharton *could* have glossed Lily's expulsion as a ritualistic sacrifice (as she does Ellen Olenska in the backward-looking *Age of Innocence*), she paints Lily instead as a modern accident victim caught in forces far more impersonal, contingent, and ruthless—and, in the end, makes her an actual fatality. Unlike Ellen Olenska, Lily's vulnerability to Bertha's social power is finally an economic vulnerability. If she is to travel at all, Lily must travel on someone else's yacht, according to someone else's itinerary. As a result, she is in the wrong place at the wrong time and, as the scandal of Bertha's affair begins to surface, Lily grasps that she will not be able to be a bystander. It is precisely because she is *standing by*, a body on the margins of the plans and power of the rich, that she will take the force of the crash. When the scandal hits, Bertha virtually throws her overboard: she announces to the dining party in Monte Carlo that "Lily is not going back to the yacht" (*N*, 227). As deliberate as are Bertha's actions, Lily's fate is not a structured, ritual punishment (like Ellen's nineteenth-century expulsion) but an incidental harm, the indifferent destruction that comes to the accident victim. Lily and Selden's diffuse fears about train wrecks and metaphorical crashes are realized in the wake of the Dorsets' yachting trip and the callously wielded power it makes visible on the social scene.

Little wonder, then, that Wharton's evocations of rapid transport become signs of the social recklessness and potential for destruction in a mass society. The narrator calls the Gormers' journey to Alaska a "tumultuous progress across their native continent," a phrase that allows the forward motion of mechanized travel to signify the agitated, ungoverned energies of modernity that make the overtones of "progress" ironic if not wholly false (*N*, 247). Figuring nouveau riche society as "the rush of travellers," Wharton condemns a world that "scarcely slackened speed—life whizzed on with a deafening rattle and roar" (*N*, 244).

Yet, while the novel indicts this "life" as crass and thoughtless, it is hard to deny that the energies signified in the "possible crash"—motion, power, suspense, the anticipation of novel sensations and arresting sights—are the very energies that give the novel its dramatic tension and excitement. It is hard to deny, in other words, that Wharton herself recognizes and indeed *uses* the modern currents of feeling that Selden and Lily both register as the sense of impending accident. This tone of anxious anticipation is the novel's keynote. Generated as it is through evocation of mechanical speed, the "possible crash" as a structure of feeling can be said to transform—to modernize—the genre in which Wharton wrote. The nineteenth-century novel of manners was built on the close examination of local social life, the contained worlds of Jane Austen's parishes and George Eliot's country towns. In *House of Mirth*, intercontinental travel and the evocation of travel disaster make us see social worlds not as self-contained locales but as communities cut through by larger, far more impersonal governing forces. In Wharton's fiction, the questions of most concern are no longer social regulation and marital resolution but reckless pleasure and potentially fatal risk.

Thinking about matters of risk in Wharton's fiction, however, may well give us pause. Compared to the vast majority of people who inhabit the lands that travelers merely visited, the wealthy had the means to protect themselves from the most serious kinds of harm. Like Selden's escape from New York through the re-opened Caribbean route, the journeys of wealthy travelers taking flight from personal disaffections or romantic failures followed a set of military and economic routes that were the grid, as it were, for the global powers in Wharton's era. Her characters often flee their sense of personal risk or loss, the merely metaphorical "crash," by making literal journeys along these intercontinental routes, tracing paths in which losses and upheaval were far more likely to fall on the poor or on native populations than on the leisure-class travelers. How then should we read the irony that in Wharton's works the dread associated with modern risk is felt so strongly by the class least in danger of physical harm?

Wharton's fiction can be said to enact a distribution of risk, a careful managing of the modern sense of danger through a narrative process that is both revealing and evasive. In contrast to earlier narratives in the genre, the stakes in Wharton's novels of manners are dizzyingly high. When Lily Bart flirts with Lawrence Selden, she also flirts with real poverty and eventually with the question of her own survival. When the much-married Undine Spragg uses up a husband, the result is usually cataclysmic, a suicide or the abandonment of a child. The gentler ironies attending courtship and marriage in Austen's novels have given way to harsh, sometimes strange incongruities and startlingly destructive forms of kinship: compulsive serial divorces (*The Custom of the Country, The Glimpses of the Moon*), bizarre intergenerational love triangles (*The Mother's Recompense*), and forms of incest (*Summer, The Children, Twilight Sleep*). Though these novels tend to focus on the affluent, Wharton can be said to reintroduce internal class lines by depicting extreme consequences that fall overwhelmingly on the most economically vulnerable: children and single women. Even the most socially polished woman can, like Lily Bart, find herself facing privation and physical threat. A very young and poor woman like Charity Royall in *Summer* is doubly at risk. The downward mobility and the sexual vulnerability that shadow the lives of so many of Wharton's women make the inequities of modern conditions visible within the white middle and leisure classes.

At the same time, however, these internal fault lines can be said to obscure as much as they reveal. Absent from Wharton's novels is any appreciable recognition of the people most at risk in modernity: the poor and the colonized populations for whom travel routes represent labor rather than leisure and imperial intrusion rather than escape. I shall return later to these absent populations when I discuss Wharton's nonfiction writings on early twentieth-century globalization. First, however, it is instructive to consider the way Wharton's novels acknowledge— perhaps not fully consciously—an internal impulse to redistribute modern threats and vulnerability. The process of redirecting risk, of displacing or exaggerating or transforming a sense of threat, is one of the activities undertaken by Wharton's characters—and, necessarily, by Wharton's readers as well.

Once again, the "possible crash" is a pivotal trope in this regard. Like the narrator, Selden in *House of Mirth* views Lily as someone headed for a smash up. But it is significant that the novel's most complex rendering of *Selden's* position is also rooted in the trope of the travel accident. Selden practices a technique of "personal detachment," as the narrator calls it, designed to protect him from romantic feelings he wishes to keep at a distance (N, 195). When he sees Lily as a woman "on the brink of a chasm," his concern for her is also a feeling of self-protective removal from her plight (N, 200). He is, as it were, on the other side of the chasm. But even his sense of detachment carries a trace of the emotional risk he wishes to acknowledge only in Lily's life: "The feeling he had nourished and given prominence to was one of thankfulness for his escape: he was like a traveller so grateful for rescue from a dangerous accident that at first he is hardly conscious of his bruises. Now he suddenly felt the latent ache, and realized that after all he had not come off unhurt" (N, 195). As the passage suggests, the practice of viewing others as potential victims of an unseen physical harm ("on the brink") may betray one's own sense of threat. The habit of detachment may be entangled in a wish to disavow feelings of vulnerability.

As Wharton's readers, we can never quite escape this habit of mind, either. Like a car accident, the extreme, sometimes astonishing spectacles in Wharton's novels are able to shock at the same time they prompt a complex form of interest, a readerly fascination or even pleasure. The sight of the social wreckage and bizarre forms of harm evoke our sympathy at the same time they trigger relief and a reassuring interest in destructiveness that can be enjoyed from a protective distance. Like Selden, we are made to see characters on the brink. Yet also like Selden, our very interest as readers-spectators is also an ironic sign of our shared sense of the "general insecurity" that is Lily Bart's vulnerability to economic and social power, an insecurity felt by so many of Wharton's women and children (N, 201). Tellingly, the trope of the traveler at risk returns in Wharton's later works as almost an authorial tic. In *The Mother's Recompense* (1925), for instance, when evoking the crisis of the protagonist Kate Clephane, the narrator returns again and again to the trope of the travel accident as if by compulsion. Kate is compared to a "traveller" who has "skirted an abyss" and glimpsed "the depth into which she had not fallen"; to a "traveller" on a "ledge above a precipice"; and finally to a "traveller" who has "fallen asleep in the snow" and wakes to great pain (NW, 623, 670, 710). The structure of feeling Wharton identified with the anticipation of an accident captures a convergence of dread and fascination pervasive in modern life. For Wharton, the freedoms symbolized by travel are simultaneously the threats, personal as well as social, that she saw at the heart of modernity.

Responsiveness to Wharton's fables of the "possible crash," then, may be a measure of readers' own mix of relief and distress at modern conditions. The novels' reliance on managing a diffuse sense of risk makes visible what social theorists have identified as the central problem driving modern systems, the felt need to master unpredictable harm.[17] By offering readers a complex meditation on risk management—directing feelings of dread and analyzing the sentiment of "thankful escape"—Wharton's fiction makes use of energies of felt danger and a desire for control that were circulating unevenly through the "perpetual modern agitation" of her era.

National, International, Global

In one important respect, I have suggested, Wharton obscured the profound changes signified in the modern culture of travel.

Though she saw destructive effects in modern commercializa-
tion, Wharton was largely blind to the damage that global travel
inflicted on colonized peoples. This blindness is thus the unstable
ground on which Wharton's sense of internationalism was
founded. Her sophisticated sense of the international is, we
might say, a cover or alibi for her inattention to the global. If a
position of detachment can mask feelings of vulnerability (as
with Selden), by the same token, Wharton's sense of leisure-class
vulnerability could blind her to the far more pervasive risks facing the poor populations, risks that go largely unnoticed in her
picture of modernity.

In an essay of 1927, Wharton cited the motor car as one of the
machines to "internationalize the earth." Mechanical power and
modern commodities had created a "new order of things," an
order Wharton found both absorbing and repelling. "The whole
world has become a vast escalator, and Ford motors, and Gillette
razors have bound together the uttermost parts of the earth."
But as the American brand names suggest, for Wharton this international "order" was also national, the result of a distinctly
American process of commercial globalization. "The universal
infiltration of our American plumbing, dentistry, and vocabulary
has reduced the globe to a playing-field for our people; and
Americans have been the first to profit by the new facilities of
communication which are so largely of their invention and pro-
motion" (*UCW,* 156–57). Wharton's picture of this commercial
global order as an Americanized order is crucial, since it is the
source of both blindness and insight in Wharton's understanding
of modernity. By casting the "new class of world-compellers" as
Americans, driven by distinctively American excesses (*N,* 803),
Wharton analyzed as largely destructive the "infiltration" of the
globe by U.S. interests. "We have, in fact, internationalized the
earth, to the deep detriment of its picturesqueness, and of many
far more important things" (*UCW,* 156).

At a moment when most Americans greeted U.S. expansion as
an unequivocal force of progress, then, Wharton's view was far
more wary and critically discriminating. But while this way of
reading globalization prompted a disapproving view of American commercial powers, then, Wharton's critique rested on a dis-

tinction that allowed her to embrace European empires as America's opposite, as global orders that cultivated rather than destroyed the things Wharton found most important. Yet this crucial distinction—between America and Europe, between empires that raze and those that preserve—was not only a political distinction but also an aesthetic one. The criterion for telling the difference was for Wharton the criterion of beauty: while Americanization destroys beauty, European imperialism reveres and protects it. Art and beauty are the key to her understanding of global politics, a fact that put art and artists more deeply within the sphere of the political than Wharton was otherwise prepared to admit.

To understand these interrelated criteria, we need to begin with Wharton's sense of the beginning: her own transatlantic childhood. Wharton describes herself in her memoir, *A Backward Glance*, as "the offspring of born travellers" (*NW,* 807). Her deepest sensibilities, as she saw it, were formed by the "happy misfortune" that forced her parents to leave for Europe when she was a very young child in order to live more economically abroad than was possible in New York in the years after the Civil War. Living and traveling in Europe, Wharton believed, imprinted on her for life a "background of beauty and old-established order" (*NW,* 817). And from the first Wharton conceived this order of beauty through an opposition to New World "ugliness." In an autobiographical piece "Life and I," Wharton writes of her return from her early years abroad that "I shall never forget the bitter disappointment produced by the first impressions of my native country. I was only ten years old, but I had been fed on beauty since my babyhood, & my first thought was: '*How ugly it is!*' I have never since thought otherwise, or felt otherwise than as an exile in America" (*NW,* 1080–81).

Significantly, though, Wharton eventually came to see a "pathetic picturesqueness" in the New York world of her youth. As she described it in her memoir, this was a beauty she perceived only after world war and modernization brought about its "total extinction." But the moment when Wharton sees the "compact [American] world of my youth" as one of beauty is also the moment she identifies that vanished America with Europe. This lost

American world is defined not only in opposition to modern technology ("telephones, motors, electric light, central heating . . . , X-rays, cinemas, radium, aeroplanes and wireless telegraphy were not only unknown but still mostly unforeseen") but is also remembered as a transatlantic outpost of "an old tradition of European culture" (*NW*, 780–81).

America and Europe, then, are less geographic places for Wharton than they are movable sites of contrasting aesthetic value. Seeing a belated beauty in nineteenth-century New York makes that spot a lost island of European culture. By the same token, Wharton saw the "standardizing" practices of modern American trade opening the world to vast commercial "infiltration." What Wharton called "the growth of modern travelling facilities" meant the dissemination throughout the world of a set of commercial habits that she associated with the national culture of the United States. Indeed, Wharton saw "the modern American as a sort of missionary-drummer selling his wares and inculcating his beliefs from China to Peru" (*UCW*, 156–57). The results were for Wharton largely lamentable, even though the drama of American commercial imperialism was the subject she urged as worthy of serious fiction. But the most striking thing about the way Wharton cast global trade as American is the way that it permitted her to locate a national explanation for what were far more complicated global processes. Conceiving global trade as American allowed Wharton to separate cultivated travel—the source of her own aesthetic perceptions—from a destructive commercial travel, when in reality both art and commerce (like the Europeans and Americans who largely controlled them) were quite literally traveling in the same global circles.

In her memoir, for instance, it is Americans who pursue "feverish money-making" and get rich in "railway, shipping or industrial enterprises" (*NW*, 827). For these Americans, travel means cash and movement means profit. Even leisure travel for the rich American is merely a displaced form of acquisitiveness, an insatiable appetite for novelty. Wharton's *Custom of the Country* offered a fully drawn portrait of moneyed Americans as a "new class of world-compellers" who were also world travelers (*N*, 803). In this novel, which follows the transatlantic adventures of the divorcée Undine Spragg, Wharton explored the "taste for modernity" that theorist Walter Benjamin identified both with fashion and with travel. An analysis of fashion, Benjamin argued, "throws light on the significance of the trips that were fashionable among the bourgeoisie during the second half of the [nineteenth] century." The most "trifling symptoms" of fashion, even the "switch from a cigar to a cigarette," reflect an enthrallment with the "tempo of modern life," the "yearning for quick changes in the qualitative content of life." Like travel, fashion is finally an attraction to speed, a "switching—at high frequency— of the tastes of a given public." Benjamin thus concurred with the sociologist Georg Simmel that the essential drive behind fashion "is fully manifest in the passion for traveling, which, with its strong accentuations of departure and arrival, sets the life of the year vibrating as fully as possible in several short periods."[18]

Travel, in short, gives speed—gives a vibrating "life"—to time itself. Though Benjamin and Simmel saw the twin passions for fashion and travel as characteristic of bourgeois culture generally, Wharton's *Custom of the Country* presents the merger of feminine fashion and intercontinental travel as a distinctively American phenomenon. What attracts Undine to Europe is not only the literal fashions of Paris couture but also the fashionable hotels where Americans gather and enclose themselves in a luxe life of their own making. Undine's restlessness represents an appetite for sheer novelty, for change in everything from dresses to husbands, that the novel identifies as characteristically American.

As more than one critic has observed, while Undine's cultural ignorance makes her nothing like Edith Wharton, there is still something about the character's voraciousness and love for the "rush of physical joy" that echoes portraits of Wharton offered by some of her contemporaries (N, 754). And in her memoir, Wharton herself owns up to the "state of euphoria" she enjoyed for over two months when she indulged in a chartered yachting trip in the Aegean. Although she stresses that the trip was an uncharacteristic extravagance ("my prudence vanished like a puff of smoke"), she also describes her travel as a wondrous excess of joy akin to the excessive wealth of the rich industrialist. On "that magical cruise nothing ever seemed to occur during the day to diminish my beatitude, so that it went on rolling up like the interest on a millionaire's capital" (*NW*, 1058–59). Mobility and money, Wharton saw, were interchangeable. Tellingly, Wharton used some of the proceeds of her first novel to buy her beloved Panhard motor car. To illustrate the novelist's "motor-mania," one critic points to Wharton's "graphic account of a near-fatal accident suffered by a friend, in which her profoundest horror is reserved for the destruction of 'the beautiful car.'"[19]

But in contrast with these portraits drawn by friends—and perhaps in part because they contain truth—Wharton tended to present herself not as a restless traveler but as someone far more rooted and home-centered. In her letters, her memoirs, and even her photographs, Wharton emphasizes her devotion to personal dwelling places—to gardens and rooms and local surroundings. Put another way, Wharton recasts herself from an American traveler to a settled expatriate, a transformation that converts transatlantic travel into a form of dwelling, a rooted way of life. In her descriptions of "the compact and amiable little world" of her social circle in prewar Paris, Wharton's life seems to stand as an antidote to the rootlessness of modernity (*NW*, 978). Whereas London society reminded Wharton of the rush of travel—"the stream of new faces rushing past me often made me feel as if I were in a railway station rather than a drawing-room"—Paris represented an increasingly rare continuity of social relations, a place for the cultivation of intimate and enduring human ties (*NW*, 980). France was a place where Wharton cultivated not only lasting friendships but also the domestic arts of gardening and home decoration, first in her Paris townhouse and later in the country home of Pavillon Colombe she purchased after World War I.

These ties distinguished Wharton from most American tourists and even from the younger, flashier Paris expatriates such as Fitzgerald and Hemingway. Yet to accept at face value Wharton's description of her Paris circle as a small society of homey Old World seclusion would be to overlook the astonishing degree to which members of this "amiable little world" directed power in the world at large. Frederick Wegener has examined the political writings of many who belonged to Wharton's coterie in the Faubourg Saint Germain and concludes that "most of those who frequented the salons to which she belonged were affiliated in some fashion with French colonial enterprise."[20] The French journalists, diplomats, and writers in her circle were some of the chief architects of the empire erected by the Third Republic. Similarly, Wharton's American intimates in Paris were strong proponents of U.S. expansionism and wrote some of the most influential works in favor of solidifying an American empire. The American scholar Archibald Coolidge, for instance, whom Wharton credits with having introduced her to Parisian literary circles, gave a lecture series at the Sorbonne that later became his pro-imperial volume *The United States as a World Power.* Wharton's one-time lover, the political journalist Morton Fullerton, wrote a series of articles urging the United States to become a "predominant" power in the Caribbean. Naval superiority in the Atlantic and Pacific, Fullerton announced, was necessary in order to fulfill the nation's "destiny." In *Problems of Power* (1913), the book Fullerton published from his articles, he declared that Americans "are marching to the step of an imperial movement."[21]

The closed circle of Wharton's friends and acquaintances, then, turns out to have possessed a remarkable global reach. It was through this "little world" that Wharton met General Hubert Lyautey, a leading figure in the French expansion into Indochina, Madagascar, and Algeria. When Lyautey was serving as the Resident-General of the French Protectorate in North Africa, he invited Wharton to travel through Morocco under the auspices of his colonial office. Wharton's account of that trip, her travel book *In Morocco* (1920), might be described as an aesthetic revisioning of the facts of empire. Although Wharton prized the continuity of social relations she found in her Parisian society, the imperial relations these men and women promoted globally, of course, brought discontinuities of the most profound kind. Wharton recognized the contradiction, if obliquely. Her own attempt at a resolution in her Morocco book, however, elided as much as it admitted. Wharton acknowledged the destructive effects of colonialism only to set that destruction in opposition to an imperial "appreciation" for beauty, a force of aesthetic preservation and discernment that Wharton located in French colonial rule.

Unlike imperial enthusiasts such as Fullerton or her friend Paul Bourget, Wharton never justified European expansion in the name of progress. In fact, Wharton puts the notion of the colonizer's modern "improvements" under the scorn of quotation marks: "Before General Lyautey came to Morocco," Wharton writes, "Rabat had been subjected to the indignity of European 'improvements,' and one must traverse boulevards scored with tram-lines, and pass between hotel-terraces and cafés and cinema-palaces, to reach the surviving nucleus of the once beautiful native town" (*IM*, 182). The greatest sin of the "modern European colonist," Wharton insists, is the "harm" he does to "the beauty and privacy of the old Arab towns" (*IM*, 22).

However, just as the destruction of beauty is for Wharton the most damning fact about colonialism, so too does aesthetic value become Wharton's chief criterion for defending the most recent "French intervention" in North Africa (*IM*, 22). For Wharton, General Lyautey is exceptional because of his exceptional sensibility: he possesses "a sense of beauty not often vouchsafed to Colonial governors" (*IM*, 23). In Wharton's Morocco book, French military intervention is represented as a force deployed largely for aesthetic preservation. Elaborating Lyautey's cultural qualifications for colonial rule, Wharton writes that "a keen feeling for beauty had prepared him to appreciate all that was most exquisite and venerable in the Arab art of Morocco, and even in the first struggle with political and military problems he found time to gather about him a group of archeologists and artists who were charged with the inspection and preservation of the national monuments and the revival of the languishing native art-industries" (*IM*, 221). Wharton doesn't deny France's colonial occupation so much as fold it into a curatorial role that is preoccupied with preserving national treasures that Moroccans themselves are unfit to protect. Rhetorically, the "French administration" in Wharton's book is elided with "the Ministry of Fine Arts," and Lyautey is less a colonialist than a connoisseur. "Were the [colonial] experiment made on artistic grounds alone," Wharton writes, "it would yet be well worth making" (*IM*, 158).

"Artistic grounds," then, become for Wharton the Moroccan cultural territory that only select Westerners value and thus can rightfully possess. Wharton's travel book is a map of the same artistic geography, surveying the aesthetic grounds of enlightened French rule. Yet Wharton also seems to know just how precarious are these "grounds" for a defense of colonialism. Her Preface acknowledges that Wharton's own travel had been contingent upon military occupation ("the next best thing to a Djinn's carpet, a military motor, was at my disposal every morning"). At the same time, she attempts to distinguish her travel from a debased tourism sure to ruin Morocco through "the corruption of European bad taste." Wharton's Preface recognizes that the uniqueness of her brand of travel lies in the fact that she visited in "the brief moment of transition between [Morocco's] virtually complete subjection to European authority, and the fast approaching hour when it is thrown open to all the banalities and promiscuities of modern travel" (*IM*, viii). The Preface sounds a note of melancholy that the rich "mystery" of Moroccan culture will "inevitably vanish" with the coming onslaught of Western travelers (ix). But the same wistfulness belies Wharton's own suppressed knowledge that the artistic grounds on which she justifies colonial subjection will culminate in little more than routinized sites for an army of tourists.

Kinship in Transit

In a peculiarly telling sentence from her memoir, Wharton writes that "at the end of the second winter in New York, I was married; and thenceforth my thirst for travel was to be gratified" (*NW,* 853). The sentence virtually erases her marriage from the account of her life. Any expected mention of a courtship, wedding, or honeymoon (not to mention a husband) has been swallowed up in the space marked by the terse semi-colon. The first clause is passive ("I was married"), while the second joins the fact of her marriage not to the gratifications of love, sex, or companionship but to the excitement and satisfactions of travel. This rather curiously constructed sentence was no doubt Wharton's attempt to sidestep with proper discretion the misery that was her failed marriage to Edward ("Teddy") Wharton. But the sen-

tence also tells a truth about Wharton, the truth that travel was
for her a passion and a mobile institution, a kind of substitute for
marriage that ordered her relations to people and places.

The grammar conjoining a marriage, an elided divorce, and a
passion for travel in this sentence illustrates a central feature of
Wharton's later fiction. In these novels, the weave of departures
and returns that make up her characters' perpetual traveling provides a striking picture of modern marriage and kinship. The institution of the family was changing as rapidly as any other social
institution in this time. Anthony Giddens notes that modernity
introduces a dynamism into human relationships, an instability
that brings both ruptures and potentially freeing innovations.[22]
Divorce, new kinds of sexual latitude, women's increasing autonomy from men, untraditional forms of family and association—all are instances of a "dynamism" as characteristic of the
modern as is the speed of motor cars. Wharton's ambivalence
about such dynamism is plain enough, both in her life and her
fiction. With caution and a marked anxiety, Wharton traded on
the freedoms from traditional family and gender strictures that
modernity was making available to women of wealth, and she
finally divorced Teddy in 1913. Yet these dynamic features of
modern sexuality and family, in turn, become the objects of a
deft, funny, and often penetrating scrutiny in Wharton's novels.
Behind her most pointed moments of satire we can read a
disavowal, an attempt to indict a recklessness she wanted to distinguish from her own chosen life as a divorcée. Yet the disavowal
itself is also an indirect acknowledgment that Wharton knew
from the inside, as it were, the exhilaration as well as the damage
that could come from ruptures in conventional family structures
and more locally rooted ways of life.

Wharton found an ingenious way to capture this dynamism in
fiction by severing the conventional marriage plot from local
place and supplanting it with stories of divorces, remarriages,
abandonments, and adoptions that transpire across time and
space. Wharton's narratives of the affluent Americans that
"inter-married, inter-loved and inter-divorced each other over the
whole face of Europe" together distill one of her chief insights
about modernity, her understanding that modern travel is a kind

of index to the radical change within marriage and family. The ability in travel to rapidly exchange closeness for distance and to combine estrangement with intimacy reflects the mobile nature of modern kinship ties. Marriage and even blood relations are detachable, transplanted, improvised.

To this end, the travel plots of her later novels often deliberately induce a kind of disorientation in her readers as an initiation into the unsettled and often unsettling relations among the characters. Wharton's 1928 novel, *The Children,* opens on board an ocean liner bound for Italy. From his deck chair Martin Boyne observes a collection of children who defy his attempts to unravel their relation to one another and to the "little-girl-mother" who cares for them (*C,* 38). Martin's confusion is our own, as children with differing accents, coloring, and last names behave as siblings. Their baffling presence on the steamship eventually becomes the most telling fact about their family identity. Crossing the Atlantic without any parent, the group of heterogeneous children is the product of myriad marriages, divorces, affairs, and remarriages among adults from at least three continents. The ocean liner is thus an appropriate host to children who owe their relation to siblings and "steps"—indeed, owe their own lives— to the couplings and breakups that are inseparable from their parents' incessant travel. Similarly, the striking absence of any mother or father on board reflects Wharton's emphasis on the losses and disruptions that can come with modern mobility. Where do these children belong and to whom? These puzzles only deepen into more existential questions as the novel explains the complex "matrimonial chess-board" that is the children's varied parentage (*C,* 11).

The novel also poses a further question: Are "the children," in fact, children? Like Henry James in his *What Maisie Knew,* Wharton reconsiders what we understand as the nature of childhood. In the placeless context of travel, age and identity are no longer aligned. The oldest of the group, Judith Wheater, is variously "a playmate, mother and governess all in one" and Martin has difficulty conjecturing her age (*C,* 37). The more Martin saw of her, the narrator notes, "the more difficult he found it to situate her in time and space." Identity has become changeable and indistinct: "Whatever she was, she was only intermittingly" (*C*, 36). This mutability of the otherwise certain identities of kinship and age becomes increasingly charged as the middle-aged Martin unwittingly falls in love with Judith. He acts on his unacknowledged desire by agreeing to guide and protect the children as a "father." As others force him to confront his sexual love for the teenage girl, Martin becomes enraged and then resigned, withdrawing from a world out of joint. In *The Children*, the vicissitudes of travel not only figure for us a new distance between parent and child but also forge new intimacies that shade into the taboo of incest.[23]

Wharton's families and lovers, then, supply fables of the "restructuring" of social relationships across the large-scale dimensions of time and space that Giddens identifies with modernity. In Wharton's world, kinship is geography, a spatial reordering of the responsibilities and rights of the generations and the routes of intimacy and sexual access. Rather than offering a haven from a commercialized culture (as in domestic novels) or a resolution to class tensions (as in novels of manners), the family is a central site for the explosive forces unleashed during the "take-off period" of global modernization. Absorbing these forces, the family in Wharton's fiction is transformed by strains of vertigo, satirical farce, and an increasingly literalized vision of incest. As I show below, these pressures culminate in characters' personal dislocations, through an individual "restructuring" of intimacy that is both compelling and frightening, and that eventually produces for certain characters the rupture of actual violence.

Modern dislocation has a specific site in *The Mother's Recompense* (1925). Wharton both begins and ends the narrative in a French Mediterranean town that is a colony for "uprooted, drifting women" (*NW*, 570). The unnamed Riviera resort is an archipelago for the social exile of women who had, as it were, traveled too much: in this "female world" (*NW*, 553), an international collection of adulterers and divorcées do their time for having fled marriages or traveled as mistresses. Kate Clephane, Wharton's American protagonist, had escaped from the "thick atmosphere of [her husband's] self-approval and unperceivingness" by agreeing to set sail from New York for the West Indies on another man's yacht (*NW,* 562). As the gossips put it, Kate had "travelled" with "another man" (*NW,* 583). It is clear that for Wharton, as for Kate herself, the real transgression was Kate's temporary abandonment of her young daughter Anne. Soon after she fled her marriage, Kate had returned to reclaim her child from her husband's family but found that mobility was no longer on her side: upon arrival she was told that the Clephane family had left with little Anne "in a private car for the Rocky Mountains" (*NW,* 563).

With exile and abandonment as backdrop, however, *The Mother's Recompense* begins by holding out the possibility of their redemption. The novel opens with travel as a trope of homecoming: the ruling Clephane matriarch has died and Kate receives a telegram from her daughter asking her to sail back for New York. When an elated Kate descends on "the gang-plank of the liner" in the New York port, she feels herself "born again" (*NW,* 596). She has been delivered, as it were, from a homelessness of geographical and family exile. What she discovers, however, is a terrible distortion of kinship rather than the redemption of a mother and her daughter. Kate learns that Chris, her former and much younger lover from her days in France, has been courting Anne in New York, unaware that Anne is Kate's daughter. The prospect of a marriage between Anne and Chris is the horrific "recompense" awaiting Kate upon her return to New York society.

Kate's decision to flee her husband for Europe, then, eventually gives rise to a quasi-incestuous triangle with her daughter and former lover. Distance in space collapses into a damaging hypercloseness in human relations. The secret that Kate's daughter might unwittingly marry Kate's onetime lover brings "instantaneous revulsion" to anyone who suspects it (*NW,* 717). Wharton conveys these distortions of kinship through a sense of the physical nausea of rapid transit: in one scene in which Kate rushes out of New York by train, her state of alienation in time and space is so profound that it is literally sickening to her. From this vantage, the world is nothing but "meaningless traffic" (*NW,* 650).

At the same time, however, Wharton's kinship stories are more than merely cautionary. That is, they not only measure risks and warn of dangers, but they also imagine a modern kinship that holds the possibility for altogether new forms of intimacy. When family relationships are chosen rather than merely inherited, Wharton suggests, they carry the promise of a reciprocity or pure affinity free from the petty tyrannies that mar traditional family relationships. Kate regains her status as a mother, for instance, only because Anne invites her to resume it, and as a result, Kate conceives of their tie as a relation of "perfect companionship." She "could not picture herself as having any rights over the girl" (*NW*, 606, 607). The depth of her love finally compels Kate to relinquish even her cherished role as a mother and to return to her European exile. The freedom of modern kinship, then, its foundation in consent rather than in birthright, offers a tantalizing vision of unalloyed love. Only when relations are freely chosen can they have the affective depth that seems to stimulate Wharton's imagination. In contrast to her mockery of the adults, who produce the motley "tribe" in *The Children*, for instance, Wharton reserves a profound if tenuous heroism for the children in their determination to assert the status of family against all other claims. It is precisely the absence of any clear legal or even blood relation that makes their choice to love and protect each other a poignant exception to the debased forms of kinship pervading the novel.

Wharton's portrait of family, then, is fundamentally ironic: the radical instability of the modern family, its institutional fragility, is precisely what creates the possibility for believable bonds of love. In her *Glimpses of the Moon* (1922), for instance, it is only the pervasiveness of divorce that reintroduces the option of marrying for love. Nick and Susy Lansing, both without wealth of their own, undertake an "experiment" to marry for only as long as they can live on the wedding gifts and hospitality of their rich friends (*GM*, 1). By agreeing to relinquish the other when either of them had the opportunity of marrying for money, they rely on divorce to license their temporary marriage. In some respects, Wharton holds out their bond as an attenuated form of love, a mere "bargain" to "stick to" when secure luxury later beckoned (*GM*, 327). Yet the novel finally suggests that such an extraordinary if not perverse agreement is, in fact, the proof of an exceptional intimacy: the couple's "free-masonry of precocious tolerance and irony" is in the end the reader's only guarantor of authentic love in a world of dislocation (*GM*, 17).

A proleptic agreement to divorce, in other words, is the only way of contracting real love. Such ironies are permanent features of Wharton's modernity, where human relations and identities are rootless and mercurial; the Lansings circulate "among people so denationalized that those one took for Russians generally turned out to be American, and those one was inclined to ascribe to New York proved to have originated in Rome or Bucharest" (*GM*, 46). Among this set, creatures shaped by modern "detachment and adaptability," their essence is realized most vividly in their twin appetites for changing partners and travel locations (*GM*, 47). Yet though Nick and Susy's eventual renunciation of their special understanding is a critique of the impermanence of modern marriage, they really only escape this critique because they recognize in each other a superior adaptability to the ungrounded nature of modernity. Their finally confirmed marriage, in other words, is not a return to marital tradition but a glimpse of its uncertain future.

In *The Children* and *The Glimpses of the Moon*, then, the improvised familial bonds in modernity can offer a "troubled glory," at least for the lucky few (*GM*, 364). Yet the most self-conscious Wharton novel about modernity, *Twilight Sleep* (1927), also contains her darkest portrait of modern intimacy. In *Twilight Sleep*, the usual finesse of Wharton's social satire has been deliberately converted into blunt-edged narrative sarcasm. The modern adaptability of Mrs. Pauline Manford, for instance, is manifest in her reliance on a succession of debased fads, from the sham spiritualism of her guru the "Mahatma," to the "eurythmic exercises" she practices to reduce hip size. The norms assumed by domestic realism—the naturalness of the nuclear family, the pull of the marriage plot—are so far removed from the Manfords' world as to be wholly strange if not forgotten. Indeed, the normative category of the family can be said to reappear in the metaphor of the freak show: Mrs. Manford "was used to such rapid adjustments [in her beliefs], and proud of the fact that whole categories of contradictory opinions lay down together in her mind as peacefully as the Happy Families exhibited by strolling circuses" (*TS*, 20).

Even more starkly than her other late novels, then, Wharton's *Twilight Sleep* presents modernity as distortion. The Manford drawing-room looks "more like the waiting-room of a glorified railway station than the setting of an established way of life," and modern mobility has begun to appear limiting rather than freeing or seductively risky (*TS*, 30). The "breathless New York life" of ocean liners and motor travel has created a static world of mass-produced discontent:

> Today [Mrs. Manford] really felt it to be too much for her: she leaned back [in her car seat] and closed her lids with a sigh. But she was jerked back to consciousness by the traffic-control signal, which had immobilized the motor just when every moment was so precious. The result of every one's being in such a hurry to get everywhere was that nobody could get anywhere. She looked across the triple row of motors in line with hers, and saw in each (as if in a vista of mirrors) an expensively dressed woman like herself, leaning forward in the same attitude of repressed impatience, the same nervous frown of hurry on her brow. (*TS*, 100–01)

Significantly, though, the affinities of kinship in this world still look like the best—perhaps the only—refuge for human feeling and fellowship. In the "oddly-assorted" Manford family, divorce and remarriage have actually produced a wider extension of mutual family sentiment. Pauline Manford and her two husbands "had been drawn into a kind of inarticulate understanding by their mutual tenderness for the progeny of the two marriages" (*TS*, 49). Indeed, one young woman's *refusal* to grant her husband a divorce is the novel's yardstick for measuring acts of cruelty. But, as if to exploit the reader's relief at finding "mutual tenderness" in the Manfords' checkered kinship, Wharton gradually undermines the shared affection of this "dual family" through a relationship of quasi incest (*TS*, 165).

When Dexter Manford falls in love with his stepson Jim's wife, even the regenerative relations of family succumb to what one character calls the "slippery sliding modern world" (*TS*, 52). Dexter deceives himself that his feelings for Lita are brotherly. They share "the same free and friendly relation which existed, say, between Jim and Nona [Dexter's daughter]," he tells himself, in a reflection that does more to bring doubt upon the mutual fondness of the Manfords than to exonerate Dexter (*TS*, 255). The narrator glosses the thought as Dexter's "sense of having just grazed something dark and lurid," a metaphor of danger whose overtones reverberate with the fact that he is at this moment driving Lita at high speed in his private motor (*TS*, 256). With his hands on the steering wheel, he refrains from touching her. But pages later, the near miss becomes a "crash" when he throws off constraint and acknowledges his desire: "'Lita—' He put his hand over hers. Let the whole world crash, after this . . ." (*TS*, 301).

In the novel's climactic scene, the violent trope of the "crash" is realized in the literal violence of a gunshot that shatters the family. During a stay at the Manfords' country house, Pauline's first husband, Arthur Wyant, attempts to kill Dexter for his betrayal of Jim, Wyant's son. But in the nighttime attack, Wyant manages only to shoot and injure Nona Manford, Jim's half-sister. Prostrate and bleeding, Nona makes her radically ambiguous plea: "It was an accident. Father—an accident!" (*TS*, 355).

Accidents, we know, are never merely the products of chance in Wharton's fiction. In a Wharton narrative, rather, the accident is a violent symptom of modern conditions. The spectacle of an accident can cover up those conditions at the same time it registers their force and potential for damage. Real or imagined, the accident is a sign of the velocities of change, the extraordinary power, and the resulting potential for destruction that accelerated in Wharton's era. In *Twilight Sleep*, Wharton makes the complexities of modern kinship into the scene of a wreck. Nona's hysterical claim that the shooting was an "accident" burdens her with the work of collective disavowal that frees the rest of the family for the "remedy of travel" prescribed "when rich people's nerves are out of gear" (*TS*, 362). While Nona lies immobile, the Wyants and Manfords scatter from Vancouver and the Rockies to Ceylon and Egypt.

Strikingly Anthony Giddens chooses for his distillation of modernity the same recurring image of the "possible crash" that governs Wharton's fiction. Rejecting Max Weber's icon of the restrictive "iron cage," Giddens stresses that the conditions of modernity are expressed much more acutely in an image of speed. For Weber's image, Giddens writes, "I suggest we should substitute that of the juggernaut,"

> a runaway engine of enormous power which, collectively as human beings, we can drive to some extent but which also threatens to rush out of our control and which could rend itself asunder. The juggernaut crushes those who resist it, and while it sometimes seems to have a steady path, there are times when it veers away erratically in directions we cannot foresee. The ride is by no means wholly unpleasant or unrewarding; it can often be exhilarating and charged with hopeful anticipation. But, so long as the institutions of modernity endure, we shall never be able to control completely either the path or the pace of the journey.[24]

In Giddens's view, speed and dread, exhilaration and violence are the phenomenology of modernity. As a novelist of the "possible crash," Wharton renders this enduring field of modern experience as acutely and poignantly as she does the vanished world of Old New York.

NOTES

1. Quoted in Claire Preston, *Edith Wharton's Social Register* (New York: St. Martin's Press, 2000), 136, 137.

2. Dale M. Bauer, *Edith Wharton's Brave New Politics* (Madison: University of Wisconsin Press, 1994), 5.

3. R. W. B. Lewis, *Edith Wharton: A Biography* (New York: Harper & Row, 1975), 247.

4. The literature on modernity is vast. Anthony Giddens, *The Consequences of Modernity* (Stanford: Stanford University Press, 1990), presents something of a primer; Jürgen Habermas, *The Philosophical Discourse of Modernity* (Cambridge, MA: MIT Press, 1987), and Arjun Appadurai, *Modernity at Large: Cultural Dimensions of Globalization* (Minneapolis: University of Minnesota Press, 1996), offer philosophical and global approaches respectively.

5. Roland Robertson, *Globalization* (London: Sage, 1992), 25–31.

6. Giddens, *The Consequences of Modernity,* 21.

7. Studies of Wharton and travel include Sarah Bird Wright, *Edith Wharton's Travel Writing: The Making of a Connoisseur* (New York: St. Martin's Press, 1997) and Mary Suzanne Schriber, "Edith Wharton and Travel Writing as Self-Discovery," *American Literature* 59 (May 1987): 257-69.

8. Appadurai, *Modernity at Large,* 2.

9. Philip S. Bagwell, *The Transport Revolution from 1770* (London: Batsford, 1974), 107.

10. Michael J. Freeman and Derek H. Aldcroft, eds., *Transport in Victorian Britain* (New York: Manchester University Press, 1988), 232.

11. William Henry Flayhart III, *The American Line, 1871–1902* (New York: W. W. Norton, 2000), 225.

12. Ibid., 289–93.

13. F. Lawrence Babcock, *Spanning the Atlantic* (New York: Knopf, 1931), 186.

14. Flayhart III, *The American Line,* 132, 226–39.

15. The episode appears in chapter 6 of Kenneth Grahame, *The Wind in the Willows* (1895; rpt., New York: Scribner's, 1965).

16. Bagwell, *The Transport Revolution,* 202.

17. Giddens describes this impulse as central to modernity in chapters 1 and 4. For a critique of Giddens that also extends "risk management" to cultural texts, see Elaine Freedgood on specific strategies of containment in Victorian writing. *Victorian Writing about Risk: Imagining a Safe England in a Dangerous World* (Cambridge: Cambridge University Press, 2000).

18. Walter Benjamin, *The Arcades Project* (Cambridge: Harvard University Press, 1999), 77–78.

19. Preston, *Social Register,* 136–37.

20. Frederick Wegener, "'Rabid Imperialist': Edith Wharton and the Obligations of Empire in Modern American Fiction," *American Literature* 72 (2000): 788.

21. Quoted in Wegener, "'Rabid Imperialist,'" 786–87.

22. See chapters 1 and 4 in Giddens, *The Consequences of Modernity.* For a more developed discussion of the relations between modernity and kinship, see his *Transformation of Intimacy: Sexuality, Love, and Eroticism in Modern Societies* (Stanford: Stanford University Press, 1992).

23. In *American Literary Realism, Critical Theory, and Intellectual*

Prestige, 1880–1995 (Cambridge: Cambridge University Press, 2001), Phillip Barrish discusses the centrality of incest in Wharton's later work and offers an incisive reading of the theme in *Twilight Sleep* (97–127).

24. Giddens, *The Consequences of Modernity*, 139.

Wharton and Art

Eleanor Dwight

In the early 1930s, Edith Wharton, successful novelist and expatriate woman of letters, was writing her memoirs. She was living in France, in her eighteenth-century pavilion near Paris in summer, and in winter in her medieval hill-top château overlooking the town of Hyères and the Mediterranean. Both residences with their gardens were as close to perfection as her sense of beauty and good taste could make them. Looking back to her childhood—the years spent in Europe between the ages of four and ten and later in fashionable New York City—she would identify her paramount quality as an innate visual sense.

During the years Wharton lived abroad as a child, she had been enraptured by the beauty of the art, architecture, and landscape. European sites—Rome as seen when walking with her mother or the townscapes of Paris and Florence viewed from a hotel window—were to her a revelation. She absorbed vivid memories and had acquired a mental storehouse of pleasing images and a lifelong standard of beauty. In her youth, comprehensive reading in art and art history, particularly of Ruskin, gave an intellectual ballast to her childhood enthusiasm for European art and kept her aesthetic sense alive, while she was, in her view, trapped in the ugliness of the city of her birth. After her marriage, yearly pilgrimages to the continent renewed and heightened her knowledge and love of art and architecture. Brilliantly pictorial and carefully structured with balanced architectural forms, her fiction from the outset reflected this firmly held aesthetic developed early on.

Like many others of her time and background, Wharton so completely identified art with traditional European culture that she was unable to appreciate American art or to respond to modern European art.[1] Impervious to the efforts in the post–Civil War period manifested in museum founding, art criticism, and exhibitions to create an artistic climate in America comparable to that in Europe, she extolled European art of the past in her early fiction, praising the Italian Baroque style and later French art and culture, while she scathingly criticized American aesthetic insensitivity.

The effects of Wharton's early encounters with European art can be found in the artistic preferences that she gives to her characters, as well as the manner in which she describes them. In several of her works, Wharton uses the theme of portraiture to look into a character's nature. Her characters are often either sitting for an artist or conceiving of themselves as visual objects. Throughout her writing, Wharton carefully highlights the physical appearance of her female characters and the importance that their society places on female beauty.

Childhood Attitudes toward Art

As Wharton tells it in her memoir, "Life and I," "I always saw the visible world as a series of pictures, more or less harmoniously composed, & the wish *to make the picture prettier* was, as nearly as I can define it, the form my feminine instinct of pleasing took" (*NW,* 1071). From childhood, she had a rare "visualizing gift," and, as she wrote in her longer memoir, *A Backward Glance,* she could remember indefinitely in all their detail, "rooms and houses— even those seen but briefly, or at long intervals" (*NW,* 805).[2] A bookish and solitary child, she was anxious to make sense of a confusing world. By internalizing her artistic observations, she ordered her own world and separated herself, she felt, from the ordinary experience of life. Wharton's response to art and beauty placed her among a class of people who cared for *"les choses de l'esprit"* (FW, 49). She cherished her life of the imagination, "a life of dreams & visions, set to the rhythm of the poets, & peopled with thronging images of beauty" (NW, 1083), and it brought her at once relief and a sense of isolation from others.

Wharton's early response to art can be found in her first novel, *The Valley of Decision* (1902), in the experience of Odo Valsecca. Although he will mature into a dynamic, intellectual man who later inherits the throne of an eighteenth-century duchy Wharton names Pianura, as a boy Odo is introspective, lonely, and sensitive, finding refuge in his love of art and companionship in paintings. Although related to the ruling family, Odo grows up among peasant children in the village of Pontesordo. Feeling different from them and strange in his surroundings, he sees the frescoes in the family chapel as worlds he would like to enter. The chapel at Pontesordo was "indeed as wonderful a story-book as fate ever unrolled before the eyes of a neglected and solitary child" (V, 1:4). Later as a young man, Odo moves to Turin, the "Paris of Italy," and becomes the protegé of Benedetto Alfieri, a renowned architect who gives him a taste for the classical, as Edith learned from her own family friend Egerton Winthrop.

Wharton also paints her own picture in "The Fullness of Life" (1893), a story about an intensely visual and intellectual young woman, who has a brilliant vision when she is sitting in the Church of Or San Michele in Florence. The vision separates her from her less sensitive husband, who is sitting unmoved next to her.

When, as a teenager, Wharton returned to France with her parents in the early 1880s searching for a healthy climate for her ailing father, she rapturously encountered the paintings in the Louvre. She felt that "first rush of sensation before the Giorgione, the Titian & the Mona Lisa," as if "all the great waves of the sea of Beauty were breaking over me at once"(NW, 1094). The young Edith not only reacted to art, but she also developed a prejudice for European art and architecture. Having acquired "that background of beauty and old-established order," she could never see her native New York City measuring up to "the nobility and harmony of the great European cities" (*NW*, 817). She preferred the paintings of high Renaissance masters like Titian and Leonardo da Vinci to any that she could see in her native New York, not yet the center for museums and great collections.

New York's Art Scene during Wharton's Childhood

Many Americans and foreign visitors would agree that before the end of the nineteenth century, New York and other large American cities were aesthetic wastelands compared to their European counterparts. In 1880, Oscar Wilde was impressed by the energy and "real experience" of the men, but not by their art or literature. In Chicago he noticed "millions and millions of dollars sunk in public buildings, but I failed to find one architectural triumph."[3]

For art education and inspiration Americans traveled to Europe. William Merritt Chase proclaimed when he was sent to study abroad in the 1870s by a group of St. Louis businessmen, "My God, I'd rather go to Europe than to heaven." American novels like Henry James's *Roderick Hudson* (1875) showed the attraction of Europe's artistic heritage to aspiring young American artists. But some American intellectuals like Henry Adams complained: "All through life we had seen the American on his knees to the European." Howells noted in *A Foregone Conclusion*, "A painter must be a very poor sort of American—his first thought is of coming to Italy."[4]

In the nineteenth century, New York was struggling to come of age as a cultural center. The National Academy of Design, modeled after the Royal Academy in London, had been founded in New York in 1825 to mount yearly exhibitions of the work of living American artists and to offer art classes and lectures. The Richard Morris Hunt Tenth Street Studio building provided quarters for painters and sculptors to live, work, and exhibit, but when Wharton returned from her first European sojourn in 1872, the Metropolitan Museum was still in its downtown location at

128 West Fourteenth Street. Civic leaders were jubilant when ground was broken in Central Park in 1874, and the museum opened its elaborate new quarters uptown six years later.[5]

At fifteen, Edith was taken to the Capitol Building in Washington to see the large paintings of Revolutionary War scenes in the Rotunda by the eminent American painter, John Trumbull, two of which included images of her great grandfather, Ebeneezer Stevens, her favorite ancestor, a general of artillery during the war. In *A Backward Glance,* she remembers her disappointment: "I was vaguely sorry to have any one belonging to me represented in those stiff old-fashioned pictures, so visibly inferior to the battle-scenes of Horace Vernet and Detaille"—which she had absorbed as a child (*NW*, 782).[6] She disdained American art and history and did not care that John Trumbull was an important figure in both the English and American art world.

Wharton records visits to a number of New York's cultural centers during the 1870s. She enjoyed going with her father to services at Cavalry Church at the corner of Gramercy Park, to performances at Wallack's Theatre, and to the opera at the old Academy of Music. Church and the theatre, however, were the only bright spots in an otherwise dreary cultural landscape. "Looking back across the blurred expanse of a long life, I see them standing up side by side, like summits catching the light when all else is in shadow" (*UCW*, 283). Although she may have been taken to art exhibits at the National Academy of Design, then near her home on Twenty-third Street, she remembered only the "inferior" art works that hung on the walls of the brownstone houses inhabited by her parents' friends. Many bought poor copies of didactic European masterpieces while traveling abroad—a "Mary Magdalen cloaked in carefully waved hair, or a swarthy group of plumed and gaitered gamblers doing a young innocent out of his last sequin." Her mother had several of "these 'awful warnings,' a Domenichino, I think, darkened the walls of our dining room, and Mary Magdalen, minutely reproduced on copper, graced the drawing-room table." Wharton did share her mother's taste for Colonial furniture—at Newport "a fine lot of highboys and lowboys" and "sets of the graceful Colonial Hepplewhite chairs. It is a pity she did not develop this branch of her collecting mania and turn a deaf ear to the purveyors of sham Fra Angelicos and Guido Renis" (*UCW*, 280–81).

Polarizing her reactions to Europe and New York—exalting the former as an ideal wonderland and denigrating the latter as "intolerable ugliness"—became a life-long attitude. Everything in America was contrasted with its European counterpart, as she found a happy if lonely refuge in her father's library, poring over volumes by British art critic John Ruskin and others that would help her retrieve her childhood memories of Europe. Ruskin's descriptions, conjuring up images full of light and movement appealed to her: "His wonderful cloudy pages gave me back the image of the beautiful Europe I had lost, & woke in me the habit of precise visual observation. . . . As an interpreter of visual impressions he did me incomparable service" (*NW*, 1084).

Italian Period

Although her marriage to Edward (Teddy) Wharton in 1885 was to be unhappy, it gave Wharton the freedom to develop her aesthetic and intellectual interests: "At the end of my second winter in New York I was married; and thenceforth my thirst for travel was to be gratified" (*NW*, 853). Although Teddy's intelligence could never match hers, the couple did share the pleasure of travel in Italy or France, their destination a shrine or ruin, a church or monastery, which might catch Edith up in another exhilarating artistic experience. She was now able to fulfill the images of the beautiful art she had yearned for in her New York years. The Whartons visited peasant shrines on mountain tops in Piedmont and Lombardy, and Edith became expert on the byway sights within the less well-known cities like Parma and Milan, and reveled in the ambiance of Venice and Florence and their surroundings. They also returned to Rome, where she became enamored of the "style de parade" Baroque architecture.[7]

Although many Americans, like her parents, went abroad for health reasons or to live more graciously and economically, Wharton was among those drawn to Europe by a spirit of discovery and a desire for artistic enjoyment. Like other travelers of her generation, she saw landscape as art in the "picturesque" tradition. As she writes about the approach to Orvieto, "the nearer slopes are clothed in olive and cypress, with castles and monasteries jutting from their ledges, and just below us the sight of an arched bridge across a ravine, with a clump of trees at its approach, touches a spring of memory and transports us from the actual scene to its pictured presentment—Turner's 'Road to Orvieto'" (*IB*, 145–46).

Wharton would capture her passionate feeling for Italian art in her Italian essays. In "An Alpine Posting Inn" (1905), she and her companions are at Splügen, a small village in the Alps, and must choose whether to return to the coolness of Switzerland or journey southward into the blistering heat of the Italian August. Her question, "Was it better to be cool and look at a waterfall, or be hot and look at St. Mark's," answers itself. While one coach will go back to "the region of good hotels, pure air and scenic platitudes," the other will "climb the cold pass at sunrise and descend by hot windings into the land where the church steeples turn into *campanili*, where the vine, breaking from the perpendicular bondage, flings a liberated embrace about the mulberries, and far off beyond the plain, the mirage of domes and spires, of painted walls and sculptured altars, beckons across the dustiest tracts of memory" (*IB*,14).

Wharton's travel essays praise the art that daily enriches the life of the Italian, left intact in its native setting. She writes of seeing a painting by Romanino in a little church in Brescia. As the sacristan pulled back the curtains to reveal the picture, he cried, "'È stupendo! È stupendo!'. . . . In its presence one thinks with a pang of all the beautiful objects uprooted from their native soil to adorn the herbarium of the art-collector. . . ." (*IB*, 37).

When she brought her travel essays together for publication in *Italian Backgrounds* (1905), she added the title essay, which uses the metaphor of the traditional religious paintings to explain her attitude toward savoring Italy. Most travelers see only Italy's foreground—the famous monuments, paintings, and sculptures. Only a few—like herself, Wharton boasts—explore the background regions claimed by the true lover, whose intimacy with

Italy has been earned through devoted study.[8] Although convention required the artist of these devotional paintings to place the
Holy Family in the foreground flanked by saints and angels in
prescribed dress and attitudes, in the background he was free to
express his personality, to depict "not what some one else has
long since designed for him, in another land and under different
conceptions of life and faith, but what he actually sees about
him, in the Lombard plains, in the delicately-modeled Tuscan-hill
country, or in the fantastic serrated landscape of the Friulian
Alps" (*IB*, 174).

Wharton's travels, which engaged her visual acuity so actively,
provided rich material for her writing. As Sarah Bird Wright has
pointed out, "the cultural capital" her travels produced "became
a constant resource for her fiction."[9] Her Italian travel essays
between 1894 and 1904 record her enthusiasm for Italian art and
cultural history and were the source material for *The Valley of
Decision*. This ambitious historical novel examines the complex
political and social problems in an Italian duchy just before
the French Revolution, as well as the art that surrounds her
characters.

Having seen and described images and ideas during her years
of European travel, Wharton now became the guide to Americans who she felt needed better taste. Her first "how-to" book,
The Decoration of Houses (1897), preached an architectural style of
decorating: Wharton favored simple but classically proportioned
rooms derived mainly from eighteenth-century French models,
accentuating symmetry and harmony. Once the strong geomet-
ric architectural framework was established, then the highlight-
ing of certain beautiful artifacts was possible.[10] The second
book, *Italian Villas and Their Gardens* (1904), advised Americans on
how to cultivate brilliantly designed formal gardens.

Wharton not only preached precepts of garden and house design, but she also practiced them herself. In 1900, in Lenox, Massachusetts, she bought land on a hill overlooking Laurel Lake
and built her spacious "cottage," The Mount, modeled on an
impressive English country house. In it she created the well-
proportioned rooms she had visualized in *The Decoration of
Houses*. On the grounds she gradually realized a variety of land-

scape designs, illustrating principles she would champion in *Italian Villas and Their Gardens*.

A contemporary visitor admired Wharton's picture-making abilities used in making her gardens. Looking out at the grounds from The Mount's terrace, the observer was struck by the magnificent background view "of the nearer and farther hills for miles, with half a dozen lakes flashing to the sun." The shrubbery curved "like an approaching wave," and edged the lawns nobly. In each of the double sunken gardens down the hill was a central fountain "surrounded by geometrically shaped beds separated by narrow gravel paths and planted with brilliant flowers of contrasted hues." When one looked down at these two lower gardens from the terrace, "the glory of their colouring actually vibrate[d] in the sunlight: Yet framed as they [were] in spacious green, they [did] not clash with the distant prospect."[11] By the time she began to consider writing fiction about New York society, Wharton had developed an aesthetic refined during her energetic European travels, her creative house, and garden efforts, and her books on travel, house, and garden design.

Novelistic Tendencies

When *The Valley of Decision* was reviewed in 1902, critics noted that the story seemed overwhelmed by details of setting and lifestyle; in short, the "background" upstaged the characters: "The characters are clearly and conscientiously drawn, the drama in which they play a part deals with vital questions of life and liberty and human happiness; and yet they leave us cold; they fail for the most part to touch the keynote of responsive sympathy." The explanation lay "in the author's obvious willingness to subordinate her characters to the exposition of her main theme, the picture of Italy as a whole."[12] Wharton had overwhelmed her reader with details of churches, peasant shrines, and architectural wonders. She could not resist reproducing the ambiance of the towns she loved and had her hero Odo visit—like Venice, Turin, Florence, Rome and Naples—and expressing her joy in the art she had studied for so long.

Despite its faults, *The Valley of Decision* was good preparation for Wharton's later fiction. It heightened an already keen visual sense and helped her to become a pictorial novelist. By the time she finished *The House of Mirth* three years later, she had mastered the art of arranging fictional elements—background and foreground, characters, settings, and details—into a happier relation to each other. In later works she describes settings with great care, but the details of dress and decoration that she so carefully employed to make her historical novel authentic are articulated with a lighter hand. One scene she became adept at evoking was a kind of sumptuous spectacle, in which the main character is pictured among a collection of people, all situated before an imposing building, creating a tableau like the Italian paintings she had observed by such artists as Giovanni Bellini or Vittore Carpaccio or the rituals of government and church she had described in her first novel.[13]

In the opening scene of *The House of Mirth* (1905), the homogeneity of a crowd of commuters in Grand Central Station highlights the beauty of Wharton's heroine, Lily Bart, in a way that promotes her novel's theme. In *The Age of Innocence* (1920), Ellen Olenska first appears as a stranger in her exquisite dark blue velvet Empire gown, her décolletage attracting the gaze of men among the opera audience. The individual woman is thus set, tableaulike, against a dynamically populated backdrop in order that both her physical beauty and her place in the society be illuminated for the reader.[14]

Wharton's pictorial sense also enabled her to describe houses, clothes, and other details of what we today call "lifestyle" in order to flesh out a character. Much has been written about how the houses of her characters, like Ellen Olenska's little house on West Twenty-third Street, Mrs. Mingott's grand townhouse, and Anna Leath's French château, are extensions of their owner's personality.[15] Clothes too make the woman, as Ellen Olenska chooses dresses that identify her as a rebellious outsider, and the impoverished Lily Bart flaunts her spendthrift nature by wearing Doucet and Paquin gowns she can't afford. These details, so aptly described, are examples of Wharton's "visualizing gift," which she believed to be essential for the novelist. George Eliot's

Romola, a historical novel set in Italy, suffered, she opined, because its distinguished author did not possess it: "[Eliot's] letters from Italy show her curious insensibility to qualities of atmosphere, to values of form and color. And for this reason her Florence, for all its carefully studied detail, remains a pasteboard performance."[16]

Although Wharton never developed a comprehensive artistic theory as a basis for her criticism, she continued throughout her career to bring art into her fiction. She repeatedly frowned at the lack of art in the lives of Americans and admired the way it enriched the lives of Europeans. In *The Valley of Decision*, she had pictured a society that, although troubled, lived in the context of beauty. Unlike America, where art was a luxury for the well-off, Italy, she believed, offered art to all. The Italian peasant can enjoy and learn from great churches with their altarpieces and frescoes and from mountain shrines with their dioramas illustrating the Stations of the Cross. They can also learn the history of their duchy by observing the architectural monuments from the past. Once he becomes duke, Wharton's hero, Odo Valsecca, lives in a palace with a wing designed by Borromini. He hangs a Venus by Giorgione in his bedroom. Setting her story in the eighteenth century enabled Wharton to refer to these great artists as part of the living past. Like Henry James, however, she was aware of "the contrast between the fecundity of the great artistic period and the vulgarity there of the genius today." As James observed, little in the way of interesting Italian art was actually being produced at the end of the nineteenth century.[17] The aesthetic climate therefore is Wharton's fantasy: she would like everyone to have the same strong response to the art she found most beautiful.

Fictional Criticism of the New York Art Scene

Throughout her fiction, Wharton tells her readers that one of the weaknesses in this flawed upper-class New York society is its philistine attitude toward art. She uses art as a metaphor to show that a society that cares only for surface and appearance dimin-

Edward Harrison May, Edith Jones, *1881. Courtesy of the American Academy of Arts and Letters, New York City.*

Fernand Paillet, Miniature of Edith Wharton, 1890. The New-York Historical Society.

Photograph of John Singer Sargent painting at Fenway Court, Isabella Stewart Gardner Museum, Boston.

ishes its members and reduces life to a competition based on wealth. Collecting Old Masters or building mansions copied from European models are status symbols acquired by the nouveau riche for prestige, not for the profound artistic response that Wharton herself experienced or the sense of national pride that she assumed a European feels. Although Wharton later acknowledged the improved cultural situation in turn-of-the-century New York, in 1905 she refused to ascribe any value to the new Europe-inspired architecture and art collections. Perhaps jaded by watching millionaires in Newport create their palazzi next to each other on small seaview plots, Wharton recognized only the showy and vulgar efforts of the newly rich, despite exquisite American public buildings like the Boston Public Library and the Metropolitan Museum, that were starting to appear, and worthy art collections like Mrs. Jack Gardner's and J. P. Morgan's. [18]

To make her points about the frivolous society of the rich, Wharton explored the relationship of the inner self to its outward image. Using the theme of portrait painting in two short stories, "The Portrait" (1899) and "The Moving Finger" (1901), she shows how the outward appearance and its expression on canvas both express and falsify the "real self." In "The Portrait," a corrupt political boss (possibly modeled on Boss Tweed) is indicted during the painting of his portrait and must flee with his face unfinished. Lillo, the painter, watches as, during their painting sessions, the daughter comes to realize her father's flawed personality. Lillo finishes the portrait without further sittings but hides the vulgarity that he doesn't want the daughter to see.

Wharton's characters describe Lillo's approach to portraiture painting. While other artists depict the surface, Lillo "does the depths; they paint the ripples on the pond, he drags the bottom." When painting a small, but overdressed personality, Lillo faces another problem—in "his portraits of fine ladies in pearls and velvet," what appears is "a little naked cowering wisp of a soul sitting beside the big splendid body, like a poor relation in the darkest corner of an opera box" (*CSS*, 1:174). One can speculate that Wharton's view of how to delineate female character in her novels is reflected in her admirable creation Lillo. Like Wharton's friend, painter John Singer Sargent, Lillo succeeds with his brush in creating a portrait that reveals character—even "the little naked cowering wisp of a soul" within "the big splendid body"—just as Wharton does with her pen.

In "The Moving Finger" (1901), Wharton creates a fascinating triangle—husband, wife, and portrait painter—who are entangled by their admiration for each other and Mrs. Grancy's portrait. Mrs. Grancy, the vivid and beautiful second wife of a diplomat, is painted by Claydon, who claims the resulting work is not only his masterpiece but also is the essence of Mrs. Grancy herself. After her death, the narrator discovers that Claydon has altered the portrait on Ralph Grancy's urging to make her image appear older. "The bright hair had lost its elasticity, the cheek its clearness, the brow its light" (*CSS*, 1:307). The face on the canvas becomes the widower's companion. Ten years later when the husband seems to be dying, Claydon alters the painting again—placing in Mrs. Grancy's eyes the knowledge of her husband's death. Claydon eventually inherits the portrait and changes it back to its original state. He feels that he owns one side of Mrs. Grancy—"her beauty; for no one else understood it" (*CSS*, 1:312). Here, Wharton is showing the power of a woman's beauty—either real or depicted in paint—while playing off fictional precedents like *Pygmalion* and *The Portrait of Dorian Gray*.

The House of Mirth, Wharton's first novel to treat upper-crust New York society, appeared in 1905. It was highly praised, particularly for its heroine Lily Bart, an impoverished socialite, who engages the reader's sympathy, despite her yearning for the material luxury that characterizes the taste of New York's wealthy set and despite the compromises she must make to satisfy her yearning.[19] While contemporary critics concentrated on *The House of Mirth*'s moral issues and its criticism of a cruel society, more recently the novel has been read for its artistic themes.

In *The House of Mirth*, Wharton further explores themes found in "The Moving Finger." She uses these themes to accentuate her belief that, among other things, a frivolous society makes narcissists of its women. Choosing as a central character a woman who is spectacularly beautiful but unsure of her value to herself and others, Wharton employs portraiture as a useful metaphor for Lily's dilemma. She examines the differences and similarities between Lily's "real" and observed self, her private and public image, and her success and failure in meeting society's expectations of appearance and behavior. Another theme that runs throughout the novel is the authentic versus the inauthentic response to art. One inauthentic response involves the collector's wish to see a woman as a pretty object for his collection.

Wharton uses words to paint many revealing portraits of Lily. In the novel's opening scene in Grand Central Station, Lily ap-

pears amid the crowd of suburban travelers: "Her vivid head, relieved against the dull tints of the crowd, made her much more
conspicuous than in a ball-room, and under her dark hat and veil
she regained the girlish smoothness, the purity of tint, that she
was beginning to lose after eleven years of late hours and inde-
fatigable dancing" (*N*, 3). Several pages later Wharton pictures
Lily as she sits in Selden's apartment. He finds that "it was so
pleasant to sit there looking at her, as she lifted now one book
and then another from the shelves, fluttering the pages between
her fingers, while her drooping profile was outlined against the
warm background of old buildings" (*N*, 11). Several times her
face is framed in a mirror. As Cynthia Griffin Wolff points out,
Lily continually shows herself off, as on the train when she
"arranged herself in her corner with the instinctive feeling for effect which never forsook her" (*N*, 18).[20]

The culmination of these scenes is the tableaux vivants performance at the party at the Wellington Brys's. These performances—in which fashionable society posed as figures in paintings or sculptures—were a popular form of entertainment at the
end of the nineteenth century. At the Walhalla, a hall on Canal
Street, less-refined displays of tableaux vivants—women representing sculptures of figures like Venus, Psyche, or the Greek
Slave—would be displayed for an admission fee, to the accompa-
niment of badly played violin and piano music. At the Franklin
Theatre on Franklin Square, one could see an equally eclectic
group of images, including *The Three Graces, Venus Rising from the
Sea, The Rape of the Sabines,* and *The Greek Slave.* As Dell Upton
writes, "Tableaux Vivants openly addressed the strong erotic
content that respectable critics and viewers saw but euphemized
in such statues as the *Greek Slave* or Palmer's *White Captive,*" and
these exhibits had a sexy, peep show quality to them.[21] Although
Lily may intend only to appear beautiful through her exact portrayal of the painting, she also appeals to the erotic appetites of
men in her audience. Wharton uses the ritual not only to record
a social history but also to comment on the objectification of
women in this trivial society.

Wharton has Lily choose Joshua Reynolds's painting of a
woman carving her lover's initials on a tree for her performance,

so that the simple classical lines of her flimsy costume show off her beautiful figure to best advantage. By creating the image of this eighteenth-century artist, who painted women as idealized abstractions, Lily now appears not as the complicated, real-life person she is, but as a work of art whose value is determined by the viewer. When Lawrence Selden observes Lily in this guise, he enters into one of those transcendent moments in which real life disappears altogether. As Wharton writes, "to the responsive fancy [tableaux vivants] may give magic glimpses of the boundary world between fact and imagination" (*N*, 140). Selden can easily yield to such "vision-making influences," and when he sees Lily in her ravishing beauty, he only sees what he wants to see: an illustration of an abstract concept that he is sure is the "real Lily Bart, but divested of the trivialities of her little world, and catching for a moment a note of that eternal harmony of which her beauty was a part" (*N*, 142).

There are a number of collectors in the novel: Perry Gryce collects Americana; Lawrence Selden collects old books; and Simon Rosedale will surely collect Old Masters in a slow, decorous fashion (unlike the unnamed millionaire whose meteoric rise and fall ends with the sale of his gallery of masterpieces in order to pay his creditors). Lily's aunt Mrs. Peniston with a copy of the *Dying Gladiator* in bronze and a "seven-by-five painting of Niagara" is an example of the Old New Yorkers with bad taste in art that the author had observed during her childhood (*N*, 105). Lily's friends and relatives lack the "authentic" appreciation Wharton values and practices herself.

French Aesthetic

By the time Wharton took up residence in Paris in the winter of 1907, she had developed an enthusiasm for the French way of living, culture, and aesthetic standards that would stay with her for the rest of her life. Now frequenting the salons of articulate, interesting French intellectuals, Wharton felt she was among equals who saw art as "part of life," the same way she did. The process had begun with motor excursions through France with

Henry James and others, the basis for another book of travel essays, *A Motor-Flight Through France* (1908).

Wharton worked on her novel *The Custom of the Country* from 1907 to 1913, the years she was relocating herself—gradually giving up her house in Lenox and making France her permanent home. Not surprisingly, the novel is full of criticism for America and praise for France. Again, shallow Americans value art, not for its beauty or moral qualities but for its status. Being painted by a fashionable portrait painter is another prize for the social climber, along with having a house on Fifth Avenue, a good box at the opera, and the right social invitations. The beautiful Undine Spragg is pictured repeatedly as if in a portrait. In one scene, she is seated before a mirror, illuminated by artificial light that shows off her stunning looks, her greatest asset:

> Celeste, before leaving, had drawn down the blinds and turned on the electric light, and the white and gold room, with its blazing wall-brackets, formed a sufficiently brilliant background to carry out the illusion. So untempered a glare would have been destructive to all half-tones and subtleties of modelling; but Undine's beauty was as vivid, and almost as crude, as the brightness suffusing it. (*N*, 635)

One theatrical display of Undine's narcissism occurs when her full-length portrait by the dandyish painter Claud Walsingham Popple is unveiled to a socially prominent group of New Yorkers. Popple and his clientele illustrate Wharton's general view of society painters and their subjects: not only does Popple subordinate "art to elegance" and keep his studio "tidy enough for a lady to sit for him in a new dress," but he is also esteemed for being the only painter "who could 'do pearls'" (*N*, 745). When Undine's likeness is received by a group that she is pleased to attract, the reader is told that "not one of the number was troubled by any personal theory of art: all they asked of a portrait was that the costume should be sufficiently 'lifelike', and the face not too much so; and a long experience in idealizing flesh and realizing dress-fabrics had enabled Mr. Popple to meet both demands" (*N*, 750). The assembled observers also lament the fact that an important fancy dress ball is one of the casualties of a Wall Street financial disaster. Undine complains that she had taken much trouble with her dress. She was to go as the Empress Josephine, after the Prudhon portrait in the Louvre, and the dress, already fitted and partly embroidered, might not be returnable to the dressmaker. Wharton knew well the fancy dress balls that were favorite pastimes of the newly rich, who little appreciated the art that inspired their frivolous and spendthrift entertainments.

When Undine marries Raymond de Chelles, she is at first impressed by his sincere involvement with French masterpieces. His family had "a real castle, with towers, and water all round it, and a funny kind of bridge they pull up" (*N*, 813). They also had family portraits and Boucher tapestries given to the family by Louis XV. Undine later finds these objects extremely dull when she is entrapped in the same castle and at the mercy of her mother-in-law, in a kind of genteel poverty, since her husband is the second son in this aristocratic family. She wants to sell the Boucher tapestries, finding cash much more appealing than the deep feelings of family and national pride that the tapestries might inspire. When Undine finally remarries Elmer Moffatt, now reported to be "one of the six wealthiest men east of the Rockies," she is given as wedding presents a necklace and tiara of pigeon-blood rubies that once belonged to Marie Antoinette and a house in New York that is an exact copy of the Pitti Palace in Florence. Wharton is again poking fun at the extravagance of millionaires whose behavior she had witnessed in New York and Newport.[22]

Now living in France, Wharton took up wholeheartedly what she saw as French attitudes toward the visual arts. In France, she felt, everyone was gifted with taste. According to Wharton, "the essence of taste is suitability. . . . It expresses the mysterious demand of eye and mind for symmetry, harmony and order." "That a thing should be in scale—should be proportioned to its purpose—is one of the first requirements of beauty, in whatever order. Suitability—fitness—is, and always has been, the very foundation of French standards" (*FW*, 41). In France, as in Italy, Wharton noted that aesthetic beauty can be a profound part of one's daily life. "It would be difficult for any one walking along the Quai Malaquais, and not totally blind to architectural beauty, not to be charmed by the harmony or proportion and beauty of composition of a certain building with curved wings and a small central dome that looks across the Seine at the gardens of the Louvre and the spires of Saint Germain l'Auxerrois" (*FW,* 45).

Later Themes

After the Great War, Wharton's fiction continued to treat artistic themes. In *A Son at the Front* (1923), one of the main characters is a sympathetic portrait painter, and *The Age of Innocence* (1920) focuses again on portraiture. In the latter novel, she expressed again New York attitudes toward art in the 1870s. Newland Archer realizes that in New York creative people have little social value:

> [He] had been aware of these things ever since he could remember, and had accepted them as part of the structure of the universe. He knew that there were societies where painters and poets and novelists and men of science, and even great actors, were as sought after as Dukes; he had often pictured to himself what it would have been to live in the intimacy of drawing rooms dominated by the talk of Mérimée . . . of Thackeray, Browning or William Morris. But such things were inconceivable in New York, and unsettling to think of. (*N,* 1097–98)

In *The Age of Innocence* many painters are mentioned, and one suspects that paintings had remained in Wharton's memory since childhood and helped her visualize the period when she wrote the novel in 1919. In this kinder view of her home city, she records the different artists who were society's acceptable portrait painters at the time. Daniel Huntington, who painted many prominent Americans (including women in Wharton's own Jones and Stevens families), has painted Mrs. van der Luyden, a leading society matron. Perhaps as insincere flattery, the painting is proclaimed "as fine as a Cabanal" (*N,* 1056), a much better

French painter who painted Wharton's friend Olivia Cutting. These paintings portray the women the way society likes to see them: usually better looking than they actually are, prosperous, and decorative.

Many of Wharton's beautiful women fall beneath the gaze of both society and the artist. But is any of them, like their creator, an artist herself? As critics have noted, in *The Age of Innocence* Wharton makes her heroine Ellen Olenska not only an art object but also a creative woman, an artist in the art of life. Wharton took years to make the transformation from debutante and young married socialite to creative artist, and her fiction deals over and over with young people trying to make their own transition into maturity. Ellen is perhaps closest to Wharton's percept, "As life is an art . . . so woman is the artist" (*FW*, 112). As Elizabeth Ammons writes, "Ellen is not an artist in any narrow, sheerly production-oriented sense of the word. She does not paint, sing, write, dance, or act—although as a child she did most of those things. . . . As an artist Ellen's medium is life itself. She moves into her aunt's dilapidated house on unfashionable West Twenty-third Street and, without commotion or a lot of money, changes it into something original."[23]

In 1924, with the writing of *False Dawn*, part of the *Old New York* quartet, Wharton returned to the subject of Italian touring and art collecting. The novella is yet another satire of New York society and its attitude toward art. Halston Raycie sends his son Lewis to Europe to buy a fashionable collection of paintings. Lewis is instructed to return with works of art by the finest names in Italy: perhaps "a Domenichino, an Albano, a Carlo Dolci, a Guercino, a Carlo Maratta—one or two of Salvator Rosa's noble landscapes." Mr. Raycie wants to compensate for the fact that America lacks works of great genius. "Where are our Old Masters?" he asks (*NW*, 335). Although Mr. Raycie turns out to be a narrow-minded fool, whose goal is to impress his friends and neighbors with a gallery of well-known Italian art, his son is an intelligent and romantic young man who discovers the world beyond New York and is not afraid to embrace it.

In Italy, he meets a man modeled after Wharton's beloved Ruskin, who will become his mentor. Ruskin announces with certainty that Lewis is one of the fortunate who like Wharton does possess "the seeing eye," the ability to see beyond the ordinary (*NW*, 341). The two travel to Venice together and visit a tiny church where Lewis's eyes are opened to the stunning beauty of a Carpaccio fresco. He forgets about the master works of the Italian artists his father named. Lewis returns home with crates of unknowns from the early Italian Renaissance: a Giotto, a Piero della Francesca, a Carpaccio and others. His father is horrified. The Raycie gallery never opens and Lewis is eventually cut from his father's will with only a small allowance. But Lewis continues to believe and sets up a gallery of early Christian art in his home. Unfortunately, public interest doesn't keep the gallery open for long.

Fifty years later, a distant cousin inherits the paintings. She has no idea of their value and sells the collection to buy pearls and a Rolls Royce, never realizing that she had owned one of America's most valuable collections of primitive Italian art. In this story of changing artistic taste, Wharton uses the early American collectors, Thomas Jefferson Bryan and James Jackson Jarves, as models. Bryan's collection eventually made its way to The New-York Historical Society and Jarves's to Yale University.[24]

Bernard Berenson, Wharton's great friend and expert on Italian art, validated art works for the firm of Joseph Duveen, advising many American collectors of Renaissance and Baroque paintings. In Wharton's thirty-year friendship with Berenson, the two shared many intellectual interests, *"les choses de l'esprit."* But when they traveled together and visited the galleries in Germany in the summer of 1913, he found her aesthetic approach to paintings "anecdotal." He felt that she, as a novelist, was looking for the good human story in a painting, not its inherent beauty, a criticism that was not valid: although Wharton had an instinct for the good story, she also recognized the aesthetic qualities of a painting.

Although Wharton had little good to say about the arts in America, several expatriate artists, such as John Singer Sargent and Walter Gay, expressed very well the world she wrote about. Like Wharton, Sargent spent his childhood years in Europe, learning French and Italian and becoming familiar with European art and culture. As adults, both Wharton and Sargent alternated their primary work—writing fiction and painting portraits—with travel. She wrote travel essays, and he painted holiday scenes in Switzerland, Italy, and Spain.

Sargent's first success as a painter was the showing of his *Oyster Gatherers of Cancale* in the salon in 1878. Having moved to London after the scandal caused by his provocative and brilliant portrait, *Madame X*, he came to America to do portraits in 1887, just about the same time a complimentary article written by his friend Henry James was published in *Harper's*.[25] Many of Edith Wharton's friends were painted by Sargent, like Egerton Winthrop, Elizabeth Winthrop Chanler, Theodore Roosevelt, Edward Robinson, and Florence Vanderbilt Twombly. The confident, urbane, and often self-satisfied faces which look out from his portraits are very much those of the inhabitants of Edith Wharton's real and fictional worlds. They are well dressed, usually posed with one or two props—which suggest their privileged station in life—and are painted with discernment. Sargent used some of the techniques of contemporary Impressionist painters, but, as a critic has noted, his sensibility belonged to the past and he "was the spiritual contemporary of Reynolds and Gainsborough."[26]

It was Wharton who led the move to commission Sargent to paint a famous portrait of her friend Henry James for his seventieth birthday, three years after Sargent had vowed "no more mugs." Sargent preferred travel sketches, watercolors, and other genre pieces. In the spring of 1912, James posed for Sargent, and the result became famous. As Leon Edel describes it:

> Sargent painted him in a characteristic pose, his left thumb catching his striped and elegant waistcoat. He is wearing a bow tie and starched collar, and a watch chain dangles across the ample embonpoint. . . . For the rest, the picture fades into chiaroscuro; the full highlight accentuates the great forehead, the eyes half-closed but with all their visual acuteness; and the lips formed as if the master were about to speak. James is caught in one of the moments of his greatness—that is, a moment of "authority."[27]

Wharton's friend Walter Gay was another American painter who chose to live in France. A fourth-generation New Englander, he came to Paris at twenty in 1876 and joined the French-American art world, making friends with Sargent, Whistler, Degas, and Cassatt. He is best known for the versions of eighteenth-century French interiors that he began painting in the mid-1890s.[28] He painted many settings familiar to Wharton: the Villa Sylvia in the south of France, home of the Ralph Curtises (a setting she used for her 1908 short story, "The Verdict"); the Palazzo Barbaro in Venice, owned by the senior Curtises; the salon of Comtesse Rosa de Fitz-James; the Hôtel de Crillon; and rooms within Wharton's Pavillon Colombe.

Walter Gay's reaction to modern living was typical of many expatriate Americans, including Wharton. She lived out her life in France in settings like Gay's paintings, which preserved, as Wharton's intimate friend Daisy Chanler describes it, "a bygone world, a setting of a human life more sensitive, more finished, than the life we are able to lead among noisy machines and machine-made objects; an age when things were made by skillful workmen with tools fitted to their hands, not turned out by factories where men are the servants of powerful automata."[29]

There were many reasons that Wharton chose France as her last home. As Judith Saunders has noted, she admired French social conventions, and as a foreign resident she could avoid "actually suffering under their grip." Her status as a foreigner gave her a kind of freedom and separateness that helped her as a creative person.[30] At the same time, Wharton's last years in France were conspicuously filled with the artistic atmosphere she had loved since childhood. Living in houses where the beauty of details was completely under her control, she re-created an ambiance of the past, particularly at Pavillon Colombe with its classical architecture, formal garden, and lovely pool designed by Hubert Robert. Some friends felt, however, that she was too rigid and overdid aesthetic perfection. Percy Lubbock once wrote: "Her house, her garden, her appointments were all perfect—money, taste and instinct saw to every detail; yet the sense of a *home* was not there, and I think that perhaps it is a quality one always missed in her surroundings."[31]

Just as knowledge of French and Italian art had been invaluable to Wharton's personal outlook and development as a novelist and critic of America, it played a large role in her decision to live abroad. Not long before she died in 1937, Wharton returned three times to Italy, where she renewed her enthusiasm for Rome and the Italian art that had shaped her tastes during her earlier days as a writer. Until her death, Wharton continued to savor her own way of seeing the world, living a life enriched by contacts with the French and Italian beauty of the past, including the art she had loved since childhood.

NOTES

1. In 1906, the year before Wharton began to spend winters on the rue de Varenne in Paris, Pablo Picasso painted his famous Cubist portrait of American writer Gertrude Stein. Paintings of the innovative Impressionist school were being bought by discerning American collectors. When Edith Wharton was living her last years in France, modernism was raging in its exciting forms and would eventually make New York, the city she had seen as so aesthetically backward, the artistic capital of the world.

2. Besides her visual precocity, and her tendency to want *"to make the picture prettier,"* Wharton had a "secret sensitiveness to the landscape." As she notes in "Life and I" about Europe's beautiful landscapes, art, and architecture, when she was between the years of four and ten: "my visual sensibility seems to me, as I look back [almost seventy years], to have been as intense then as it is now" (*NW*, 1071–72).

3. Lloyd Lewis and Henry Justin Smith, *Oscar Wilde Discovers America* (New York: Benjamin Blom, 1967), 183.

4. William Merritt Chase, qtd. in Russell Lynes, *The Art-Makers* (New York: Dover, 1970), 425; Henry Adams, *Education* (New York: Library of America, 1983), 319; William Dean Howells, *A Foregone Conclusion*, in *Novels, 1875–1886*, ed. Edwin Harrison Cady (New York: Library of America, 1982), 119.

5. Wharton describes the Metropolitan in its new Central Park location in *The Age of Innocence*, with Archer commenting, "Some day, I suppose, it will be a great Museum" (*N*, 1262). Ellen and Archer's meeting in front of the Cesnola Collection is anachronistic,

however, because the novel is set in the mid-1870s and the museum did not open in Central Park until 1880. By the time Wharton returned to New York from Europe, the Metropolitan had purchased paintings by several Old Masters—Rubens, Van Dyck, Hals, Poussin, Guardi, Tiepolo—but had not yet established an Italian Renaissance collection that could rival those in Europe.

6. The Trumbull paintings depicted the surrenders of Burgoyne and Cornwallis. Vernet came from a family of French painters and was known for his renderings of horses and battle scenes. He was an ardent Bonapartist, and his chief commission was the Gallery of Battles at Versailles, painted for Louis Philippe. Jean Baptiste Édouard Detaille was a French painter who studied under J. L. E. Meissonier and served in the Franco–Russian War. His experiences enabled him to paint strikingly graphic portrayals of warfare. He became famous for his portraits of soldiers and precise, realistic execution of details. Wharton's negative reaction to the paintings, expressed later in life, might reflect attitudes formed in adulthood rather than at fifteen.

7. With husband Teddy and such friends as Egerton Winthrop and Paul and Minnie Bourget, Wharton made yearly trips to Europe, joining in the popular American pastime for the well-off and cultivated at the end of the nineteenth century. She would eventually join the set that included the Curtises, who rented the Palazzo Barbaro in Venice. She also met art critic Vernon Lee and other expatriate Americans, who settled near Florence, like Bernard Berenson and his wife Mary, who were just becoming known in the world of American collectors. She met Henry James for the first time in Venice, where she famously tried to impress him by wearing a fashionable hat. In contrast to this group's connoisseurship, very rich Americans like the Vanderbilts saw Europe as a place to find models for their enormous houses in New York or Newport and as an artistic field to plunder in order to aggrandize their images of wealth and power.

8. Each Italian city also has its foreground and background. The "background" sights in some cities are the "continuation, the amplification of the central 'subject'; in others, its direct antithesis" (*IB*, 179). This metaphor was probably inspired by Ruskin and Anna Jameson. For example, Ruskin recognized that artists painted "what they have seen and felt from early childhood. . . . The madonna

of Rafaelle was born in the Urbino mountains, Ghirlandajo's is a Florentine, Bellini's a Venetian. . . . Expression, character, types of countenance, costume, colour, and accessories are, with all great painters whatsoever, those of their native land." See John Ruskin, *Modern Painters*, vol. 3 of *The Works of John Ruskin*, ed. E. T. Cook and A. Wedderburn (London: George Allen; New York: Longmans, Green, 1903–1912), 3:229.

By the late 1890s and early 1900s, the woman who as a little girl had so loved the writings of Ruskin now broke with him to savor her passion for the animated and decorative art of the Baroque. In her essay, "Picturesque Milan," Wharton praises a number of churches, buildings, and painters that were not favorites of the art critic who praised the Gothic. The ingenue had become the expert: "[Milan] is rich in all that makes the indigenous beauty of Italy, as opposed to the pseudo-Gothicisms, the transAlpine points and pinnacles, which Ruskin taught a submissive generation of art critics to regard as the typical expression of the Italian spirit" (*IB*, 155). Wharton also praised the work of Tiepolo in Venice. As Rosella Mamoli Zorski writes, she found in Venetian art "a joie de vivre" that helped her to escape "from the stifling conventions of the New York society she was to portray so bitterly and accurately the following year in *The House of Mirth* (1905) and then *The Age of Innocence* (1920). . . . One seems to sense a sort of personal identification with a world where freedom and enjoyment were celebrated, a world that did not exclude sexual and sensuous relationships, a world that the dark and oppressive atmosphere of the Victorian nineteenth century could not tolerate or admire" ("Tiepolo, Henry James and Edith Wharton," *Metropolitan Museum of Art Journal* 33 [1998]: 218).

9. Sarah Bird Wright, "Refracting the Odyssey: Edith Wharton's Travel Writing as the Cultural Capital of Her Fiction," *Edith Wharton Review* 13, no. 1 (Fall 1996): 23.

10. Wharton's conviction that European art and architecture were superior to their American counterparts was on her mind in the late 1890s, when she was working on *The Decoration of Houses*. In an address entitled "School Room Decoration," given at age thirty-five to those connected with the Newport schools for which she volunteered, she maintained that beautiful surroundings were not just an aesthetic but a moral necessity. "Our object in decorating the schoolrooms is not to turn all schoolchildren into painters and

sculptors or to teach them history, but to surround them with such representations of beauty as in older civilizations the streets, the monuments and galleries of almost every city provide." In America "the conditions are unfavorable to the development of taste. We must teach our children to care for beauty" (*UCW,* 57–58). Ugliness, the result of indifference, disorder, and evil, must be banished from a child's environment. "In art, as in literature and in conduct, the child must be taught to care only for the best. It is as easy to buy a plaster cast or a photograph of some really great work of art as a foolish pink and white chromo. . . . Don't indulge your pupils in a diet of trashy prettiness" (*DH,* 61). See also Mary Blanchard, *Oscar Wilde's America: Counterculture in the Gilded Age* (New Haven: Yale University Press, 1998), 81, for an alternate reading of Wharton's Eurocentric decorating schemes.

11. Hildegarde Hawthorne, "Gardens of Well-Known People," in *The Lure of the Garden* (New York: Century, 1911), 135–36.

12. James W. Tuttleton, Kristen O. Lauer, and Margaret P. Murray, eds., *Edith Wharton Contemporary Reviews* (New York: Cambridge University Press, 1992), 52.

13. In *The Valley of Decision,* Wharton creates a tableau setting for her heroine. "The eyes of the impatient audience" await Fulvia, the heroine, in the great council chamber: "A pause followed and then Fulvia appeared. Against the red-robed faculty at the back of the dais, she stood tall and slender in her black cap and gown. The high window of painted glass shed a paleness on her face, but her carriage was light and assured as she advanced to the President and knelt to receive her degree" (*V,* 2:276).

14. Wharton even pictures herself in scenes in which a beautiful girl is the center of attention. In her memoirs, "Life and I" and *A Backward Glance,* written in her seventies, she remembers precise details of the "pleasing" white satin bonnet she wore as she strolled along Fifth Avenue with her father and cousin. The child's luxurious trappings thus serve to delight and pacify the eyes of what are almost always male viewers (*NW,* 1071).

15. See Marilyn R. Chandler, *Dwelling in the Text* (Berkeley and Los Angeles: University of California Press, 1991), 149–81, and Eleanor Dwight, *Edith Wharton: An Extraordinary Life* (New York: Harry N. Abrams, 1994), 169–71.

16. Edith Wharton, *Untitled fragment,* Wharton Archives, Bei-

necke Library, Yale University, New Haven, Conn. Wharton's knowledge of European art and architecture also influenced the structure of her novels, which are architectural in form. The episodic novel of manners like *The House of Mirth* and *The Age of Innocence* is made up of tightly plotted, balanced, and symmetrical parts. Within this framework, Wharton was free to capture feelings and the complexities of human psychology. A parallel to this way of organizing her novels can be found in her later gardens in France. Within a tight structure like her walled potager with espaliered fruit trees on the walls at Pavillon Colombe, she found the freedom to plant masses of brilliantly colored annuals and perennials.

17. Henry James, "Italy Revisited," in *Italian Hours* (New York: Horizon Press, 1968), 157.

18. In *A Backward Glance,* Wharton writes that in the years of the new century, the artistic milieu had improved. "With the coming of the new millionaires the building of big houses had begun, in New York and in the country, bringing with it (though not always to those for whom the building was done) a keen interest in architecture, furniture and works of art in general. The Metropolitan Museum was waking up from its long lethargy, and the leading picture dealers from London and Paris were seizing the opportunity of educating a new clientèle, opening up branch houses in New York and getting up loan exhibitions" (*NW,* 894). Although aware of this changing situation, she gives her nouveau riche characters little part in any sincere appreciation of the art available in New York's public and private places.

19. Tuttleton, Lauer, and Murray, *Reviews,* 120. A reviewer in *Literary Digest* remarks that "the force and value of *The House of Mirth* lie in the pitiless psychological description of a beautiful young woman, Lily Bart, and of the forces and tendencies of 'Society.' "

20. Cynthia Griffin Wolff also suggests that the schools of art at the time—society portraiture by such artists as Abbott Thayer and John Singer Sargent, murals, and art nouveau depictions—all viewed women as decorative and demanded certain appropriate behavior. For most women, these demands were superficial, but for someone as narcissistic and vulnerable as Lily, they are harmful and diminishing.

On the tableaux vivants in *The House of Mirth,* see Cynthia Griffin Wolff, "Lily Bart and the Beautiful Death," in Edith Wharton, *The*

House of Mirth, ed. Elizabeth Ammons (New York: Norton, 1990). See also Reginald Abbott, "A Moment's Ornament: Wharton's Lily Bart and Art Nouveau," *Mosaic: A Journal for the Interdisciplinary Study of Literature* 24, no. 2 (Spring 1991): 73–91. Helen Killoran discusses Lily's portraits in *Edith Wharton: Art and Allusion* (Tuscaloosa: University of Alabama Press, 1996), 25–26.

21. Dell Upton, "Inventing the Metropolis: Civilization and Urbanity in Antebellum New York," *Art and the Empire City: New York, 1825–1861* (New York: Metropolitan Museum of Art, 2000), 40.

22. While Wharton makes the Boucher tapestries the objects coveted by greedy Americans in the novel, other Americans were fascinated by the new art. In 1913, Gertrude Stein, the Havemeyers, and Mary Cassatt were buying the canvases of Manet, Matisse, Degas, and Picasso. The situation in the novel reflects on the American millionaires Wharton had known in New York and Newport.

23. Elizabeth Ammons, "Cool Diana and the Blood-Red Muse: Edith Wharton on Innocence and Art," in *The Age of Innocence*, ed. Carol J. Singley (Boston: Houghton Mifflin, 2000), 401.

24. Adeline Tintner, "False Dawn and the Irony of Taste Changes in Art," *Edith Wharton in Context: Essays on Intertextuality* (Tuscaloosa: University of Alabama Press, 1999), 158.

25. See Lynes's discussion of Sargent, *The Art Makers*, 431–37.

26. Allan Gowans, "Painting and Sculpture," qtd. in Woolf, "Lily Bart and the Beautiful Death," 322.

27. Leon Edel, *Henry James: A Life* (New York: Harper & Row, 1985), 685.

28. Gary A. Reynolds, *Walter Gay: A Retrospective* (New York: New York University, Grey Art Gallery, 1980).

29. Margaret Terry Chanler, *Autumn in the Valley* (Boston: Little Brown, 1936), 116.

30. Judith Saunders, "Edith Wharton, Gertrude Stein, and France: The Meanings of Expatriation," *Edith Wharton Review* 9, no. 1 (Spring 1992): 5.

31. Percy Lubbock, *A Portrait of Edith Wharton* (New York: Appleton Century Crofts, 1947), 40.

Wharton and the Age of Film

Linda Costanzo Cahir

A surprisingly large number of Edith Wharton's works—her short stories, novels, novellas, and even her autobiography—have been adapted to film and television. While the temptation in explaining this anomaly is to take the high road and presume that Wharton's extraordinary writing talents and her acute capacity to analyze American society compel the attention of filmmakers, it would be more accurate to state that Wharton's popularity on screen typifies a simple principle of cinematic production: certain literary works lend themselves more naturally to the *economic* function of the screen. Edith Wharton's writing has the functional qualities that filmmakers traditionally seek.

Producers and financiers of film foremost favor and scout for strong narrative realism, and they value upscale properties, like Wharton's writings, because they confer an immediate integrity on any movie based on such a source. Wharton, specifically, appeals to cinematic translation because of the solid materiality of her writing, a quality that translates well into the visual medium of moviemaking. Her precise rendering of period detail complements film's great strength: the capacity to convey an abundance of visual information efficiently. Wharton delivers, in highly visual and interestingly particularized ways, an inside view of the American ruling class of the late nineteenth and early twentieth centuries, with its ironclad social bonds and unassailable rules of comportment, kinship, and taste—the obeisance required by the society's pressures and forms. Her settings and her clean linear narratives with well-constructed story lines and rounded, differentiated characters have a popular market appeal. Unfortunately, however, when adapted to the screen, these complexities of character and plot are often reduced, and storytelling, in the simplistic mass market model, rather than nuances of meaning becomes the driving force.

By Hollywood standards, Edith Wharton was and remains of commercial interest. As early as 1906, Wharton was not only a critically praised author but also a popular one. Her novels became best-sellers nationwide. Capitalizing on the popularity of her fiction, Hollywood began making films of her books. The first movie based on a Wharton work is the 1918 Metro silent film version of *The House of Mirth* (1905). Within five years, Paramount produced the silent 1923 film version of *The Glimpses of the Moon* (1922); and the following year, 1924, Warner Brothers released its silent film version of *The Age of Innocence* (1920).[1] It is significant that the three major Hollywood studios, Metro Pictures Corporation, Paramount, and Warner Brothers, all had produced, within six years of each other, silent film versions of Wharton's novels. However, as Scott Marshall, in his pioneering and important Wharton filmography, explains, "Unfortunately, all three of these early silent movies are considered lost films, and although major performances and directors were involved, it is difficult to evaluate their quality or their faithfulness to the original text."[2]

The earliest surviving Wharton film is *The Marriage Playground* (1929, Paramount), based on Wharton's novel *The Children* (1928). As Kathleen Fitzpatrick notes, the film was produced during a very brief, yet distinctive, period in American film history, the point at which "talkies" were emerging[3] and prior to the institution of the stricter and more formal Hays Production Code of the 1930s.[4] The film betrays the flaws of early sound. The camera, creatively moved, angled, and situated in late silent films, becomes more inert here, attempting, primarily, to record the actors mouthing their lines, as they are positioned to be heard by the microphone. As a result, throughout *The Marriage Playground*, the composition of frames seems static and redundant, creative cuts are rare, and visual images are functional rather than expressive.

Wharton's novel, *The Children*, tells the story of Martin Boyne, unmarried and solitary, and the effects that his chance meeting with the offspring of his old Harvard friend, Cliffe Wheater, have on the rest of his life. The children, seven in all, are in the care of their governess and their oldest sister, Judith, not their parents, and they are an odd amalgam of the Wheaters' (Cliffe's and Joyce's) various marriages. In contrast to the irresponsible, monied, slapdash lifestyle of their parents, the children are determined to remain together as a stable family; and their worthy desire slowly compels Boyne to become involved in their cause. His involvement with them deepens, and, quite startlingly to him, Martin Boyne, age forty-seven, realizes that he has fallen in love with the unusually mature and sensible, but fifteen-year-old, Judith Wheater, who relies on him for stability, coherence, integrity, and emotional steadiness, much in the same way that Boyne has relied on Rose Sellars. Martin Boyne, adrift most of his life and deplete of significant human relationships, is seeking what the children seek, and, being so much a child himself, he has never really reached emotional maturity.

Boyne's efforts to keep the family of children intact are kind-hearted but ineffective. At the end of the novel, the children have been dispersed, hither and yon, and the great sorrow is not that they are scattered, but that they have forgotten how vital it once was to remain together. On the book's last page, Martin Boyne ends situated where he began: "a lonely man," standing on the deck of a ship (*C*, 347). However, the experience of the children has changed him, made him more cognizant of his inherent isolation, and deepened his understanding of self, painfully so.

Despite thin reviews of the book, *The Children* was the September 1928 Book-of-the-Month Club selection and earned Wharton a sum in excess of $95,000. Attempting to capitalize on the book's popularity, Famous-Lasky Corporation (soon to become Paramount) purchased the film rights to *The Children* from Wharton for $25,000.[5] With that heavy fee, the studio presumed that it was free, as it legally was, to alter Wharton's text in any way seen fit. Their film, retitled *The Marriage Playground*, is unabashed in its bid for audience popularity and commercial success. Consequently, the movie often detaches itself from the somber tones and thematic complexities of Wharton's work. It is guilelessly and unapologetically rompish, at points, and driven far more by the amusing, the urbane, and the droll than by the regrettable plight of the children. Wharton's darker implications, her undertones of sexual unorthodoxy, and her complexities of character, times, and emotions are fully eviscerated from J. Walter Rubin and Doris Anderson's script. In *The Marriage Playground*, "Judy" (never "Judith") is a blithe, (nearly) eighteen-year-old (played by Kay Francis, who was twenty-nine at the time). The unwholesome age difference between Judith Wheater and Martin Boyne (played by Fredric March, who was, then, thirty-one), that is so unsettling in the book, is conveniently narrowed. The two are simply made more age-appropriate; and, it is Judy, not Martin, who does the romantic pursuing, declaring her love for him several times throughout the movie. The couple marry, happily so, and the family of children is preserved. Cliffe and Joyce Wheater, transmogrified into a couple with emotional insight, remarry in the full and splendid understanding that they are meant to be together. Throughout the film, love and marriage are a playground on which happy endings are manufactured. The ending is blissful, Hollywood style.

That ending, however, is antithetical to Wharton's work, and the extremes of *The Marriage Playground*'s reconstruction of plot waste the cardinal complexities and prepossessing subtleness of Wharton's ideas to an absurd, if not infuriating, degree. What is gained, however, is that in *The Marriage Playground*, produced just prior to the inception of the Production Code, a freedom of expression common to this short era is visible, "permanently locking in the lingo, manners, and values of their moment."[6] For what it says about the age in which it was made and for the manner in which the popular culture was assimilating Wharton at the time, *The Marriage Playground* is a worthy film.

A second film of *The Children* was produced in 1990. Directed by Tony Palmer and starring Ben Kinglsey (Martin Boyne), Kim

Novak (Rose Sellars), and Siri Neal (Judith Wheater), the film attempts a faithful adaptation of Wharton's book. What results from such punctilious orthodoxy, as often does in literal translations of books into film, is a movie that is frozen in fatigue. The subversive gestures, often necessary to create worthy film translations of literature, the boldness of filmmaking that carries us to the domain of discovery, is fully missing here, and at best, the movie is little more than a polite and restrained homage to its parent text.

The first laudable film based on a Wharton work is *The Old Maid*. Edith Wharton's novella, *The Old Maid*, disguises itself as a sentimental tale of hoopskirts and corsets. The stock offerings of the sentimental tale are all present: a fallen yet virtuous woman, a roguish man, a cold and spiteful female adversary, familial settings, tortured virtue, betrayed trust, and heightened emotions. The protagonist, Charlotte Lovell, bears a child (Clementina/Tina) out of wedlock. Caught in social interdicts and guided by love for her daughter and a sense of honor superior to all ordinary passions, she places her child in the home of her respectfully married cousin, while she herself plays the role of Tina's spinster aunt. Charlotte's private woes, suffered in quiet dignity, buttonhole us and demand the emotional response sentimental literature traditionally exacts of its readers.

In the tradition of the sentimental novel, words are not left alone to bear the weight of meaning. They are assisted by other amplifying devices—exclamation points, dashes, capital letters, ellipses, and italics, all of which occur to an immoderate and altogether un-Whartonian degree in *The Old Maid*. The book sacrifices a certain dignity of punctuation and dramatic corporeality in a blatant effort to appeal to our sentiments.

However, Wharton uses the conventions of the sentimental narrative to construct a relentlessly unsentimental work. The sentimental ethos sends dangerous codes to women, Wharton warns us. Often, it lauds a woman's patient and mute renunciation of life carried out in high service to love and virtue. This sentimental ideal, for Wharton, exists as a destructive mythology that reduces life to a joyless task and ultimately smothers the animus. The archetypal protagonist of sentimental fiction is the suffering and defenseless woman of fervent female virtue, who is either happily rewarded by marriage and children or ennobled by a redemptive death. However, in *The Old Maid*, neither of the two female protagonists meets the high sentimental end. Delia Ralston, naive and defenseless in her youthful ideas about marriage, slowly discovers that her marriage represents a forfeiture of life, of spirited freedom, and vibrant aspirations. Charlotte Lovell's renunciation of life, virtuous by sentimental standards, becomes, by Wharton's standards, an unredemptive death in life, as she lives in proximity to, but fully alienated from that which she loves most, her own daughter. At the novella's end, Tina promises her "mother" (her Aunt Delia) that she will bestow upon her "Aunt Charlotte" (her mother) her departing kiss as she leaves on her honeymoon. While ostensibly touching, the kiss is patronizing and darkly ironic. Nothing has changed. The gesture is all surface and ephemera. Tina's kiss, unbeknownst to her, is fraught with the secrets, denials, hypocrisies, and guilt that have defined the book's *two* triangular relations: Charlotte, Delia, and Clem's followed by Charlotte, Delia, and Tina's. After Tina's honeymoon departure, Charlotte will remain in the Ralston house. In the end, all she has is the life-in-death continuance of cohabitation with Delia.

Charlotte Lovell clearly is cast in a sentimental tradition that glorifies motherhood and the feminine impulse to sacrifice all for the child. But, as written by Wharton, Charlotte is a mother with a past, a character who, like the rogues of sentimental literature, has ventured into forbidden sexual terrain. Charlotte was the seducer not the seduced, and in her one bold, unnarrated, sexual pursuit of Clem Spender, she rebelled against the sentimental ethos that condemns such behavior in women. Vibrant, impulsive, and self-assured, she represents the attempt at a new female ideal, albeit a failed attempt, since Charlotte Lovell ultimately ends pinned fast in Wharton's immemorial social web.

The Old Maid follows Charlotte Lovell's despair. By the end of the story, Charlotte is an old woman, "enigmatic and inaccessible" (*NW*, 437). She is a stranger to her daughter, Tina, the one person with whom she wants to make meaningful contact. Uncommunicative (except to Delia), solitary, and acutely private, the once charming and vibrant Charlotte ages into a bitter and misanthropic old maid, whom her own daughter thinks of as an inconvenient fixture in the otherwise merry Ralston household. Far afield of the freeing, happy-ending reversals common to sentimental novels, *The Old Maid* illustrates society's crushing imposition of conformity and sacrifice, of the worst sort, on its members, who are beset by a vision of something more.

Charlotte stands as an exemplar of spirited but constrained femininity, who instigates an unconventional liaison, but does so tastefully behind the scenes, whose dark and curious masculine appearance emerges as far more provocative than Delia's conventional feminine beauty, whose restrained surface hints at deep yearnings, and who always has to maneuver within the corseted restrictions of society. As such, she expresses a part of the American zeitgeist that found articulation in the genre known as "women's films" of the late 1930s and early 1940s.

A prime and important example of this genre is *The Old Maid* (1939), a film, which like the Wharton novella on which it is based, employs the specific conventions of the sentimental tradition. In handsome and judicious translation of the book's literary amplifying devices (its exclamation points, dashes, capital letters, ellipses, and italics), the movie employs cinematic devices to achieve the same heightening results. To an immoderate degree, dramatic fadeouts, hard cuts, atmospheric lighting, stylized acting, overwrought gesturing, and heightened music are used.

Because the plot involves an illicit affair and the illegitimate child who resulted, Edith Wharton battled censorship in trying to publish *The Old Maid* in 1921. In a similar situation, Warner Brothers, from 1935 to 1939, had to battle the Production Code Administration, headed by Joseph Breen, for clearance for the film's production. As the record of correspondence between the studio and Breen, as well as internal memos of the Production Code Adminstration (PCA) demonstrate, approval was to be forthcoming because of the "compensating moral values" that the draft-script ensured, more specifically, that "sacrifice and retribution are paramount in that the mother gives up all for her indiscretion."[7] Before final PCA approval was awarded, however, many specific details had to be negotiated.

One such detail is that the film subtly recasts the novel's setting from 1850s New York to Philadelphia at the time of the
American Civil War. Clem Spender (George Brent), rebuffed by
Delia Lovell (Miriam Hopkins) on her wedding day to Jim Ralston, enlists in the Union army and spends his final day and
evening with her cousin Charlotte Lovell (Bette Davis). The next
afternoon, he heroically departs for the battlefield (none of the
Ralston men enlists). He dies serving a virtuous cause, with the
film's PCA-pleasing implication that, had he lived, he would have
returned and done right by his new family. The film includes two
key scenes between Clem and Charlotte: their return to Charlotte's home after having passed the infamous evening together
and their farewell on the train platform, as Clem is about to em-
bark for war. While both scenes are kept constrained, the more
notable one is the farewell scene. In compliance with PCA demands, in this particular exchange Clem and Charlotte's passion
and fears are held in abeyance; their conversation hints of mo-
mentous things unsaid; and their parting kiss is kept polite. The
scene is simply beautiful. To the actors' and director's credit
(Edmund Goulding), the sequence is more fully charged with
emotion because of the manner in which the emotions lay unex-
pressed. The audience presumes the couple's restraint is a necessary response to the rigid rules of conduct imposed by their hov-
eringly rigid world of decorum. However, in a letter from Joseph
Breen to Jack Warner, Breen insists that the scenes between the
two characters should not "show Charlotte and Clem in embrace" and that they must be "exceedingly careful with the fade-
out, so that it does not indicate a sex affair."[8] Ironically, the off-
camera constraints imposed by Breen's office, invisible to the
audience, heighten the sexual tension and lingering pathos of
this sequence.[9]

Wharton's *The Old Maid* is suffused with the language of double meanings, words unsaid, and coded conversations; and while
these are literary nuances that do not translate well into the
medium of film and are often omitted in production, the beauty
of this movie is that we see, writ elegantly in the details of long,
full-screen close-ups and meticulously framed, dynamic two-
shots,[10] Delia's jealous furor, Charlotte's ongoing pain, the great

and slow toll that her sacrifice takes upon Charlotte's spirit and her body, and the subterranean hell that dwells beneath the outwardly merry Ralston household. In the beauty of its visual composition, this film has a moving power.

In direct contrast to the power of Warner Brothers' *The Old Maid*, RKO's 1934 version of *The Age of Innocence*[11] is a thin, spiritless, and aseptic movie which, upon release, was described in *The New York Times* as "a painstaking but emotionally flaccid photoplay."[12] Less an adaptation of Wharton's novel than a diminution, the film was an attempt to capitalize on the enduring success of Margaret Ayer Barnes's 1928 stage version of Wharton's novel. In casting Irene Dunne (Ellen Olenska) and John Boles (Newland Archer), Pandro S. Berman, the film's producer, hoped to rekindle the box office voltage that the two had created earlier in *Back Street* (1932). However, Berman seemed to see little more in Wharton's novel than the same sort of adulterous, sudsy scandal that made *Back Street* so successful. *The Age of Innocence*, too rooted in the time in which it was produced and too driven by the urgency of commercial success, never attempts to rethink Wharton's novel as the material of film. It is void of any genuine emotion. Told in flashback, with an elderly Archer relating the tragic love story to his grown grandson, the narrative frame is a contrivance, serving no real end except to state the obvious (the differences between generations) in a film that lacks sincerity and visual interest.

In contrast to the 1934 *The Age of Innocence*, Martin Scorsese's 1993 screen version is all visual interest. "The object of the film was authenticity, absolute authenticity," stated Robin Standefer, a research designer for the film. To this end, Standefer further explains:

We researched all the places Wharton knew in New York, all the interiors, all the furniture, the sleeping habits, the beds, the art. We recreated 500 paintings for all the rooms. In one passage, Wharton talks about some obscure Italian paintings. I talked with the Met, and we decided she must have meant the work of a group of Italian Impressionists called *I Macchiaioli*, so we sent for the paintings and reproduced them for the banquet scene. . . . There are seven dinner scenes in the movie. Each of them represents a family, and the differences in design suggest the differences in the families. It was extraordinarily subtle and complex.[13]

Scorsese demanded an exacting attention to historical authenticity throughout all aspects of the production. The locales, the furniture, the china, the food preparation and presentation, the music, the costumes, the etiquette, and the manner of speech and articulation were rigorously researched and superintended by experts in each of the fields.[14] *The Age of Innocence* is a technically masterful film of sequence-by-sequence beauty, nearly unfailing in its compositional choices and visual density, an expert collaboration between the director and the cinematographer, Michael Ballhaus. Scorsese's sense of sequencing is prime, as he juxtaposes shots of turmoil and order, fecundity and sterility, ardor and ice. Throughout the film, there is the enchanting feeling that this is what the world Wharton describes must really have looked like.

The film is filled with internal references to other matters. In a matte shot of busy New York City, a store sign appears for "Schoonmaker's Painting Supplies," in deference to Scorsese's editor of duration, Thelma Schoonmaker. While Newland waits for Ellen outside a Boston hotel, the name "Lily Bart" can be seen on a nearby window; and, at May and Newland's first dinner party, Archer's staring at the elegant twist of Ellen's hair is a tribute to a similar scene in Alfred Hitchcock's *Vertigo*, a film in which the protagonist (James Stewart) is in love with two women (both played by Kim Novak), one, knowable and safe, and the other, mysterious and erotic.

Martin Scorsese is known for starting with concrete and specific topics. He explores small, limited subjects, from which a wider significance emerges. In the case of *The Age of Innocence*, he claims that what drew him to the project was "the idea of a love story that couldn't be fulfilled, two people caring for each other so much but having a responsibility and obligation to other people and to a way of life."[15] The great misfortune of Scorsese's *The Age of Innocence*, however, is that the film never expands beyond his initial concept of it as an ill-fated love story. It stands strongly as a beautiful minutia of execution, but one from which no wider Whartonian import ever emerges.

In Wharton's work there is a brutal collision between the lyrically literal and the bitterly ironic in her calling Old New York an age—a place and a time—of innocence. Ellen Olenska is caught in the pull. She loves Newland Archer for the Old New York authentic rectitude and integrity he embodies (he is a direct contrast to her corrupt husband), yet she is somberly cognizant of that same society's quietly destructive willingness to repress, coerce, and choke any member who challenges its values. Newland Archer is also ambivalent toward the innocence of the age. Through Ellen, Newland comes to see society's lethal hypocrisy, even as he longs for the two of them to live among the abiding refinements and virtues of that age. Both understand that to have each other is to violate the values that they share (their dilemma is complex); and both are victimized by a society pernicious in its insistence on empty conformity. The film never explores Wharton's ambivalence toward her topic, and, while it proclaims itself a love story, it never makes inquiry into the nature of Ellen's and Newland's love for one another. Known for being inquisitive, audacious, and innovative, Martin Scorsese abandons those qualities in this film that is just too polite toward the society that Wharton acerbically indicts.

While Scorsese's film fails to probe the delicate layers and depths of Wharton's text (it simply never makes us think), it is a work of intelligent, cinematic refinement, visually lovely and interesting. In trumpeting contrast to *The Age of Innocence* is *Ethan Frome* (1993), a bleakness of mediocrity. The first theatrical film by John Madden, an English stage and television director, *Ethan Frome* displays the flaws of a first venture in a new medium. Madden's cinematic style is diligent but quotidian. Visually, the film is prosaic and unimaginative, as the camera largely functions throughout the entire movie to show us who is speaking or to stress how cold Starkfield winters really are or to "present a New England the way tourists remember it."[16] Vincent Canby describes the movie as a "sad and solemn little film that never has a life of its own." He further adds, "The delicate, mysterious

Wharton precision is gone. . . . Take away Wharton and all that's left is a synopsis."[17]

This synopsis film opens with a stationary, long shot of Starkfield, as a stark field. In the distance, a figure walks into the frame. It is Ethan Frome (Liam Neeson), exaggeratedly deformed, as he drags and twists and gyrates tortuously into full screen. Frome's deformity looks cartoonized and, consequently, strips the character of the inherent sense of dignity and potency that Wharton's Frome possesses. Wharton's narrator first sees Frome and is compelled by the "powerful look he had" (*NW*, 63). The film's first view of him makes no such pronouncement, and, despite Liam Neeson's efforts, his Frome never mounts to more than a lamentable, unfortunate soul who suffers from one very bad decision. The character is flattened by Richard Nelson's spiritless screenplay, concerned solely with plot, and, in consequence, the film is fully emptied of the majesty of pain that belongs to Wharton's Ethan Frome.

Ethan Frome entered the public domain in 1989, and while four other production companies announced plans at the time to film it, American Playhouse Theatrical Films was the only one to complete the project (Miramax Films became the distributor). The film was shot in Peacham, Vermont, and the house selected as Frome's farmhouse was one that had been uninhabited since the early 1900s. Commenting on the location, Madden stated, "We had horrendous problems trying to film in a space the size of the farm, but on screen you [get] the claustrophobia and restriction depicted in Wharton's novel."[18] The movie aspires to depict scenes just as they appear in Wharton's novel. This tenaciously faithful adherence to Wharton's novel makes its one plot alteration seem even more jarringly odd and radical: Ethan Frome and Mattie Silver (Patricia Arquette) consummate their love in Frome's farmhouse one evening.

In Wharton's book Ethan Frome is a vastly solitary soul, who prefers imaginative escape over the mundanity of life in Starkfield. Continually occupying a dream-life that is better than his real one, Frome, despite repeated opportunities, cowers before any act that would improve his circumstances. His passivity allows him to remain insular, outlying, and securely detached from the materiality of his milieu. His vision-life provides an enticing repose, a numbing inertia that Frome finds addictively comfortable. As Cynthia Wolff writes, "It is always easier for Frome to retreat from life into a 'vision.' . . . As always, the uncompromised richness of the dream is more alluring than the harsher limitations of actual, realized satisfactions."[19]

Frome does not want the temporary physical satisfaction or the real-world intimacy that a sexual assignation with Mattie would provide. Matters are much more complex with him, but the filmmakers are either too unpracticed or too distrusting of an audience's capacity to follow depths of meaning to explore Frome's aching intricacies. Instead, they give the audience what they think we should see and would enjoy: soft-hued lamplight, openmouthed kisses, and gentle sex, a pedestrianization of Frome's complexity, a silliness of indignity. It is not the tampering with Wharton's text that is objectionable in this amended scene—many great literature to film translations are the product of radical alterations of the parent text. Here it is the film's supercilious manner, in all its prurient, dumbing-down transparency that is so unfortunate. John Madden's *Ethan Frome* takes wine and turns it into water.

In curious contrast to *Ethan Frome* is the more venturesome 1981 adaptation of *The House of Mirth*, produced on a small budget for television through the joint underwriting of the National Endowment for the Humanities, Exxon Corporation, and the Corporation for Public Broadcasting. Directed by Adrian Hall from a script he coauthored with Richard Cumming, the production features a commendable performance by Geraldine Chaplin as Lily Bart. In reviewing it for *The New York Times*, John J. O'Connor quite aptly describes the production as "less a literal dramatization than an impressionistic interpretation."[20] Shot in Rhode Island in only twenty-eight days and with a running time of only 82 minutes, *The House of Mirth* is a lean but imaginative production that utilizes brevity of scenes, soft-focus, voice-overs, and incongruous camera set-ups in creative ways. (Reminiscent of the work of Federico Fellini, a traditional society wedding scene is shot through a distorting lens.) The production, odd in its way, is nevertheless thought-filled, sure-footed, and commendable.

The House of Mirth was adapted once more in a film[21] directed by Terence Davies and produced by Olivia Stewart, a highly creative, collaborative team who have worked together on four feature films over more than fifteen years.[22] The movie was made on the comparatively small budget of $8 million. Filmed in just nine weeks in June and July of 1999, it was shot largely in Glasgow, Scotland, where the Glasgow City Chamber (William Young's masterpiece), the Kelvingrove Museum, the Theatre Royal, and several imposing mansions authentically re-create turn-of-the-century New York. The cast features Gillian Anderson as Lily Bart, in a lovely, credible, and solid performance. Eric Stoltz plays Lawrence Selden, in the film's most singular weakness: his performance flattens Selden's character to the clear-cut and banal. Also featured are Anthony LaPaglia, strong and convincing as Simon Rosedale, and Laura Linney, quietly emphatic and subtly complex as Bertha Dorset.

In addition to directing the film, Terence Davies also wrote the screenplay, which is an intelligent, engaging, and, at intervals, witty integration of his own language with Wharton's.[23] The film's story consistently follows the novel's and most plot alterations are negligible and done, understandably, in service to the time-constraints of a theatrically released film. These alterations include Wharton's characters, Gerty Farish and Grace Stepney, being combined into one composite character and Lawrence Selden lacking the shades, tinges, and tints of character and the prevailing plot value that he has in the book.

The screenplay is logically constructed and compact. Moreover, it is a meticulously detailed blueprint for efficient filming, as it includes inordinately thorough directions for camera placement, camera movement, and cuts. Thus, more than a story with dialogue, Terence Davies's screenplay is an intricate, creative, visual map, instrumental in keeping production costs down through an implied shooting schedule that is thoroughly and efficiently planned. His screenplay shows a distinctive talent: this writer/director's capacity *to see*, to envision in exacting detail, the completed film long before the camera ever turns on.

The film itself is intrinsically stunning in its compositional beauty. Davies is known for his gently exquisite visual style, which is painterly here, as he consciously attempts to employ film's equivalents of the kind of beauty seen in the paintings of John Singer Sargent and Jan Vermeer. Visually pleasing, the film is also substantive. Terence Davies has very definite ideas about Wharton's novel and he brings his interpretive position of her work to this film. He explains, "With Edith Wharton, the gloves are off and there's blood on the walls. . . . The glittering facade of New York Society at the turn of the century only thinly veils a compassionless world of savage humor and cruelty."[24] In slowly modulated sequencing, Davies depicts the utterly savage cruelty beneath the genteel facade of Wharton's society. The film is clean, honest, intelligent, and bold. Davies's boldness may seem transgressive to readers of Wharton's book who hold that any movie's plot-distorting, interpretive alterations of her novel are, de facto, taboo. While Davies's film, overall, is true to Wharton's novel, he does amend one significant scene.

"I'm at the end of my tether," Lily poignantly confesses to Grace Stepney. In consequence, feeling she has no alternative, Lily goes to the Dorsets' house for the sole purpose of extorting them with Bertha's old love letter to Lawrence Selden. In adding this scene, one that clearly is not in Wharton's book, the film alters—arguably, radically—Wharton's notion of her own character. Wharton's Lily does not use the letters to her advantage; she is made of finer stuff. However, for Davies, the singular, most pronounced element in Wharton's novel is not the triumph but the defeat of Lily's nobler self. Most dominantly, Davies sees in Wharton's novel the aching ambit and depth of society's horrid, appetitive—almost cannibalistic—capacity to destroy, fully and without compunction, a thing of vulnerability and beauty. He shows, in full tones, the excruciating extent of that destruction. Everything beauteous about Lily—everything—is stripped away, corroded, and laid to waste. This version of *The House of Mirth* is so deeply tragic.

The film has the disturbing power of art; days later, it rushes up and overwhelms. It is a movie of emotional reach, a cry of passion, a slow-paced disclosure of disgust. There is nothing commonplace and nothing extraneous in this film, which, while it may rankle some because of its plot alterations, makes us think

The House of Mirth: *Lawrence Selden (Eric Stoltz) and Lily Bart (Gillian Anderson) engage in an afternoon's dalliance. Three Rivers Production and Sony Pictures Classics, 2000.*

about alternate ways of reading Wharton's text and viewing her characters.

Like Terence Davies's movie, Edith Wharton's writing has the disturbing power of art; however, far too often, when translated to film, Wharton's capacity to disturb is muted by filmmakers, whose talents are not up to the complexities of the task or by the industry's money-making motive, which overwhelms all other concerns. However, there are commendable film translations of Wharton's works and moments of rarified beauty within given films, when the filmmakers get it right—Martin Scorsese's Newland Archer, in the privacy of a carriage, erotically touching the gloved, inner wrist of Ellen Olenska; Edmund Goulding's Charlotte Lovell, keeping a strange vigil, as she waits all alone for her daughter to return from a dance; and Terence Davies's transition from America at the end of the season to Monte Carlo, a sequence replete with Lily's futile longings. In those moments and through those films, Wharton's work is illuminated, the text is made brighter by the insight, talent, meditation, and vision of prodigiously gifted filmmakers, who commendably translate Wharton's writing, while they simultaneously depart from her text sufficiently, to create provocatively independent works of art.

NOTES

1. *The House of Mirth*, Dir. Albert Capellani, Metro Pictures Corporation, 1918; *The Glimpses of the Moon*, Dir. Allan Dwan, Paramount, 1923; *The Age of Innocence*, Dir. Wesley Ruggles, Warner Brothers, 1924.

2. Scott Marshall, "Edith Wharton on Film and Television: A History and Filmography," *Edith Wharton Review* 13, no. 2 (1996): 17.

3. The first film to use synchronized sound as a means of telling a story was *The Jazz Singer*, which opened on Broadway, October 5, 1927.

4. Kathleen Fitzpatrick, "From *The Children* to *The Marriage Playground* and Back Again," *Literature/Film Quarterly* 27, no. 1 (1999): 45.

5. R. W. B. Lewis, *Edith Wharton: A Biography* (New York: Harper & Row, 1975), 484.

6. Thomas Doherty, *Pre-Code Hollywood: Sex, Immorality, and Insurrection in American Cinema* (New York: Columbia University Press, 1999), 16.

7. Vincent Hart, memo to Joseph Breen, January 22, 1935, *The Old Maid* file, PCA Collection, AMPAS Margaret Herrick Library, Beverly Hills, California.

8. Joseph Breen, letter to Jack Warner, December 21, 1938, *The Old Maid* file, PCA Collection, AMPAS Margaret Herrick Library, Beverly Hills, California.

9. A second off-camera, real situation in the filming of *The Old Maid* arguably worked to the film's advantage. The vitriol that exists on screen between the fictional Delia Ralston (Miriam Hopkins) and Charlotte Lovell (Bette Davis) was heightened by the off-screen, real enmity that existed between the two women. Two episodes in Davis's and Hopkins's lives fueled the furor that existed between them. First, Miriam Hopkins had starred in the Broadway version of *Jezebel* (1933), which was most unsuccessful. When the film was cast, Hopkins was passed over in favor of Davis. The film was immensely popular, and for her performance in it, Davis won the Academy

Award for Best Actress (1938). Second, while filming *The Sisters* (1938), Bette Davis had a brief affair with the film's director, Anatole Litvak, who was Miriam Hopkins's husband at the time. Hopkins became fully aware of the affair. Several months later, production began on *The Old Maid* (1939), making painfully true to life the fictional Charlotte/Delia/Clem triangle.

10. Also called an "American shot," a two-shot is, generally, a three-quarter, medium, or close shot in which two people occupy the frame. This shot allows the viewer to see characters responding to one another from various stances and camera angles.

11. *The Age of Innocence*, Dir. Philip Moeller, RKO, 1934.

12. "Wax Flowers and Horse Carts," *The New York Times*, October 19, 1934, p. 27, col. 1.

13. Martin Scorsese and Jay Cocks, *"The Age of Innocence": A Portrait of the Film Based on the Novel by Edith Wharton*, ed. Robin Standefer (New York: Newmarket, 1993), 400.

14. "Production Notes for *The Age of Innocence*" (New York: Columbia Pictures, 1993), 6–12.

15. Standefer, 468.

16. Vincent Canby, "Liam Neeson in Lead of Wharton Classic," *The New York Times*, March 12, 1993, sec. C, p. 8.

17. Canby, "Liam Neeson," 8.

18. Roberta F. Green, "Ethan Frome," in *Magill's Cinema Annual: 1994*, ed. Frank N. Magill (Pasadena, CA: Salem Press, 1994), 90.

19. Cynthia Griffin Wolff, *A Feast of Words: The Triumph of Edith Wharton* (New York: Oxford University Press, 1977), 176–77.

20. John J. O'Connor, "TV: The New York of Edith Wharton," *The New York Times*, November 2, 1981, sec. C, p. 22.

21. *The House of Mirth*, Dir. Terence Davies, Three Rivers Production and Sony Pictures Classics, 2000.

22. In addition to *The House of Mirth*, their collaboration produced the highly regarded *Distant Voices, Still Lives* (1985), *The Long Day Closes* (1992), and *The Neon Bible* (1995).

23. Terence Davies, *The House of Mirth Screenplay*, second draft (London: Three Rivers Ltd., September 30, 1997).

24. "Production Notes for *The House of Mirth*" (New York: Sony Pictures Classics, 2000), n.p.

ILLUSTRATED
CHRONOLOGY

| Wharton's Life | Historical Events |

1862: Edith Newbold Jones born January 24 at 14 W. 23rd Street, New York City, the third child of Lucretia Stevens Rhinelander and George Frederic Jones.

1866–72: In order to economize during post–Civil War recession, family moves to Italy, Spain, and France. Captivated by Europe.

1868: Taught to read by father; begins "making up" stories.

1870: Contracts severe case of typhoid fever.

1861–65: U.S. Civil War.

1864: Fyodor Dostoevski publishes *Notes from Underground.*

1865: President Abraham Lincoln assassinated.

1866: Transatlantic cable invented.

1868: Louisa May Alcott publishes *Little Women*; Elizabeth Cady Stanton and Susan B. Anthony first publish *The Revolution*, a women's rights periodical. First commercial typewriter patented.

1869: Transcontinental railroad completed.

1870–1900: Gilded Age in U.S. history.

1871: Charles Darwin publishes *The Descent of Man.*

1872: New York Metropolitan Museum of Art opens to the public.

1876: Alexander Graham Bell patents the telephone.

1877: Reconstruction ends. American Museum of Natural History opens in New York City. Rutherford B. Hayes becomes president.

1878: Henry James publishes *Daisy Miller.*

Edith Jones, 1870, age 8, during her family's residence in Europe. Courtesy Lilly Library, Indiana University, Bloomington.

Fifth Avenue north of 27th Street, ca. 1875. In her memoir, Wharton described this neighborhood of her childhood, with its tree-lined streets and brownstones, as "a little world, so well-ordered and well-to-do." Collection of The New-York Historical Society.

Tennis at Newport, 1870s. Introduced in the United States in 1873, the game gained rapid popularity among the upper and middle classes. The Newport Historical Society (P45).

1872–75: Family returns to New York City from Europe. Summers at family's Pencraig Cottage, Newport, Rhode Island. Reads avidly in father's library; contends with mother's prohibition against reading novels. Begins lifelong friendship with sister-in-law Mary (Minnie) Cadwalader Jones.

1876: Begins first novella, *Fast and Loose*.

1878: Family privately publishes her book of poems, *Verses*.

1879: Makes social debut.

Edith Wharton, 1880, age 18. Courtesy Lilly Library, Indiana University, Bloomington.

1879: Henrik Ibsen publishes *A Doll's House*.

1880: Joel Chandler Harris publishes *Uncle Remus*.

1881: James Garfield becomes president; is assassinated. Chester Arthur becomes president. Henry James publishes *The Portrait of a Lady*. One in twenty-one U.S. marriages ends in divorce.

1883: Brooklyn Bridge completed. Standard U.S. time zones established.

1884: Mark Twain publishes *The Adventures of Huckleberry Finn*.

1884–88: Suffragettes form Equal Rights party; nominate woman candidate for president.

1885: Emile Zola publishes *Germinal*. Grover Cleveland becomes president. Automobile invented.

1889: Vincent Van Gogh paints *The Starry Night*. Benjamin Harris becomes president.

1890: Sherman Anti-Trust Act passed. The motion picture developed.

1891: International copyright law is established.

1880: Poems appear in *Atlantic Monthly*.

1882: Father dies at age 61 in Cannes. Returns to Newport with mother. Briefly engaged to Harry Stevens. Travels with mother to Paris.

1883: Meets Walter Berry, who becomes lifelong intimate, at Bar Harbor. Bostonian Edward (Teddy) Wharton visits Bar Harbor and begins courtship.

1884: Hires Catherine Gross, who becomes her companion and housekeeper for more than forty years.

1885: Marries Teddy Wharton in April at Trinity Chapel, New York City.

1885–88: Spends time in New York City, Newport, and Europe. Becomes acquainted, through friend Egerton Winthrop, with Darwin and other writers on evolution.

1888: Splurges with Teddy on four-month Aegean cruise. Receives large inheritance from distant relative.

1889: Rents small house on Madison Avenue. Poems accepted by *Century*, *Harper's*, and *Scribner's* magazines.

Egerton Winthrop, *by John Singer Sargent. Wharton credits this family friend, "the lover of books and pictures, the accomplished linguist and eager reader," with having "first taught my mind to analyze and my eyes to see." Courtesy Lilly Library, Indiana University, Bloomington.*

Edith Wharton, ca. 1889. The Yale Collection of American Literature, Beinecke Rare Book and Manuscript Library, Yale University.

1891: First story, "Mrs. Manstey's View," published in *Scribner's*. Purchases home near 78th Street. Works on long story, "Bunner Sisters." Suffer bouts of nausea, fatigue, and breathing difficulty, which persist through the decade.

1892: *Scribner's* rejects "Bunner Sisters."

1893: Buys Newport estate, Land's End; hires Boston architect Ogden Codman, Jr., to decorate its interior; entertains novelist Paul Bourget and his wife. *Scribner's* accepts three stories; editor Edward Burlingame suggests a short story collection.

1893: Chicago World's Columbian Exposition. Grover Cleveland again becomes president.

1894–95: Sino-Prussian War.

1895: Stephen Crane publishes *The Red Badge of Courage*. Elizabeth Cady Stanton publishes *The Woman's Bible*. H. G. Wells publishes *The Time Machine*.

1896: In *Plessy v. Fergueson*, U. S. Supreme Court upholds doctrine of separate but equal.

1897: William McKinley becomes president.

Land's End, Newport. Wharton purchased the home in 1893 and renovated and landscaped it with the help of architect Ogden Codman, Jr. She disliked "the vapid water-place amusements" of Newport but "loved Land's End, with its windows framing the endlessly changing moods of the misty Atlantic, and the night-long sounds of the surges against the cliffs." The Yale Collection of American Literature, Beinecke Rare Book and Manuscript Library, Yale University.

1893–1904: Publishes thirty short stories in *Scribner's, Century, Youth's Companion, Hearst's, Lippincott's, Harper's, Collier's,* and *Atlantic Monthly* magazines.

1894: Burlingame rejects story, "Something Exquisite" (later "Friends"). Writes Burlingame with doubts about her literary talent. Travels in Tuscany; makes original art discoveries that she describes in an article in *Scribner's*. Meets art critic Vernon Lee (Violet Paget). Asks for extension to complete story collection. Becomes distant from mother, who resides in Paris.

1895: Sends "The Valley of Childish Things, and Other Emblems" with ten other fables to Burlingame, who rejects the collection.

1898: First show of American Impressionist painters.

1898–99: Spanish-American War.

1899: Kate Chopin publishes *The Awakening.* Coca-Cola first bottled. Sigmund Freud publishes *The Interpretation of Dreams.*

1900–20: Progressive Era in U.S. history.

1900: Theodore Dreiser publishes *Sister Carrie.* L. Frank Baum publishes *The Wonderful Wizard of Oz.* Five-cent cable cars operate between Broadway and Lexington Avenue, New York City; one hazardous corner is known as Dead Man's Curve. The Old Company, Detroit, begins to mass-produce automobiles, but many Americans prefer bicycles.

Fifth Avenue north from 35th Street, ca. 1894–95. By century's end, the once placid residential neighborhood of Wharton's youth was bustling with commerce. Collection of The New-York Historical Society.

1897: Publishes successful book on interior design, *The Decoration of Houses*, with architect Ogden Codman.

1898: Battles illness and suffers breakdown, for which she follows Dr. S. Weir Mitchell's rest cure. Writes and revises stories.

1899: Publishes first collection of stories, *The Greater Inclination*, with Scribner's; reviews and sales are positive. Settles with Teddy in Washington for four months. Walter Berry becomes close friend and advisor. Begins extensive correspondence with Sara Norton, daughter of Harvard professor Charles Eliot Norton. Travels in Europe during summer, joined by Bourgets. Returns to Newport in September. Visits Lenox, Massachusetts, in fall.

1900: Publishes *The Touchstone*; it sells 5,000 copies in the first year. Again travels in Europe with Bourgets. Spends summer and fall in Lenox. Begins work on *The Valley of Decision*. Sends her work to Henry James, who offers encouragement.

1901: Publishes second volume of stories, *Crucial Instances*. Purchases Lenox property and hires architect to design house, The Mount; oversees extensive landscaping and gardening. Mother dies at age 76 in Paris. Her inheritance is placed in trust with husband and brother Harry as cotrustees.

1901: President William McKinley is assassinated. Theodore Roosevelt becomes president. Guglielmo Marconi develops the radio.

1902: Henry James publishes *The Wings of the Dove*. Joseph Conrad publishes *Heart of Darkness*.

1903: W. E. B. Du Bois publishes *The Souls of Black Folks*. Orville and Wilbur Wright fly an airplane 852 feet in 59 seconds. Ford Motor Company is established.

1904: First subway opens in New York City.

1905: Albert Einstein proposes theory of relativity.

1906: Upton Sinclair's *The Jungle* leads to passage of food inspection laws. Marie Curie becomes first female professor at the Sorbonne, Paris.

1907: Electric washing machine is invented.

1908: Featuring tight skirts and no petticoats, "Directoire," or sheaf gowns, arrive from Paris. The forty-seven story Singer Building becomes the tallest skyscraper.

*Postcard of The Mount, Wharton's Lenox, Massachusetts, home, completed in
1902. With her handwritten note to friend Charles Eliot Norton, Harvard professor
of fine arts, 1906. By permission of the Houghton Library, Harvard University.*

1902: Publishes two-volume novel, set in eighteenth-century Italy, *The Valley of Decision*. Declines to review *Wings of the Dove*, eschewing James's late style. Teddy suffers a nervous collapse.

1903: Publishes novella, *Sanctuary*. Meets art critic Bernard Berenson. Travels in Italy. Sells Land's End. Summers in Lenox.

1904: Publishes *The Descent of Man and Other Stories* and *Italian Villas and Their Gardens*. Buys her first car and tours Europe; tours England with Henry James. Entertains James and other friends at The Mount.

1909: Gertrude Stein publishes *Three Lives*. William Howard Taft becomes president. New York City garment workers strike for higher wages and better working conditions. W. E. B. Du Bois founds the NAACP. Robert Peary reaches North Pole.

1910: 8.7 million immigrants have arrived since 1900. U.S. population is 91.9 million.

1911: Franz Boaz publishes *The Mind of Primitive Man*. Sherman Anti-Trust Act orders dissolution of Standard Oil Corporation. Marie Curie wins Nobel Prize in Chemistry.

Edith Wharton, novelist Henry James (rear), husband Teddy Wharton, and driver Charles Cook. Enamored of the automobile, Wharton often set out with James on what he called "'great loops' of exploration" over the countryside. Courtesy Lilly Library, Indiana University, Bloomington.

Edith Wharton at her desk, The Mount. Publicity photo taken for The House of Mirth (1905). Wharton's habit was to write upstairs each morning before joining guests and friends. The Yale Collection of American Literature, Beinecke Rare Book and Manuscript Library, Yale University.

1905: Publishes *The House of Mirth,* a best-seller. Publishes second travel book, *Italian Backgrounds.* Visited in New York City by Henry James. With Teddy, dines with President Roosevelt in the White House. Follows a European trip with a stay at The Mount.

1906: Heads committee to form by-laws of what becomes SPCA. Sails for France. Visits England.

Edith Wharton, Christmas, 1905. Courtesy Lilly Library, Indiana University, Bloomington.

1912: Marcel Duchamps exhibits *Nude Descending a Staircase No. 2.* Harrict Monroe founds journal *Poetry. Titanic* sinks on its maiden voyage.

1913: Willa Cather publishes *O Pioneers!* D. H. Lawrence publishes *Sons and Lovers.* Woodrow Wilson becomes president. Niels Bohr develops theory of atomic structure.

Edith Wharton and pets. Wharton owned many dogs in her lifetime and supported animal advocacy groups such as the SPCA. The Yale Collection of American Literature, Beinecke Rare Book and Manuscript Library, Yale University.

Signature du Porteur :

Edith Wharton's signature. The Yale Collection of American Literature, Beinecke Rare Book and Manuscript Library, Yale University.

1907: Publishes *The Fruit of the Tree* and *Madame de Treymes*. Rents apartment and settles in Paris. Meets London *Times* journalist Morton Fullerton. Spends winter in Paris, summer in Lenox. Motors through Europe with Teddy and Henry James. Is visited at The Mount by Fullerton.

1908: Publishes *The Hermit and the Wild Woman and Other Stories* and travel book, *A Motor-Flight Through France*. Teddy visits Arkansas spa to relieve depression and gout. Begins love affair with Fullerton.

1914–18: World War I.

1914: Robert Frost publishes *North of Boston*.

1915: Virginia Woolf publishes *The Voyage Out*. Margaret Sanger is jailed for supporting birth control.

1916: Freud begins publishing *Introductory Lectures on Psychoanalysis*. One in nine U.S. marriages ends in divorce. Henry James dies.

1917: U.S. enters World War I.

Edith Wharton, close friend Walter Berry, and an army officer during World War I. Wharton made many trips to the front; she and Berry were the first civilians to enter reconquered Alsace. The Yale Collection of American Literature, Beinecke Rare Book and Manuscript Library, Yale University.

1909: Publishes *Artemis to Actaeon and Other Verse*. Teddy suffers nervous breakdown; learns he has embezzled her trust funds. Begins lifelong friendship with Berenson. Spends a summer month in England with Fullerton.

1910: Publishes *Tales of Men and Ghosts*. Teddy enters Swiss sanitorium. Moves to 57 rue de Varenne, Paris. Love affair with Fullerton ends. Returns to New York with Teddy, who begins world cruise. Returns to Paris.

1911: Publishes *Ethan Frome*. Fails to secure Nobel Prize for James. Begins separation negotiations with Teddy. Summers in Lenox. Tours Italy; visits Berensons.

1912: Publishes *The Reef*. Tours Tuscany with Walter Berry. Sells The Mount. Visits England. Establishes permanent residence in France.

1913: Publishes *The Custom of the Country*. Obtains divorce. Becomes estranged from brother Harry. Tours Sicily with Berry. Enjoys Paris premiere of Stravinsky's *Le Sacre du Printemps*. Travels through Europe with Berenson. Attends New York wedding of niece, Beatrix Jones, and finds the city "rootless" and "overwhelming."

London Times *correspondent Morton Fullerton, ca. 1908. Wharton wrote about their love affair, "I have drunk of the wine of life at last, I have known the best thing worth knowing." The Yale Collection of American Literature, Beinecke Rare Book and Manuscript Library, Yale University.*

1920–35: Harlem Renaissance.

1920: Sinclair Lewis publishes *Main Street*. U.S. women gain the vote. League of Nations organized. Prohibition begins.

1921: Warren Harding becomes president.

1922: T. S. Eliot publishes *The Wasteland*. James Joyce publishes *Ulysses*. *Reader's Digest* founded.

1914: Tours North Africa with Percy Lubbock. Tours Spain with Berry. In Paris, establishes workrooms for displaced seamstresses. With Elisina Tyler, directs American Hostels for Refugees.

1915: War essays published in *Scribner's* appear as book, *Fighting France, from Dunkerque to Belfort.* Visits front lines often to deliver medical supplies. Organizes Children of Flanders Rescue Committee.

1916: Publishes *Xingu and Other Stories.* Edits *The Book of the Homeless* to raise money for war

1923: Harding dies; Calvin Coolidge becomes president.

1924: Adolf Hitler writes *Mein Kampf.*

1925: Virginia Woolf publishes *Mrs. Dalloway.* F. Scott Fitzgerald publishes *The Great Gatsby.* Tennessee teacher John Scopes is arrested for teaching evolution.

1926: Ernest Hemingway publishes *The Sun Also Rises.*

1927: First full-length "talkie," *The Jazz Singer,* opens. Charles Lindbergh makes solo nonstop flight across the Atlantic. Holland Tunnel, New York City, opens.

Children of Flanders house at Sevrès Lace School. One of Wharton's many WWI charities. Her relief efforts helped thousands of refugees and soldiers and earned her the French Legion of Honor. The Yale Collection of American Literature, Beinecke Rare Book and Manuscript Library, Yale University.

charities. Awarded French Legion of Honor. Launches rescue organization for tubercular soldiers.

1917: Publishes New England novel, *Summer*. Tours Morocco with Berry. Ends business relationship with Scribner's; begins to publish with Appleton. Disenchanted with manner of American Red Cross's absorption of her charities.

1918: Publishes war novel, *The Marne*. Purchases villa north of Paris, Pavillon Colombe. Brother Frederic dies.

1928: Radclyffe Hall publishes *The Well of Loneliness*. Margaret Mead publishes *Coming of Age in Samoa*. Amelia Earhart is first woman to fly across the Atlantic. Television tube invented.

1929–40: The Great Depression.

1929: William Faulkner publishes *The Sound and the Fury*. Herbert Hoover becomes president. U.S. stock market crashes. Clarence Birdseye introduces frozen foods.

1930: Sinclair Lewis wins Nobel Prize.

Pavillon Colombe, the villa Wharton purchased at the end of the war. Here, she wrote, "peace and order came back into my life. At last I had leisure for the two pursuits which never palled, writing and gardening." The Yale Collection of American Literature, Beinecke Rare Book and Manuscript Library, Yale University.

The Library, Pavillon Colombe. Wharton's style of decorating combined classical balance and elegance with comfort. The Yale Collection of American Literature, Beinecke Rare Book and Manuscript Library, Yale University.

1919: Publishes *French Ways and Their Meaning*. Leases chateau, Ste. Claire du Vieux, in Hyères.

1920: Publishes *The Age of Innocence*, which sells 66,000 copies in six months. Publishes travel book, *In Morocco*.

1921: Wins Pulitzer Prize for *The Age of Innocence*. Publishes *The Old Maid* after earlier rejections because of theme of illegitimate birth.

1922: Publishes *The Glimpses of the Moon*. Brother Harry dies.

1923: Publishes *A Son at the Front*. Film version of *Glimpses of the Moon* released. Sails to U.S. to receive honorary degree from Yale; is first woman so honored by this university.

Last formal photograph of Edith Wharton, 1921. Courtesy Lilly Library, Indiana University, Bloomington.

1924: Publishes quartet of novellas, *Old New York*.

1925: Publishes *The Mother's Recompense*, and *The Writing of Fiction*. Is first woman to receive Gold Medal from National Institute of Arts and Letters. Reads *The Great Gatsby* and invites Fitzgerald to visit.

1926: Publishes *Here and Beyond*, and *Twelve Poems*. Elected to National Institute of Arts and Letters. Cruises the Aegean Sea with friends. Travels in northern Italy with Berry. Purchases Hyères home.

1927: Publishes *Twilight Sleep*. Nominated for Nobel Prize. Walter Berry dies.

1928: Publishes *The Children*. Teddy Wharton dies. Spends a month in England. *The Age of Innocence* opens on Broadway.

1929: Publishes *Hudson River Bracketed*. Receives Gold Medal from American Academy of Arts and Letters. Suffers severe bout of pneumonia.

1930: Publishes story collection, *Certain People*. Becomes second woman elected to American Academy of Arts and Letters. Begins friendship with art historian Kenneth Clark and Jane Clark. Meets Aldous Huxley and Bronislaw Malinowski.

Edith Wharton at commencement exercises, Yale University, 1923. She was the first woman to receive an honorary Doctor of Letters degree from this institution. Yale University Manuscripts and Archives, Library.

Walter Berry, 1925. An international lawyer, he was Wharton's friend, critic, and muse. "No words can say," she wrote, "how the influence of his thought, his character, his deepest personality, were interwoven with mine." Courtesy Lilly Library, Indiana University, Bloomington.

Ste. Claire de Vieux Château, Hyères, France. The Riviera home Wharton leased in 1919 and purchased in 1926. Courtesy Lilly Library, Indiana University, Bloomington.

Edith Wharton on the east terrace of Ste. Claire, Courtesy Lilly Library, Indiana University, Bloomington.

1931: Visits England. Reunites for a time with Fullerton.

1932: Publishes *The Gods Arrive*, sequel to *Hudson River Bracketed*. Earnings are reduced because of Depression. Visits Rome with friend Nicky Mariano; becomes more interested in Christianity and Catholic Church.

1933: Publishes story collection, *Human Nature*. Housekeeper Catherine Gross dies.

1934: Publishes memoir *A Backward Glance*. Begins work on *The Buccaneers*, never finished.

1935: *The Old Maid* opens in New York and wins Pulitzer Prize for drama. Suffers first stroke; temporarily loses sight in right eye. Sister-in-law Minnie Jones dies.

1936: Publishes *The World Over*. *Ethan Frome* opens on Broadway.

1937: Suffers stroke while visiting Ogden Codman. Dies August 11. Is buried in grave adjacent to that of Walter Berry in Cimetière des Gonards, Versailles. Collection of stories, *Ghosts*, appears posthumously.

1938: Literary executor Gaillard Lapsley publishes her novel *The Buccaneers*.

Edith Wharton with friend Daisy Chanler abroad The Osprey, *a yacht she chartered in 1926 for a Mediterranean and Aegean cruise. Courtesy Lilly Library, Indiana University, Bloomington.*

1931: Pearl Buck publishes *The Good Earth*. Seventy-seven-story Chrysler Building and 102-story Empire State Building, New York City, are built.

1933: Franklin D. Roosevelt becomes president. Hitler is voted into power in Germany. Prohibition is repealed. The film *King Kong* is released.

1935–36: Italy invades Ethiopia.

1936–39: Spanish Civil War.

1939: Lapsley publishes her compilation, with Robert Norton, *Eternal Passion in English Poetry.*

1936: Margaret Mitchell publishes *Gone with the Wind.*

1938: Germany absorbs Austria.

1939: Russia invades Finland. Germany invades Poland. World War II begins.

Bibliographic Essay

Visions and Revisions of Wharton

Clare Colquitt

> True originality consists not in a new
> manner but in a new vision.
> *The Writing of Fiction (WF, 18)*

> Fashions in criticism change almost as
> rapidly as fashions in dress.
> "Fiction and Criticism" (*UCW*, 293)

The publication of her first novel, *The Valley of Decision* (1902), represented a "crucial moment" in Edith Wharton's career (*WF*, 14). By age forty, she had published four books of fiction in as many years. In her memoir, *A Backward Glance* (1934), Wharton would claim that despite the success of her first novel, at midlife she was "a drifting amateur" (*NW*, 941). Two years later, she was still adrift when, having "already promised" her next novel to *Scribner's Magazine*, but with "no date . . . fixed for its delivery," she agreed to serialize her then unfinished novel beginning in the January 1905 issue. Prior to this invitation, Wharton had made little progress on *The House of Mirth*. The challenge she faced was large: "The first chapters of my tale would have to appear almost at once, and it must be completed within four or five months!" For Wharton, "expos[ing]" her novel "to public

comment before [she] had worked it out to its climax," proved
"the severest test" she had yet undergone (*NW,* 940) and transformed the "drifting amateur into a professional" wholly dedicated to her craft (*NW,* 941).

The popular and critical success of *The House of Mirth*—first in
serial form and then as a book—firmly established Wharton's
reputation as a major figure in American letters. She had published eleven books by age forty-three, including three short
story collections (*The Greater Inclination* [1899], *Crucial Instances*
[1901], and *The Descent of Man* [1904]); two novellas (*The Touchstone* [1900] and *Sanctuary* [1903]); *The Joy of Living,* a translation of
German playwright Hermann Sudermann's *Es Lebe das Leben*
(1902); two travel books (*Italian Villas and Their Gardens* [1904] and
Italian Backgrounds [1905]); and in 1897, with Ogden Codman, Jr.,
The Decoration of Houses, a book that was to play a formative role
in "the birth of interior design in the United States."[1] Having
once "bent [herself] to the discipline of the daily task, that inscrutable 'inspiration of the writing table'" (*NW,* 941), Wharton
would go on to complete nearly fifty books before her death in
1937. Her canon ranges from novels, tales, poetry, drama, translations, critical essays, and reviews to war reportage, travel writing,
and scholarly treatises on interior decoration and home and garden design. In a career that spanned sixty years, life imitated art
as Wharton grew to resemble one of her own characters, the celebrated writer Margaret Aubyn. Like the heroine of her first
novella, *The Touchstone,* Wharton was widely esteemed as "the
most brilliant woman of her day" (*CS,* 1:164). Her most enduring
novels—*The House of Mirth, Ethan Frome* (1911), *The Custom of the
Country* (1913), *Summer* (1917), and *The Age of Innocence* (1920)—
capture and transcend particulars of time and place as they continue to speak eloquently to present-day readers of the "welter"
of our world (*NW,* 1063).

Wharton's prodigious career sprang from a creative fount that
nurtured what she described as "the secret garden" of her art.[2]
Although some scholars hold that Wharton's career began late,
in fact, she was struck by "the story-telling fever" even before she
learned to read (*NW,* 839), and in 1877, under the penname David
Olivieri, the fifteen-year-old novice completed a spirited "novel-

ette" of manners, *Fast and Loose,* which readers came to know
only when it was posthumously published a century later. Ironically, the woman who in 1923 was awarded an honorary doctor-
ate of letters from Yale University, as an "American novelist of international fame,"[3] began her publishing career as a poet and
translator.

Wharton's passion for poetry led, in 1878, to the private print-
ing of her first (and only unsigned) book of poems and translations from the German. By the time *Verses* appeared, Wharton
already dreamed of becoming a professional writer, a secret she
shared with her childhood friend Emelyn Washburn, whose father, in 1877, helped Wharton publish her translation of Heinrich
Karl Brugsch's poem, "Was die Steine Erzählen," in a new magazine. With the $50 fee she received for "What the Stones Ex-
plain," Wharton's professional career had effectively begun. Her
early poetry met with striking success. When Henry Wadsworth
Longfellow passed on a copy of *Verses* to William Dean Howells,
the latter was impressed and, in 1880, published five of her poems
in the *Atlantic Monthly.* Wharton was barely eighteen when the
first of these, "The Parting Day," appeared. Regrettably, her three
books of poetry and uncollected verse translations and poems—
the majority, like "The Parting Day," published in prominent
journals of the time—have yet to be collected in a single volume.

Following her early successes with poetry, a nine-year publishing hiatus ensued, during which time Edith Jones married Edward Wharton (in 1885) and settled into the predictable rhythms
of a leisure-class marriage, in which husband and wife had little
in common but a "love of animals and out-door life" and the
"travel-fever" that yearly led them to Europe (*NW,* 853). Particularly memorable was a Mediterranean cruise the couple took in
1888. For Wharton, "Those four months in the Aegean were the
greatest step forward in my making," not least perhaps because
the diary she kept of the cruise apparently spurred her to publish
poetry and fiction once again (*NW,* 859). In 1889, Wharton's literary career resumed with the appearance of two poems, both
published in December: "The Last Giustianini" in *Scribner's
Magazine* and "Euryalus" in the *Atlantic Monthly.* Two years later
Scribner's published her first story: "Mrs. Manstey's View." From

that moment until her death, Wharton's "story-telling fever" was unchecked. Remarkably, her finest stories were written not during a particular phase but throughout her career: from early masterpieces such as "The Muse's Tragedy," "Souls Belated," and "The Other Two" to the "Gothic" gems of her middle years, "Afterward" and "The Eyes," to the evocative tales of women and ghosts composed in her final years, notably "Pomegranate Seed," "Roman Fever" and "All Souls'," the last story she completed before she died.

Although the persons who inhabit her fiction hail from the working poor to the upper class, for many readers Wharton is best known for her consummate chronicles of "old New York," the "social aristocracy" (*NW*, 780) into which she was born and to which she paid muted tribute in *The Age of Innocence*, for which she received the Pulitzer Prize. Yet Wharton's canon also includes memorable portraits of members of the lower classes, without whose ill-paid industry "the gilded age" would have shone less bright. Particularly haunting is the early story "Bunner Sisters," the belated publication of which speaks to the vagaries of editors' tastes. Wharton completed this novella-length tale in 1892 and submitted it twice to Edward L. Burlingame, who "very kindly" rejected it for *Scribner's*, perhaps less for reasons of length, as he claimed, than for its searing critique of lives broken by drug addiction and marital abuse (*L*, 31). First published in *Xingu and Other Stories* (1916), this tale traces the unhappy history of two sisters who, like the "very small shop" they keep, seem "doomed to decline" even before they become rivals for the same man (*CS*, 2:166). The disastrous decision of one sister to refuse a marriage proposal so that her younger sibling might enjoy "the gifts of life" illumines one of Wharton's perennial themes: "the inutility of self-sacrifice" (*CS*, 2:236). A letter composed shortly before her death reveals that Wharton herself took this lesson to heart. Even when she was beset by the frailties of sickness and age, she was enthralled by "this wonderful adventure of living" and declared herself "an incorrigible life-lover & . . . adventurer" (*L*, 598).

Given the magnitude of Wharton's achievement and her popularity today, it is unfortunate that no complete collection of her works exists. As Kristin O. Lauer and Margaret P. Murray note in *Edith Wharton: An Annotated Secondary Bibliography*, "the only . . . collection of [sizeable] scope" is *The Complete Works of Edith Wharton* (1989), a 26-volume project in Japanese edited by Yoshie Itabashi and Miyoko Sasaki (36). To be sure, numerous individual editions, scholarly and not, of Wharton's novels and stories are currently in print. Of special interest in this regard are two editions of *The House of Mirth*: the historically situated Norton critical edition by Elizabeth Ammons (1990) and Shari Benstock's more theoretically oriented St. Martin's casebook (1994). Two other recent editions of oft-taught texts are equally worthy of mention: Kristin O. Lauer and Cynthia Griffin Wolff's 1995 Norton critical edition of *Ethan Frome* and Carol J. Singley's 2000 edition of *The Age of Innocence*, published in the New Riverside Series of American authors. (A Norton critical edition of *The Age of Innocence*, edited by Candace Waid, is also forthcoming.)

Despite the welcome existence of these critical editions, until a "complete" Wharton is published, many of her other titles will be more difficult to obtain (and teach). Fortunately, five Library of America Wharton volumes have to some extent offset the absence of a collected works. The first of these volumes, edited by R. W. B. Lewis in 1985, includes three of Wharton's best-known novels, *The House of Mirth*, *The Custom of the Country*, and *The Age of Innocence*, as well as her most "Jamesian" novel *The Reef* (1912). (A 1996 variant of the Lewis edition, also published by Library of America as *Edith Wharton: Four Novels*, substitutes *Ethan Frome* for *The Reef* and lists both Lewis and Wolff as editors.) With the appearance of *Edith Wharton: Novellas and Other Writings*, edited by Cynthia Griffin Wolff, seven of Wharton's novellas, among them her New England tales of greatest renown—*Ethan Frome* and *Summer*—were brought together for the first time in 1990. This volume also contains Wharton's bittersweet tale of an American in Paris, *Madame de Treymes* (1907); the four novellas originally published together as *Old New York* (1924); and the "problem" novel *The Mother's Recompense*, which traded places with *The Great Gatsby* on the bestseller list in 1925. Among the "other writings" in this volume are two works of life-writing that, like her winter's tale (*Ethan Frome*) and *Summer* (her "Hot Ethan" [*L*, 385]), complement one another: *A Backward Glance*, Wharton's "official" memoir, and the less guarded fragment "Life and I," here published in full for the first time.

One might assume from the title of the two-volume *Collected Stories*, published by Library of America in 2001, that Wharton's short fiction is readily accessible at last. Yet as Hermione Lee has recently observed, these volumes do not tell "the whole story." Whereas *Collected Stories*, expertly edited by Maureen Howard, does contain three of Wharton's lesser-known novellas—*The Touchstone, Sanctuary*, and her first major fiction on the "Great" War, *The Marne* (1918)—"twenty-two stories are omitted" (19). Nor is the earlier two-volume Scribner's set, *The Collected Short Stories of Edith Wharton*, complete. Several stories, among them "Bunner Sisters," are missing from this unannotated and now out-of-print compilation of eighty-six tales that Lewis edited in 1968. Readers who hope to glean "the whole story" of Wharton's achievements in short fiction must consult both the Howard and the Lewis editions.

Other lacunae limit our understanding of Wharton's myriad contributions in nonfiction. Indeed, until recently, with the exception of her first nonfiction title, *The Decoration of Houses*, and her last, *A Backward Glance*, Wharton's books of travel writing, literary criticism, studies of Italian villas and gardens, and her wartime essays on the "fighting" French were often difficult to locate, a situation that scholars have actively worked to redress. Heightened interest in the travel literature has resulted in several new editions, among them Mary Suzanne Schriber's 1991 edition of *A Motor-Flight Through France* (1908) and Sarah Bird Wright's 1995 compendium, *Edith Wharton Abroad: Selected Travel Writings, 1888–1920*, which contains excerpts from the six travel books Wharton published during her lifetime, as well as part of *The Cruise of the Vanadis*, the newly discovered chronicle of Wharton's 1888 Aegean cruise, edited by Claudine Lesage in 1992. Readers are also indebted to Frederick Wegener for his admirable *Edith Wharton: The Uncollected Critical Writings* (1996), which brings together "reviews, essays, literary eulogies, introductions and prefaces to her own work or the work of others," as well as miscellaneous archival material never before published (*UCW*, xv).

The nonprofit organization, Edith Wharton Restoration at The Mount, has proved a particular boon for Wharton studies. For over two decades, this organization has served as a "center for recognizing women of achievement," primary among them the creator of The Mount, the stately home in Lenox, Massachusetts, that Wharton built to her exacting specifications in 1901 and 1902.[4] In addition to raising funds to restore this national historic landmark to its former glory, Edith Wharton Restoration has, under the capable leadership of Stephanie Copeland, established a publishing program. To date, two titles have appeared: a facsimile edition of the formerly out-of-print *French Ways and Their Meaning* (1919) and Scott Marshall's exquisite *The Mount, Home of Edith Wharton: A Historic Structure Report* (1997).[5] Indeed, no mention of Wharton studies can be made without paying tribute to this longtime historian of Edith Wharton Restoration. For many years, Scott Marshall has generously shared his encyclopedic knowledge of Wharton and of The Mount with countless scholars who have journeyed to this Berkshire site.

Another pilgrimage site for Wharton scholars is the Beinecke Rare Book and Manuscript Library of Yale University, to which Wharton left her literary estate. When the Wharton holdings at the Beinecke (and at libraries elsewhere) were "opened" to scholars in 1968, outmoded portraits of Wharton toppled and new visions emerged. A watershed moment was Cynthia Griffin Wolff's discovery of the outline and fragment of the short story "Beatrice Palmato," which had apparently lain undisturbed for decades at the Beinecke. Published in Wolff's biography, *A Feast of Words: The Triumph of Edith Wharton* (1977), and in an appendix to R. W. B. Lewis's biography, *Edith Wharton: A Biography* (1975),[6] the fragment of this never completed tale contains a highly charged portrait of father/daughter love that forever upset our perception of a writer, who for much of the twentieth century was, in Vernon Louis Parrington's phrase, America's best-known "literary aristocrat." In like fashion, the uncovery of Wharton's 1908 love diary to William Morton Fullerton at the Lilly Library (Indiana University) changed our perception of Wharton's private life. First published in full in a 1994 issue of *American Literature*, "The Life Apart (*L'âme close*)" was edited by Kenneth M.

Price and Phyllis McBride and has recently been anthologized in the fourth edition of Paul Lauter's *Heath Anthology of American Literature* (2002). When, in the early 1980s, the Harry Ransom Humanities Research Center (University of Texas, Austin) became home to Wharton's love letters to Fullerton, scholars could more accurately trace what biographer Gloria C. Erlich has aptly called *The Sexual Education of Edith Wharton* (1992).

Regarding Wharton's correspondence, which is scattered in libraries across the United States and Europe, readers are indebted to R. W. B. Lewis and Nancy Lewis for their 1988 edition *The Letters of Edith Wharton.* Yet this collection of 400 letters offers at best a partial glimpse of Wharton's voluminous correspondence. Whether one accepts the Lewises' estimate that some 4,000 letters by Wharton are extant (*L* 3), or Mary Pitlick's judgment that 6,000 letters exist,[7] our record of Wharton's correspondence is incomplete. Since the publication of *The Letters of Edith Wharton,* several noteworthy editions of Wharton's letters, all to fellow writers, have appeared: Lyall H. Powers's *Henry James and Edith Wharton: Letters, 1900–1915* (1990), Daniel Bratton's *Yrs. Ever Affly: The Correspondence of Edith Wharton and Louis Bromfield* (2000), and Claudine Lesage's *Lettres à l'ami français* (2001), which includes Wharton's letters in French to Léon Bélugou.

The challenge that awaits Wharton studies is clear: a scholarly edition of the complete Wharton, including her letters, is needed. To suggest the magnitude that such an endeavor would entail, a four-part primary bibliography follows this chapter. The first sections are chronologically ordered under the headings "Books by Wharton Published in Her Lifetime" and "Posthumous Publications." The section on "Wharton's Correspondence" is ordered alphabetically by editor, the selected checklist of "Modern Collections of Wharton" by title.

Bibliography

Readers wishing to acquaint themselves with the secondary literature on Wharton face a daunting task. Even a cursory examination of the *Modern Language Association International Bibliogra-*

phy (available in print, CD-ROM, and online) makes plain that in the past thirty years Wharton scholarship has become a lively industry. Thankfully, two major bibliographies, both published in 1990, offer excellent starting places. Stephen Garrison's *Edith Wharton: A Descriptive Bibliography* provides a chronological record of the extant material history pertaining to the Wharton canon. Title- and copyright-page facsimiles complement Garrison's meticulous descriptions of the physical characteristics of "all books and pamphlets written by Wharton, including all known printings in English through 1986" (xv). Also invaluable is Kristin O. Lauer and Margaret P. Murray's *Edith Wharton: An Annotated Secondary Bibliography*, which remains the most current single-volume resource for coverage of nearly one hundred years of Wharton scholarship. Lauer and Murray, who "endeavored to include everything of importance" on Wharton through 1987 (xviii), in turn draw upon the work of other scholars. Primary among them is Marlene Springer, whose *Edith Wharton and Kate Chopin: A Reference Guide* (1976) and updated guide coauthored with Joan Gilson (1984) were superseded by Lauer and Murray's bibliography.

Prior to the appearance of Springer's reference guides, Robert E. Spiller's acclaimed *Literary History of the United States: Bibliography* (1974) was the starting point for those interested in Wharton studies. This bibliography, though no longer current, is still "the best initial source for research in American literature." Those consulting this work should be advised that the 1974 edition, "while one inclusive volume, is only partially cumulated."[8] To gain some sense of the historical reception of Wharton, readers should compare the treatment of Wharton in Spiller's original 1948 bibliography with the extensive new material in the 1974 edition. Such an exercise helps us to understand that scholars only began to give Wharton her due in midcentury.

Given the wealth of criticism that has appeared on Wharton since the late 1980s, another book-length secondary bibliography is overdue. Until such time, those wishing to keep abreast of contemporary Wharton scholarship will want to consult the *MLAIB*, the bibliographical essays appearing in the *Edith Wharton Review* (formerly the *Edith Wharton Newsletter*), and the annual volumes of *American Literary Scholarship*. It is notable that until the 1997 *AmLS* volume, Wharton scholarship was cited only in an omnibus chapter entitled "Fiction: 1900 to the 1930s." In the foreword to the 1996 volume, however, editor David J. Nordloh announced a significant departure: beginning in 1997, *AmLS* would devote a separate chapter to "Wharton and Cather" in "belated acknowledgment" of the critical stature these authors have attained. As Nordloh explains, "The past history of *AmLS* makes clear that this is not a hasty decision."[9] Indeed, with the exception of the chapter on "Whitman and Dickinson," which began in 1967, women writers have been conspicuously absent from the table of contents of *AmLS*, a situation that reflected the masculinist biases of the academy which, until the latter portion of the twentieth century, was dominated by men. The three "Wharton and Cather" essays by Elsa Nettels that have appeared to date offer judicious (and selective) reviews of current scholarship. These and other bibliographical resources, including Lawson McClung Melish's 1927 *A Bibliography of the Collected Writings of Edith Wharton*, the earliest primary bibliography extant, may be found under the bibliography section that follows this chapter.

Biography

In a recent essay on Wharton's best-known biographers, Susan Goodman acknowledges, "Writers may be among the most difficult subjects for biographies. . . . For the biographer, art always contends with life, the art of your subject, and also the art of all those who have written about the subject before."[10] The contentious nature of biography is amply apparent in the first biography to appear after Wharton's death: Percy Lubbock's *Portrait of Edith Wharton* (1947). Supposedly, Lubbock intended to assemble a pastiche of memories of Wharton by her friends and to let those memories speak for themselves. In fact, he heavily edited those accounts so as to present Wharton as cold, calculating, and imperious. Moreover, Lubbock reiterated a critical—and untrue—commonplace of the time: that as an artist Wharton was a lesser Henry James. "Justice to Edith Wharton," to cite Edmund Wilson's phrase, was not to come until some forty years after her death, when in 1975 R. W. B. Lewis's Pulitzer Prize–winning biography appeared. Followed two years later by Cynthia Griffin Wolff's probing psychological study, Lewis's biography heralded a Wharton revival that continues to this day.[11]

That revival has led to other major biographies: Shari Benstock's *No Gifts from Chance: A Biography of Edith Wharton* (1994) and Eleanor Dwight's *Edith Wharton: An Extraordinary Life* (1994). While neither biography has displaced the work of Lewis or Wolff, readers should refer to these more recent biographies when questions regarding historical accuracy arise. Benstock's meticulously researched volume has enriched our understanding of an extraordinary writer who, to borrow from Dwight, led an equally "extraordinary life." *No Gifts from Chance* provides fresh material on Wharton's friendships with women, her complicated family ties and domestic relations, and on the writer's shrewd dealings with editors and publishers. In like fashion, Dwight's crisply written biography, with over 300 illustrations, literally and figuratively offers new visions of Wharton by affording readers an "insider's" view of Wharton's privileged social and economic milieu. Sarah Bird Wright's encyclopedic *Edith Wharton A to Z: The Essential Guide to the Life and Work* is also a valuable resource for facts about Wharton's life. Hermione Lee's forthcoming biography will undoubtedly unveil another vision of Wharton. Yet even as we anticipate the next portrait of Edith Wharton, one truth remains. As Susan Goodman reminds us, "In the end, there can be no definitive biography of Wharton, because the welter will and should remain."[12]

Criticism

In *A Backward Glance*, Wharton opens her discussion of her "secret garden" by "repudiat[ing]" the assumption that her writing is "likely to be of lasting interest" (*NW*, 933). However false her modesty, Wharton was sensitive to reviewers' comments throughout her career and expressed concern that her literary legacy would endure, as a passage from a late notebook attests:

Reading most reviews of my books—the kindest as well as the
most disapproving—is like watching somebody in boxing-
gloves trying to dissect a flower. I don't mean to suggest that
my novels are comparable to flowers—real ones—but they are
certainly more nearly like them than they are like the conception of my work in the mind of the average reviewer.[13]

The 1992 publication of *Edith Wharton: The Contemporary
Reviews*, edited by James W. Tuttleton, Kristin O. Lauer, and Margaret P. Murray, makes plain that the critical reception of Wharton was "paradoxical." At the same time that "Wharton's earliest
reviewers trivialized . . . her work as that of a mere woman,
sneered at the elite class that was her material, and dismissed her
as out of touch with America," she was "simultaneously recognized as a writer of exceptional literary distinction" (ix).

The very titles given to early reviews and essays are often revealing. Vernon Louis Parrington's 1921 review of *The Age of
Innocence*, for instance, famously pronounced Wharton "Our Literary Aristocrat." In Parrington's weighty *Main Currents in American Thought*, Wharton is again paid scant attention and is discussed only in an appendix entitled "Certain Other Writers."
Asserting that she "belongs to the *ancien regime*," Parrington
holds that Wharton is "isolated in America by her native aristocratic tastes" (381). The posthumous publication of *The Buccaneers* in 1938 prompted Q. D. Leavis to scrutinize "Henry James's
Heiress" in a retrospective essay that reflected not only a preference for James but for the British novel as well. Comparing
Wharton to Jane Austen and George Eliot, Leavis concluded that
unlike these other writers, Wharton "was a remarkable novelist,"
not a great one (276). The two pages devoted to Wharton in
Robert E. Spiller's 1974 *Literary History of the United States: History*
similarly minimize Wharton's importance. According to Spiller,
she is a "court painter" (1211) who belongs more to the nineteenth century than the twentieth (1208). As "one of the last of
the old regionalists," she "is likely to survive as the memorialist
of a 'dying aristocracy'" (1211). To paraphrase Janet Flanner, for
much of the twentieth century, Wharton was yesterday.

For most readers today, however, Wharton's greatness is assumed. According to Gore Vidal, "only three or four American novelists . . . can be thought of as 'major' and Edith Wharton is one." Vidal specifically disputes the view that Wharton was second to James and regards these literary "giants" as "equals." His assessment that Wharton and James are "the two great American masters of the novel"[14] parallels Andrew Delbanco's judgment that Wharton, like James, is "required reading."

A key turning point in the evolution of Wharton's critical reception in the twentieth century was the 1953 publication of Blake Nevius's *Edith Wharton*, the first major English-language study to treat Wharton as a serious writer. Nevius frames his thoughtful study of her fiction by addressing the problem of Wharton's "decline": "It is difficult to think of a twentieth-century American novelist . . . whose reputation has suffered more from the change of interests and narrowing of emphasis in the literature of the 'thirties than has Edith Wharton's" (1). In addition to detecting what he terms "a lurking feminism" in Wharton's fiction (85), Nevius identified one of Wharton's most poignant themes: "the spectacle of a large and generous nature . . . trapped by circumstances ironically of its own devising into consanguinity with a meaner nature" (9–10).

The recuperation of Wharton's reputation, both in the United States and abroad, owes much to the Edith Wharton Society, organized in 1984. For nearly fifteen years, Annette Zilversmit, a leading figure in Wharton studies, edited what was first the Edith Wharton Society newsletter and then the *Edith Wharton Review*. Now edited by Carole Shaffer-Koros, the *Review* is an important source for contemporary Wharton criticism and book reviews, and for information about the activities of the society. Since 1987, the society has sponsored major conferences on Wharton that have attracted scholars from across the globe. Information about the society's activities and about Wharton herself may be found at the user-friendly Web site: www.gonzaga.edu/faculty/campbell/wharton.

The extensive section below on "Criticism" reflects the thriving state of Wharton scholarship today and suggests, too, the applicability of Wharton's epigrammatic wit: "Fashions in criticism change almost as rapidly as fashions in dress" (*UCW*, 293).

A bibliographer who hopes to do justice to Wharton's critics can, at best, highlight some of the main currents of Wharton criticism—from formalism, deconstruction, feminist criticism, and gender studies, to cultural studies and new historicism (and old). Yet even as fashions in criticism and theory continue to rise and fall, one fact persists: Wharton remains "of lasting interest." Moreover, as the final heading of the bibliography chapter implies, whether the visions and revisions of Wharton take the form of biography, criticism, film, opera, or fiction, "Modern Treatments" of Wharton will continue to enlarge our understanding of Wharton's life and art—and of ourselves.

NOTES

1. Theresa Craig, *Edith Wharton: A House Full of Rooms, Architecture, Interiors, and Gardens* (New York: Monacelli, 1996), 28.

2. *A Backward Glance* includes a chapter by this title in which Wharton traces the genesis of her art to "the teeming visions which, ever since [her] small-childhood . . . incessantly peopled [her] inner world" (*NW*, 933). The title is an allusion to Frances Hodgson Burnett's children's classic, *The Secret Garden* (1911), in which a lonely orphan girl discovers a magical garden where she experiences the restorative powers of nature's beauty and of newfound love.

3. This phrase is from Professor William Lyon Phelps's tribute to Wharton at the Yale University ceremony. See "Commencement, 1923," *Yale Alumni Weekly*, July 6, 1923, 1234.

4. More information about the mission and activities of Edith Wharton Restoration may be found at the beautifully designed website: www.edithwharton.org.

5. A third title now in progress, an illustrated edition of *The Cruise of the Vanadis*, with photographs by Jonas Dovydenas, is to appear in 2002, the centennial of The Mount.

6. The "Beatrice Palmato" materials are variously dated by Wharton biographers. R. W. B. Lewis, for instance, speculates that the projected story outline and the "unpublishable fragment" were written in 1935 (544), whereas Wolff argues that "Beatrice Palmato" was composed in 1919 (291).

7. Mary Pitlick, "Edith Wharton," letter to the editor, *Times Literary Supplement*, December 30, 1988.

8. Dorothea Kehler, *Problems in Literary Research: A Guide to Selected Reference Works*, 4th ed. (Lanham: Scarecrow, 1997), 18.

9. David J. Nordloh, ed., Foreword, *American Literary Scholarship: An Annual 1996* (Durham: Duke University Press, 1998), viii.

10. Susan Goodman, "Edith Wharton's Composed Lives," in *A Forward Glance: New Essays on Edith Wharton*, ed. Clare Colquitt, Susan Goodman, and Candace Waid (Newark: University of Delaware Press, 1999), 24.

11. Although Lewis's biography is still highly regarded and often cited, in 1988 two former research assistants of his (very belatedly) challenged his use of their work: Marion Mainwaring, "The Shock of Non-Recognition," *Times Literary Supplement*, December 30, 1988, 16–22, and Pitlick, "Edith Wharton."

12. Goodman, "Edith Wharton's Composed Lives," 33.

13. This passage, from the notebook Wharton began in 1924, *Quaderno dello Studente*, is reprinted here by permission of the Yale Collection of American Literature, Beinecke Rare Book and Manuscript Library, Yale University, and the Estate of Edith Wharton and the Watkins/Loomis Agency.

14. Gore Vidal, introduction to *The Edith Wharton Omnibus* (New York: Scribner's, 1978), vii, xiii, viii.

BOOKS BY WHARTON PUBLISHED IN HER LIFETIME

[Wharton, Edith]. *Verses*. Newport: C. E. Hammett, Jr., 1878.

Wharton, Edith, and Ogden Codman, Jr. *The Decoration of Houses*. New York: Scribner's, 1897.

Wharton, Edith. *The Greater Inclination*. New York: Scribner's, 1899.

———. *The Touchstone*. New York: Scribner's, 1900.

———. *Crucial Instances*. New York: Scribner's, 1901.

———. *The Valley of Decision*. 2 vols. New York: Scribner's, 1902.

———, trans. *The Joy of Living (Es Lebe das Leben): A Play in Five Acts*, by Hermann Sudermann. London: Duckworth, 1902.

———. *Sanctuary*. New York: Scribner's, 1903.

———. *The Descent of Man and Other Stories*. New York: Scribner's, 1904.

———. *Italian Villas and Their Gardens*. New York: Century, 1904.

———. *The House of Mirth*. New York: Scribner's, 1905.

————. *Italian Backgrounds.* New York: Scribner's, 1905.

————. *The Fruit of the Tree.* New York: Scribner's, 1907.

————. *Madame de Treymes.* New York: Scribner's, 1907.

————. *The Hermit and the Wild Woman and Other Stories.* New York: Scribner's, 1908.

————. *A Motor-Flight Through France.* New York: Scribner's, 1908.

————. *Artemis to Actæon and Other Verse.* New York: Scribner's, 1909.

————. *Tales of Men and Ghosts.* New York: Scribner's, 1910.

————. *Ethan Frome.* New York: Scribner's, 1911.

————. *The Reef.* New York: Appleton, 1912.

————. *The Custom of the Country.* New York: Scribner's, 1913.

————. *Fighting France, from Dunkerque to Belfort.* New York: Scribner's, 1915.

————, ed. *The Book of the Homeless* (*Le livre des sans-foyer*). New York: Scribner's, 1916.

————. *Xingu and Other Stories.* New York: Scribner's, 1916.

————. *Summer.* New York: Appleton, 1917.

————. *The Marne.* New York: Appleton, 1918.

————. *French Ways and Their Meaning.* New York: Appleton, 1919.

————. *The Age of Innocence.* New York: Appleton, 1920.

————. *In Morocco.* New York: Scribner's, 1920.

————. *The Glimpses of the Moon.* New York: Appleton, 1922.

————. *A Son at the Front.* New York: Scribner's, 1923.

————. *Old New York: False Dawn* (*The 'Forties*), *The Old Maid* (*The 'Fifties*), *The Spark* (*The 'Sixties*), *New Year's Day* (*The 'Seventies*). 4 vols. New York: Appleton, 1924.

————. *The Mother's Recompense.* New York: Appleton, 1925.

————. *The Writing of Fiction.* New York: Scribner's, 1925.

————. *Here and Beyond.* New York: Appleton, 1926.

————. *Twelve Poems.* London: Medici Society, 1926.

————. *Twilight Sleep.* New York: Appleton, 1927.

————. *The Children.* New York: Appleton, 1928.

————. *Hudson River Bracketed.* New York: Appleton, 1929.

————. *Certain People.* New York: Appleton, 1930.

————. *The Gods Arrive.* New York: Appleton, 1932.

————. *Human Nature.* New York: Appleton, 1933.

————. *A Backward Glance.* New York: Appleton-Century, 1934.

————. *The World Over.* New York: Appleton-Century, 1936.

POSTHUMOUS PUBLICATIONS

Wharton, Edith. *Ghosts*. New York: Appleton-Century, 1937.

―――. *The Buccaneers*. Ed. Gaillard Lapsley. New York: Appleton-Century, 1938. Republished in *"Fast and Loose" and "The Buccaneers,"* ed. Viola Hopkins Winner, 119–479. Charlottesville: University Press of Virginia, 1993. Also republished as *The Buccaneers* [A novel by Edith Wharton completed by Marion Mainwaring]. New York: Viking, 1993.

Wharton, Edith, and Robert Norton, comps., with collaboration of Gaillard Lapsley. *Eternal Passion in English Poetry*. New York: Appleton-Century, 1939.

Wharton, Edith. "Beatrice Palmato." In *Edith Wharton: A Biography*, by R. W. B. Lewis, 544–48. New York: Harper and Row, 1975. Republished in *A Feast of Words: The Triumph of Edith Wharton*, by Cynthia Griffin Wolff, 301-05. New York: Oxford University Press, 1977.

―――. *Fast and Loose: A Novelette by David Olivieri*. Ed. Viola Hopkins Winner. Charlottesville: University Press of Virginia, 1977. Republished in *"Fast and Loose" and "The Buccaneers,"* ed. Winner, 1–117. Charlottesville: University Press of Virginia, 1993.

Wharton, Edith, and Clyde Fitch. *"The House of Mirth": The Play of the Novel*. Ed. Glenn Loney. Rutherford, N.J.: Fairleigh Dickinson University Press, 1981.

Wharton, Edith. "Life and I." In *Edith Wharton: Novellas and Other Writings*, ed. Cynthia Griffin Wolff, 1069–96. New York: Library of America, 1990.

―――. *The Cruise of the Vanadis*. Ed. Claudine Lesage. Amiens: Sterne (Presses de L'UFR Clerc Université Picardie), 1992.

―――. "The Life Apart (*L'âme close*)." In "'The Life Apart': Text and Contexts of Edith Wharton's Love Diary," by Kenneth M. Price and Phyllis McBride. *American Literature* 66 (1994): 663–88.

―――. "Madame Lyautey's Charitable Works in Morocco." Trans. Louise M. Wills. (First published in French as "Les Oeuvres de Mme Lyautey au Maroc." *France-Maroc* [October/November 1918]: 306–08.) In "Edith Wharton on French Colonial Charities for Women: An Unknown Travel Essay," by

Frederick Wegener. *Tulsa Studies in Women's Literature* 17 (1998): 11–33.

WHARTON'S CORRESPONDENCE

Bratton, Daniel, ed. *Yrs. Ever Affly: The Correspondence of Edith Wharton and Louis Bromfield*. East Lansing: Michigan State University Press, 2000.

Gribben, Alan, ed. "'The Heart Is Insatiable': A Selection from Edith Wharton's Letters to Morton Fullerton, 1907–1915." Special Wharton issue of *The Library Chronicle of the University of Texas at Austin* n.s. 31 (1985): 7–71.

Lesage, Claudine, ed. *Lettres à l'ami français* [Letters to the French friend]. Paris: Houdiard, 2001.

Lewis, R. W. B., and Nancy Lewis, eds. *The Letters of Edith Wharton*. New York: Scribner's, 1988.

Porter, David H. "'O all you beauties I shall never see': An Unpublished Edith Wharton Letter." *Edith Wharton Review* 16, no. 2 (2000): 13–17.

Powers, Lyall H., ed. *Henry James and Edith Wharton—Letters: 1900–1915*. New York: Scribner's, 1990.

MODERN COLLECTIONS OF WHARTON

The Collected Short Stories of Edith Wharton. Ed. R. W. B. Lewis. 2 vols. New York: Scribner's, 1968.

Edith Wharton Abroad: Selected Travel Writings, 1888-1920. Ed. Sarah Bird Wright. New York: St. Martin's, 1995.

Edith Wharton: Collected Stories. Ed. Maureen Howard. 2 vols. New York: Library of America, 2001.

Edith Wharton: Four Novels [*The House of Mirth, Ethan Frome, The Custom of the Country, The Age of Innocence*]. Ed. R. W. B. Lewis and Cynthia Griffin Wolff. New York: Library of America, 1996.

Edith Wharton: New York Novels [*The House of Mirth, The Custom of the Country, The Age of Innocence*]. Fwd. Louis Auchincloss. New York: Modern Library, 1998.

Edith Wharton: Novellas and Other Writings [*Madame de Treymes, Ethan Frome, Summer, Old New York, The Mother's Recompense, A*

Backward Glance, "Life and I"]. Ed. Cynthia Griffin Wolff. New York: Library of America, 1990.

Edith Wharton: Novels [*The House of Mirth, The Reef, The Custom of the Country, and The Age of Innocence*]. Ed. R. W. B. Lewis. New York: Library of America, 1985.

The Edith Wharton Omnibus [*The Age of Innocence, Ethan Frome, Old New York*]. Introd. Gore Vidal. New York: Scribner's, 1978.

The Edith Wharton Reader. Ed. Louis Auchincloss. New York: Macmillan, 1965.

Edith Wharton: Three Complete Novels [*The House of Mirth, Ethan Frome, The Custom of the Country*]. New York: Gramercy, 1994.

Edith Wharton: The Uncollected Critical Writings. Ed. Frederick Wegener. Princeton: Princeton University Press, 1996.

The Ghost-Feeler: Stories of Terror and the Supernatural. Introd. Peter Haining. London: P. Owen; Chester Springs, Pa.: Dufour Editions, 1996.

The Ghost Stories of Edith Wharton. New York: Scribner's, 1973.

The Selected Stories of Edith Wharton. Ed. R. W. B. Lewis. New York: Scribner's, 1991.

The Stories of Edith Wharton. Ed. Anita Brookner. 2 vols. New York: Simon and Schuster, 1989.

Wharton's New England: Seven Stories and "Ethan Frome." Ed. Barbara A. White. Hanover: University Press of New England, 1995.

BIBLIOGRAPHY

Bendixen, Alfred. "Recent Wharton Studies: A Bibliographic Essay." *Edith Wharton Review* 3, no. 2 (1986): 5, 8–9.

———. "Wharton Studies, 1986–1987: A Bibliographic Essay." *Edith Wharton Review* 5, no. 1 (1988): 5–8, 10.

———. "The World of Wharton Criticism: A Bibliographic Essay." *Edith Wharton Review* 7, no. 1 (1990): 18–21.

———, ed. "A Guide to Wharton Criticism, 1974–1983." *Edith Wharton Review* 2, no. 2 (1985): 1–8.

Brenni, Vito J. *Edith Wharton: A Bibliography.* Morgantown: West Virginia University Library, 1966.

Colquitt, Clare. "Contradictory Possibilities: Wharton Scholarship, 1992–1994." *Edith Wharton Review* 12, no. 2 (1995): 37–44.

Garrison, Stephen. *Edith Wharton: A Descriptive Bibliography*. Pittsburgh: University of Pittsburgh Press, 1990.

Lauer, Kristin O., and Margaret P. Murray. *Edith Wharton: An Annotated Secondary Bibliography*. New York: Garland, 1990.

Melish, Lawson McClung. *A Bibliography of the Collected Writings of Edith Wharton*. 1927. Reprint. Folcroft: Folcroft Library Editions, 1977.

Nettels, Elsa. "Wharton and Cather." In *American Literary Scholarship: An Annual 1997*, ed. Gary Scharnhorst, 119–32. Durham, N.C.: Duke University Press, 1999.

———. "Wharton and Cather." In *American Literary Scholarship: An Annual 1998*, ed. David J. Nordloh, 113–27. Durham, N.C.: Duke University Press, 2000.

———. "Wharton and Cather." In *American Literary Scholarship: An Annual 1999*, ed. Gary Scharnhorst, 139–56. Durham, N.C.: Duke University Press, 2001.

Price, Alan. "'Far More Than They Know': Current Wharton Studies." *Edith Wharton Review* 19 (1997): 237–51.

Spiller, Robert, and others, eds. *Literary History of the United States: Bibliography*. 4th ed. rev. New York: Macmillan, 1974.

Springer, Marlene. *Edith Wharton and Kate Chopin: A Reference Guide*. Boston: G. K. Hall, 1976.

Springer, Marlene, and Joan Gilson. "Edith Wharton: A Reference Guide Updated." *Resources for American Literary Study* 14 (1984): 85–111.

Wagner-Martin, Linda. "Prospects for the Study of Edith Wharton." *Resources for American Literary Study* 22 (1996): 1–15.

BIOGRAPHY

Auchincloss, Louis. *Edith Wharton*. University of Minnesota Pamphlets on American Writers, no. 12. Minneapolis: University of Minnesota Press, 1961.

———. *Edith Wharton: A Woman in Her Time*. New York: Viking, 1971.

Bell, Millicent. *Edith Wharton and Henry James: The Story of Their Friendship*. New York: George Braziller, 1965.

Benstock, Shari. *No Gifts from Chance: A Biography of Edith Wharton*. New York: Scribner's, 1994.

Coolidge, Olivia E. *Edith Wharton, 1862–1937* [for young adults]. New York: Scribner's, 1964.

Dwight, Eleanor. *Edith Wharton: An Extraordinary Life*. New York: Harry N. Abrams, 1994.

Kellogg, Grace. *The Two Lives of Edith Wharton: The Woman and Her Work*. New York: Appleton-Century, 1965.

Leach, William. *Edith Wharton* [for young adults]. New York: Chelsea, 1987.

Lewis, R. W. B. *Edith Wharton: A Biography*. New York: Harper and Row, 1975.

Lubbock, Percy. *Portrait of Edith Wharton*. New York: Appleton-Century, 1947.

Price, Alan. *The End of the Age of Innocence: Edith Wharton and the First World War*. New York: St. Martin's, 1996.

Turk, Ruth. *Edith Wharton: Beyond the Age of Innocence* [for young adults]. Greensboro, N.C.: Tudor, 1998.

Wolff, Cynthia Griffin. *A Feast of Words: The Triumph of Edith Wharton*. New York: Oxford University Press, 1977. rev. ed. Reading, Mass.: Addison-Wesley, 1995.

Worth, Richard. *Edith Wharton* [for young adults]. New York: J. Messner, 1994.

CRITICISM

Ammons, Elizabeth. *Edith Wharton's Argument with America*. Athens: University of Georgia Press, 1980.

———. "Gender and Fiction." In *The Columbia History of the American Novel*, ed. Emory Elliott, 267–84. New York: Columbia University Press, 1991.

———. "Plots: Jessie Fauset and Edith Wharton." In *Conflicting Stories: American Women Writers at the Turn into the Twentieth Century*, 140–60. New York: Oxford University Press, 1991.

———, ed. *The House of Mirth*, by Edith Wharton. Norton Critical Edition. New York: Norton, 1990.

Balestra, Gianfranca. *I fantasmi di Edith Wharton* [Edith Wharton's ghosts]. Rome: Bulzoni, 1993.

Bauer, Dale. *Edith Wharton's Brave New Politics*. Madison: University of Wisconsin Press, 1994.

———. "The Failure of the Republic." In *Feminist Dialogics: A Theory of Failed Community*, 89–127. Albany: State University of New York Press, 1988.

Beer, Janet [Goodwyn, Janet]. *Kate Chopin, Edith Wharton and Charlotte Perkins Gilman: Studies in Short Fiction*. London: Macmillan; New York: St. Martin's, 1997.

Bell, Millicent, ed. *The Cambridge Companion to Edith Wharton*. Cambridge: Cambridge University Press, 1995.

Bendixen, Alfred, and Annette Zilversmit, eds. *Edith Wharton: New Critical Essays*. New York: Garland, 1992.

Benstock, Shari. *Women of the Left Bank: Paris, 1900–1940*. Austin: University of Texas Press, 1986.

———, ed. *The House of Mirth*, by Edith Wharton. Case Studies in Contemporary Criticism. Boston: St. Martin's, 1994.

Bentley, Nancy. *The Ethnography of Manners: Hawthorne, James, Wharton*. Cambridge: Cambridge University Press, 1995.

Beppu, Keiko, ed. *Edith Wharton's Two Worlds: America and Europe*. Tokyo: Yumi, 1996.

Blackall, Jean Frantz. "Edith Wharton's Art of Ellipsis." *Journal of Narrative Technique* 17 (1987): 145–59.

Bloom, Harold, ed. *Edith Wharton*. New York: Chelsea, 1986.

Brown, E. K. *Edith Wharton: Étude Critique* [Edith Wharton: A critical study]. Paris: Librairie E. Droz, 1935.

Cahir, Linda Costanzo. *Solitude and Society in the Works of Herman Melville and Edith Wharton*. Westport, Conn.: Greenwood, 1999.

Campbell, Donna M. "Edith Wharton and the 'Authoresses.'" In *Resisting Regionalism: Gender and Naturalism in American Fiction, 1885–1915*, 146–73. Athens: Ohio University Press, 1997.

Chandler, Marilyn R. "*The Age of Innocence*: Tribal Rites in the Urban Village." In *Dwelling in the Text: Houses in American Fiction*, 149–79. Berkeley: University of California Press, 1991.

Colquitt, Clare, Susan Goodman, and Candace Waid, eds. *A Forward Glance: New Essays on Edith Wharton*. Newark: University of Delaware Press; London: Associated University Presses, 1999.

Delbanco, Andrew. "What Would Edith Wharton Think?" In *Required Reading: Why Our American Classics Matter Now*, 155–71. New York: Noonday, 1997.

Dimock, Wai-chee. "Debasing Exchange: Edith Wharton's *The House of Mirth*." *PMLA* 100 (1985): 783–92. (Reprinted in Bloom, *Edith Wharton*, 123–37.)

Donovan, Josephine. *After the Fall: The Demeter-Persephone Myth in Wharton, Cather, and Glasgow*. University Park: Pennsylvania State University Press, 1989.

Duke, David C. "The Maelstrom of War: Wharton, Seeger, and Cowley." In *Distant Obligations: Modern American Writers and Foreign Causes*, 62–100. New York: Oxford University Press, 1983.

Dyman, Jenni. *Lurking Feminism: The Ghost Stories of Edith Wharton*. New York: Peter Lang, 1996.

Erlich, Gloria C. *The Sexual Education of Edith Wharton*. Berkeley: University of California Press, 1992.

Esch, Deborah, ed. *New Essays on "The House of Mirth."* Cambridge: Cambridge University Press, 2001.

Fedorko, Kathy A. *Gender and the Gothic in the Fiction of Edith Wharton*. Tuscaloosa: University of Alabama Press, 1995.

Flanner, Janet. *Paris Was Yesterday, 1925–1939*. Ed. Irving Drutman. New York: Viking, 1972.

Fracasso, Evelyn E. *Edith Wharton's Prisoners of Consciousness: A Study of Theme and Technique in the Tales*. Westport, Conn.: Greenwood, 1994.

French, Marilyn. "Muzzled Women." Special Wharton issue of *College Literature* 14 (1987): 219–29.

Fryer, Judith. *Felicitous Space: The Imaginative Structures of Edith Wharton and Willa Cather*. Chapel Hill: University of North Carolina Press, 1986.

Gentry, Deborah S. *The Art of Dying: Suicide in the Works of Kate Chopin, Edith Wharton, and Sylvia Plath*. New York: Peter Lang, 1998.

Gilbert, Sandra M., and Susan Gubar. "Angel of Devastation: Edith Wharton on the Arts of the Enslaved." In *Sexchanges*, 123–68. Vol. 2 of *No Man's Land: The Place of the Woman Writer in the Twentieth Century*. New Haven, Conn.: Yale University Press, 1988.

Gimbel, Wendy. *Edith Wharton: Orphancy and Survival*. New York: Praeger, 1984.

Goldman-Price, Irene C., and Melissa McFarland Pennell, eds. *American Literary Mentors*. Gainesville: University Press of Florida, 1999.

Goodman, Susan. *Edith Wharton's Inner Circle*. Austin: University of Texas Press, 1994.

————. *Edith Wharton's Women: Friends and Rivals*. Hanover: University Press of New England, 1990.

Goodwyn, Janet [Beer, Janet]. *Edith Wharton: Traveller in the Land of Letters*. London: Macmillan, 1990.

Gray, James. "'Very Important Personages': Edith Wharton, John P. Marquand, Struthers Burt." In *On Second Thought*, 83–97. Minneapolis: University of Minnesota Press, 1946.

Hadley, Kathy Miller. *In the Interstices of the Tale: Edith Wharton's Narrative Strategies*. New York: Peter Lang, 1993.

Hoeller, Hildegard. *Edith Wharton's Dialogue with Realism and Sentimental Fiction*. Gainesville: University Press of Florida, 2000.

Holbrook, David. *Edith Wharton and the Unsatisfactory Man*. London: Vision; New York: St. Martin's, 1991.

Howe, Irving, ed. *Edith Wharton: A Collection of Critical Essays*. Englewood Cliffs: Prentice-Hall, 1962.

Jessup, Josephine Lurie. *The Faith of Our Feminists: A Study in the Novels of Edith Wharton, Ellen Glasgow, Willa Cather*. 1950. Reprint. New York: Biblo and Tannen, 1965.

Joslin, Katherine. *Edith Wharton*. New York: St. Martin's, 1991.

Joslin, Katherine, and Alan Price, eds. *Wretched Exotic: Essays on Edith Wharton in Europe*. New York: Peter Lang, 1993.

Joslin, Katherine, and Annette Zilversmit, eds. Special Wharton issue of *College Literature* 14 (1987): 193–309.

Kaplan, Amy. "Edith Wharton's Profession of Authorship" and "Crowded Spaces in *The House of Mirth*." In *The Social Construction of American Realism*, 65–103. Chicago: University of Chicago Press, 1988.

Kassanoff, Jennie A. "Extinction, Taxidermy, Tableaux Vivants: Staging Race and Class in *The House of Mirth*." *PMLA* 115 (2000): 60–74.

Kazin, Alfred. "Two Educations: Edith Wharton and Theodore Dreiser." In *On Native Grounds: An Interpretation of Modern American Prose Literature*, 73–90. New York: Reynal and Hitchcock, 1942.

Killoran, Helen. *The Critical Reception of Edith Wharton*. Rochester: Camden, 2001.

————. *Edith Wharton: Art and Allusion*. Tuscaloosa: University of Alabama Press, 1996.

Kornetta, Reiner. *Das Korsett im Kopf: Ehe and Ökonomie in den*

Kurzgeschichten Edith Whartons [The corset in the head: Marriage and economy in Edith Wharton's short stories]. Frankfurt am Main: Peter Lang, 1996.

Küster, Dieter. *Das Frankreichbild im Werk Edith Whartons* [The image of France in Edith Wharton's work]. Bern: Herbert Lang; Frankfurt am Main: Peter Lang, 1972.

Laskin, David. "Henry James and Edith Wharton." Part 2 of *A Common Life: Four Generations of American Literary Friendship and Influence*, 101–88. New York: Simon and Schuster, 1994.

Lauer, Kristin O., and Cynthia Griffin Wolff, eds. *Ethan Frome*, by Edith Wharton. Norton Critical Edition. New York: Norton, 1995.

Lavergne-Peguilhen, Marietta von. *Undermining Gender, Overcoming Sex: Identität und Autorschaft bei Mary Wilkins Freeman, Edith Wharton, und Ellen Glasgow* [Identity and authorship in the work of Freeman, Wharton, and Glasgow]. Frankfurt am Main: Peter Lang, 1996.

Lawson, Richard H. *Edith Wharton*. New York: Frederick Ungar, 1977.

———. "Edith Wharton." In *American Short-Story Writers, 1880–1910*, 308–23. Vol. 78 of *Dictionary of Literary Biography*. Ed. Bobby Ellen Kimbel, with William E. Grant. Detroit, Mich.: Gale Research, 1989.

———. *Edith Wharton and German Literature*. Bonn: Bouvier Verlag Herbert Grundmann, 1974.

Leavis, Q. D. "Henry James's Heiress: The Importance of Edith Wharton." *Scrutiny* 7, no. 3 (1938): 261–76. (Reprinted in Howe, 73–88.)

Lee, Hermione. "The Unknown Edith Wharton." Review of *Edith Wharton: Collected Stories*, ed. Maureen Howard. *New York Review of Books*, October 4, 2001, 19–23.

Lindberg, Gary H. *Edith Wharton and the Novel of Manners*. Charlottesville: University Press of Virginia, 1975.

Lovett, Robert Morss. *Edith Wharton*. New York: Robert M. McBride, 1925.

Lyde, Marilyn Jones. *Edith Wharton: Convention and Morality in the Work of a Novelist*. Norman: University of Oklahoma Press, 1959.

Mainwaring, Marion. *Mysteries of Paris: The Quest for Morton Ful-*

lerton. Hanover, N.H.: University Press of New England, 2001.

McDowell, Margaret B. *Edith Wharton*. Boston: Twayne, 1976. Rev. ed. 1991.

————. "Edith Wharton." In *American Writers in Paris, 1920–1950*, 408–13. Vol. 4 of *Dictionary of Literary Biography*. Ed. Karen Lane Rood. Detroit, Mich.: Gale Research, 1980.

McGee, Diane. "In with the In-Crowd: Edith Wharton and the Dinner Tables of Old New York" and "The Art of Being an Honoured Guest: *The House of Mirth* and *The Custom of the Country*." In *Writing the Meal: Dinner in the Fiction of Early Twentieth-Century Women Writers*, 38–80. Toronto: University of Toronto Press, 2001.

Mercuri, Maria Novella. *"The Fruit of the Tree" e la narrativa di Edith Wharton* [*The Fruit of the Tree* and Edith Wharton's fiction]. Salerno, Italy: Edisud, 1990.

Michaels, Walter Benn. "Action and Accident: Photography and Writing." In *The Gold Standard and the Logic of Naturalism: American Literature at the Turn of the Century*, 215–44. Berkeley: University of California Press, 1987.

Mizener, Arthur. "Edith Wharton: *The Age of Innocence*." In *Twelve Great American Novels*, 68–86. New York: New American Library, 1967.

Moddelmog, William E. "Disowning 'Personality': Privacy and Subjectivity in *The House of Mirth*." *American Literature* 70 (1998): 337–63.

Montgomery, Maureen E. *Displaying Women: Spectacles of Leisure in Edith Wharton's New York*. New York: Routledge, 1998.

Nettels, Elsa. *Language and Gender in American Fiction: Howells, James, Wharton and Cather*. Charlottesville: University Press of Virginia, 1997.

Nevius, Blake. *Edith Wharton: A Study of Her Fiction*. Berkeley: University of California Press, 1953.

Ozick, Cynthia. "Justice (Again) to Edith Wharton." In *Art and Ardor: Essays by Cynthia Ozick*, 3–27. New York: Knopf, 1983. (First published in *Commentary*, October 1976, 48–67.)

Papke, Mary E. *Verging on the Abyss: The Social Fiction of Kate Chopin and Edith Wharton*. New York: Greenwood, 1990.

Parrington, Vernon Louis. *Main Currents in American Thought: An In-*

terpretation of American Literature from the Beginnings to 1920. 3 vols. New York: Harcourt, Brace and World, 1927–30.

———. "Our Literary Aristocrat." Review of *The Age of Innocence*, by Edith Wharton. *Pacific Review* 2 (1921): 157–60. (Reprinted in Howe, 151–54.)

Pierpont, Claudia Roth. "Cries and Whispers." *New Yorker*, April 2, 2001, 66–75.

Preston, Claire. *Edith Wharton's Social Register.* New York: St. Martin's, 2000.

Rae, Catherine M. *Edith Wharton's New York Quartet.* Lanham: University Press of America, 1984.

Rahi, G. S. *Edith Wharton: A Study of Her Ethos and Art.* Amritsar, India: Guru Nanak Dev University Press, 1983.

Ramsden, George, comp. *Edith Wharton's Library: A Catalogue.* Settrington, U.K.: Stone Trough Books, 1999.

Raphael, Lev. *Edith Wharton's Prisoners of Shame: A New Perspective on Her Neglected Fiction.* New York: St. Martin's, 1991.

Reynolds, Guy. "Re-making the Home, 1909–33: Gertrude Stein, Edith Wharton, and Mary Antin." In *Twentieth-Century American Women's Fiction: A Critical Introduction*, 38–63. New York: St. Martin's, 1999.

Rideout, Walter B. "Edith Wharton's *The House of Mirth*." In *Twelve Original Essays on Great American Novels*, ed. Charles Shapiro, 148–76. Detroit, Mich.: Wayne State University Press, 1958.

Salmi, Anja. *Andromeda and Pegasus: Treatment of the Themes of Entrapment and Escape in Edith Wharton's Novels.* Helsinki, Finland: Suomalainen Tiedeakatemia, 1991.

Saunders, Catherine E. *Writing the Margins: Edith Wharton, Ellen Glasgow, and the Literary Tradition of the Ruined Woman.* Cambridge, Mass.: Harvard University Press, 1987.

Schriber, Mary Suzanne. "Cultural Occasions: Form and Genre in the Texts of Harriet Beecher Stowe, Constance Fenimore Woolson, and Edith Wharton" and "Coda." In *Writing Home: American Women Abroad, 1830–1920*, 166–209. Charlottesville: University Press of Virginia, 1997.

———. "Edith Wharton: The Female Imagination and the Territory Within." In *Gender and the Writer's Imagination: From Cooper to Wharton*, 157–82. Lexington: University Press of Kentucky, 1987.

Showalter, Elaine. "The Death of the Lady (Novelist): Wharton's *The House of Mirth.*" *Representations* 9 (1985): 133–49. (Reprinted in Bloom, *Edith Wharton*, 139–54, and in *Sister's Choice: Tradition and Change in American Women's Writing*, by Showalter, 85–103. Oxford: Clarendon, 1991.)

Singley, Carol J. *Edith Wharton: Matters of Mind and Spirit*. Cambridge: Cambridge University Press, 1995.

Singley, Carol J., ed. *The Age of Innocence*, by Edith Wharton. Boston: Houghton Mifflin, 2000.

Smith, Christopher, ed. *Readings on "Ethan Frome."* San Diego: Greenhaven, 2000.

Spiller, Robert, and others, eds. *Literary History of the United States: History*. 4th ed. rev. New York: Macmillan, 1974.

Springer, Marlene. *"Ethan Frome": A Nightmare of Need*. New York: Twayne, 1993.

Stange, Margit. "Edith Wharton and the Problem of the Woman Author" and "Lily Bart at the Point of 'Modification.'" In *Personal Property: Wives, White Slaves, and the Market in Women*, 36–71. Baltimore, Md.: Johns Hopkins University Press, 1998.

Tichi, Cecelia. "Women Writers and the New Woman." In *Columbia Literary History of the United States*, ed. Emory Elliott, 589–606. New York: Columbia University Press, 1988.

Tintner, Adeline R. *Edith Wharton in Context: Essays on Intertextuality*. Tuscaloosa: University of Alabama Press, 1999.

Tuttleton, James W. "Edith Wharton." In *American Realists and Naturalists*, 433–50. Vol. 12 of *Dictionary of Literary Biography*. Ed. Donald Pizer and Earl N. Harbert. Detroit, Mich.: Gale Research, 1982.

———. "Edith Wharton: Social Historian of Old New York." In *The Novel of Manners in America*, 122–40. Chapel Hill: University of North Carolina Press, 1972.

———. "The Feminist Takeover of Edith Wharton." *New Criterion*, March 1989, 6–14.

Tuttleton, James W., Kristin O. Lauer, and Margaret P. Murray, eds. *Edith Wharton: The Contemporary Reviews*. Cambridge: Cambridge University Press, 1992.

Updike, John. "Reworking Wharton." *New Yorker*, October 4, 1993, 198–212.

Van Doren, Carl. *The American Novel.* 1921. Rev. and enl. ed. *The American Novel, 1789–1939.* New York: Macmillan, 1940.

———. *Contemporary American Novelists, 1900–1920.* New York: Macmillan, 1922.

Vita-Finzi, Penelope. *Edith Wharton and the Art of Fiction.* London: Pinter, 1990.

Wagner-Martin, Linda. *"The Age of Innocence": A Novel of Ironic Nostalgia.* New York: Twayne, 1996.

———. *"The House of Mirth": A Novel of Admonition.* Boston: Twayne, 1990.

Waid, Candace. *Edith Wharton's Letters from the Underworld: Fictions of Women and Writing.* Chapel Hill: University of North Carolina Press, 1991.

Walton, Geoffrey. *Edith Wharton: A Critical Interpretation.* Rev. ed. Rutherford, N.J.: Fairleigh Dickinson University Press, 1982.

Wegener, Frederick. "'Rabid Imperialist': Edith Wharton and the Obligations of Empire in Modern American Fiction." *American Literature* 72 (2000): 783–812.

Wershoven, Carol. *The Female Intruder in the Novels of Edith Wharton.* London: Associated University Presses, 1982.

White, Barbara. *Edith Wharton: A Study of the Short Fiction.* New York: Twayne, 1991.

Williams, Deborah Lindsay. *Not in Sisterhood: Edith Wharton, Willa Cather, Zona Gale, and the Politics of Female Authorship.* New York: Palgrave, 2001.

Wilson, Edmund. "Justice to Edith Wharton." In *The Wound and the Bow: Seven Studies in Literature,* 195–213. New York: Oxford University Press, 1947. (Reprinted in Howe, 19–31.)

Wolff, Cynthia Griffin. "Edith Wharton." In *American Novelists, 1910–1954,* 126–42. In Part 3: Mari Sandoz-Stark Young of vol. 9 of *Dictionary of Literary Biography.* Ed. James J. Martine. Detroit: Gale Research, 1981.

Woolf, Virginia. "American Fiction." In *The Moment and Other Essays,* 113–27. New York: Harcourt, Brace, 1947. (Reprinted in Vol. 2 of *Collected Essays,* by Virginia Woolf, 111–21. New York: Harcourt, Brace and World, 1967. First published in *Saturday Review of Literature,* 1 August 1925, 1–3.)

Wright, Sarah Bird. "Edith Wharton." In *American Travel Writers, 1850–1915,* 336–52. Vol. 189 of *Dictionary of Literary Biography.*

Ed. Donald Ross and James J. Schramer. Detroit, Mich.: Gale Research, 1998.

———. *Edith Wharton A to Z: The Essential Guide to the Life and Work.* New York: Facts On File, 1998.

———. *Edith Wharton's Travel Writing: The Making of a Connoisseur.* New York: St. Martin's, 1997.

Zilversmit, Annette, ed. *Reading the Letters of Edith Wharton.* Special Wharton issue of *Women's Studies* 2 (1991): 93–207.

MODERN TREATMENTS

Cooke, Elizabeth. *Zeena.* New York: St. Martin's, 1996.

Craig, Theresa. *Edith Wharton: A House Full of Rooms, Architecture, Interiors, and Gardens.* New York: Monacelli, 1996.

Dwight, Eleanor. *The Gilded Age: Edith Wharton and Her Contemporaries.* New York: Universe, 1996.

Dwight, Eleanor, and Viola Hopkins Winner. *Edith Wharton's World: Portraits of People and Places.* Washington, D.C.: Smithsonian, 1997.

Hill, Carol De Chellis. *Henry James' Midnight Song.* New York: Norton, 1993.

Janowitz, Jana. *A Certain Age: A Novel.* New York: Doubleday, 1999.

Marshall, Scott. "Edith Wharton on Film and Television: A History and Filmography." *Edith Wharton Review* 13, no. 2 (1996): 15–26.

———. "Media Adaptations of Edith Wharton's Work." Appendix 2 of *Edith Wharton A to Z: The Essential Guide to the Life and Work,* by Sarah Bird Wright, 287–95. New York: Facts On File, 1998. (Reprinted in Beppu, 59–80.)

———. *The Mount, Home of Edith Wharton: A Historic Structure Report.* Lenox: Edith Wharton Restoration, 1997.

Paulus, Stephen. *Summer.* Libretto by Joan Vail Thorne. Dir. Mary Duncan. Cond. Joel Revzen. Per. Margaret Lattimore, Michael Chioldi, and John Cheek. Koussevitzky Arts Center, Pittsfield, Mass. August 28, 1999.

Raphael, Lev. *The Edith Wharton Murders: A Nick Hoffman Mystery.* New York: St. Martin's, 1997.

———. *Let's Get Criminal: An Academic Mystery.* New York: St. Martin's, 1996.

Russell, Vivian. *Edith Wharton's Italian Gardens*. Boston: Little, Brown, 1997.

Scorsese, Martin, and Jay Cocks. *"The Age of Innocence": A Portrait of the Film Based on the Novel by Edith Wharton*. Ed. Robin Standefer. New York: Newmarket, 1993.

———. *The Shooting Script: "The Age of Innocence."* New York: Newmarket, 1993.

Contributors

MARTHA BANTA is Professor Emeritus of the Department of English, UCLA, and has authored numerous essays and five books, including *Imaging American Women* (1987), *Taylored Lives* (1993), and (her most recent book), *Barbaric Intercourse from Victoria to Theodore: Satiric Fantasy and the Culture of Conduct* (forthcoming). She was editor of PMLA from 1997 to 2002.

DALE M. BAUER is Professor of English and Women's Studies at the University of Kentucky. She is author of *Feminist Dialogics* (1988) and *Edith Wharton's Brave New Politics* (1994), and editor of the Bedford Books Cultural edition of "The Yellow Wallpaper" (1998). She coedited *The Cambridge Companion to Nineteenth-Century American Women's Writing* (2001). Her book in progress, "Sex Expression and American Women," studies women's writing from 1860 to 1940.

SHARI BENSTOCK is Professor of English and Associate Dean for Academic Affairs at the University of Miami. She is author and editor of ten books, including *Women of the Left Bank: Paris, 1900–1940* (1986) and *No Gifts from Chance: A Biography of Edith Wharton* (1994), which won the American literature prize for life writing from the Colonial Dames Society of America. Her recent works include the coedited *Footnotes: On Shoes* (2001) and the coauthored classroom text *A Handbook of Literary Feminisms* (2002).

NANCY BENTLEY is Associate Professor of English at the University of Pennsylvania. She is author of *The Ethnography of Manners: Hawthorne, James, Wharton* (1995) and coeditor of the Bedford Books Cultural Edition of Charles Chesnutt's *The Marrow of Tradition* (1993). Her study of the relations between popular culture and high literary culture in the late-nineteenth-century United States is forthcoming in volume 3 of the *Cambridge History of American Literature*. She has published essays on issues of race, kinship, and law in American literature.

LINDA COSTANZO CAHIR, Associate Professor of English, Centenary College, is author of *Solitude and Society in the Works of Herman Melville and Edith Wharton* (1999). She has published book chapters, commentaries, and articles in the Melville journal *Extracts*, *The Edith Wharton Review*, *Literature/Film Quarterly*, and *The Yeats/Eliot Review*. She is a trustee of The Murray Endowment Fund (of the Herman Melville Society), serves on the executive board of *The Edith Wharton Review*, and is a contributing editor for *Literature/Film Quarterly*.

CLARE COLQUITT teaches American literature in the Department of English at San Diego State University. She is coeditor, with Susan Goodman and Candace Waid, of *A Forward Glance: New Essays on Edith Wharton* (1999). She has published bibliographic essays on Wharton, as well as essays on *The House of Mirth* and on Wharton's correspondence with Morton Fullerton. She is the author of articles on Sherwood Anderson, Sarah Orne Jewett, and Rebecca West.

ELEANOR DWIGHT is author of *Edith Wharton: An Extraordinary Life* (1994) and *The Gilded Age: Edith Wharton and Her Contemporaries* (1996). Her biography of fashion editor Diana Vreeland is forthcoming. She has contributed articles and essays on literature, travel, and gardens to scholarly and popular publications. She was guest curator for the exhibition "Glancing Backward: Edith Wharton's New York," at the National Academy of Design (1994), and cocurator of "Portraits of People and Places in Edith Wharton's World" at the National Portrait Gallery (1997). She teaches literature, most recently at the New School University in New York.

CAROL J. SINGLEY is Associate Professor of English at Rutgers University-Camden. She is author of *Edith Wharton: Matters of Mind and Spirit* (1995), editor of the New Riverside edition of *The Age of Innocence* (2000), and coeditor of two collections of critical essays, *Anxious Power* (1993) and *The Calvinist Roots of the Modern Era* (1997). She has published essays on nineteenth- and early twentieth-century American writers and is completing a book on American adoption narratives.

CECELIA TICHI is the William R. Kenan, Jr. Professor of English at Vanderbilt University. She is the author of *Embodiment of a Nation: Human Form in American Places* (2001), as well as literary-cultural studies of technology, environmentalism, and American country music. She is past president of the American Studies Association.

Index